Don't Wear Your
Problems on Your Sleeve

Don't Wear Your Problems on Your Sleeve

WRITTEN AND
PRODUCED BY

SUSAN E. DURANT

COVER ART BY
SUSAN E. DURANT

Trafford rev. 02/20/2012

 www.trafford.com

North America & international
toll-free: 1 888 232 4444 (USA & Canada)
phone: 250 383 6864 ♦ fax: 812 355 4082

Contents

All of life is poetry
Its meaning is determined by how it is interpreted

INTRODUCTION

You know what the most beautiful gift in the world is? Random acts of love. You know what the most exquisite expression of that gift is? Listening.

You know what is the worst betrayal a parent can pin on the clean slate of a child's identity? Tell that child they are not who they should be. You know what is the most incriminating and fallacious proof of that accusation? Convince that child they should not feel the way they feel. You know how to cement that profanity to that infant spirit? Make sure it is clearly understood, no matter what happens, or how they feel, train them to never wear that sorrow of who they are on their sleeve.

I was born the one daughter of six children to a mother who often said; "I always wanted little boys." I was punished often and with sound reason. I was the girl among boys. I wasn't only cursed in her eyes for being a girl. I was ugly. I was cross-eyed. And I didn't act right. From a very young age, my mother insisted there was something mentally amiss about me. I could never quite figure out that final allegation. Although, looking back, being who I was in that family did make me suicidal.

I was sick often until I had my tonsils removed. I thought I was sick because I was a girl and I got my tonsils out because it was the rightful punishment for being sickly. After two terrifying eye-operations I wore glasses from the age of five. It was my whole life. My mother sang to me about how boys don't make passes at girls with glasses. When I was made to wear a patch to avoid blindness in my lazy-eye and go out to play with the neighborhood little girls, I was a monster they called me a queer and ran and hid from. I took on layers of armor for the self rejection that started before I ever left my family home. I barely touched my life yet. The only people who accepted me were my brothers. I was accused of dirtiness, beaten, and grounded for playing with them.

We had a father who was a well kept, high earning, drunken, raging, fool who called us all idiots and beat the shit out of all of us on a regular basis. I feared they'd throw me away. I loathed my prison with my parents for the way they made me hate myself. I wasn't alone in my distorted feelings. As young children we actually had meetings. We sat in a small circle and commiserated with each other. That very important bonding was both a release and a validation. But, no matter how much I bonded with my brothers, there was always kept, a defining separation. I was a girl. Since none of them wanted to be me, there was a point at which they always let me go down.

An outcast learns to cope . . . or dies.

In all my life all I ever wanted was to be loved. Boyfriends were a good distraction but, the rage I entered into the world of relationships with was a ghost of beatings and accusations of being a slut from when I played with my brothers in the backyard when we only imagined cowboys and indians and not the secrets teenagers' exchange.

My greatest lover, alcohol lifted me from the cliff of suicide. But, in seven tornado-like years, it took me to a precipice more foreboding than suicide. It was a dark, entangled web of no reprieve where suicide would be a luxury.

From alcohol I was given people who were, to the outside world, dredges of the earth. They didn't tell me who I was. They asked me to tell them who I was and they listened. Every fear, every bit of rage and sadness, and every misconstrued idea I bore, they listened to and helped me unravel. I had no idea who I was. I was terrified to find out. Fear did not stop me. I searched. When I didn't find me in my family, I tried men. When I didn't find me in men, I turned to alcohol. When I didn't find me in alcohol, I landed in AA.

In my anxious state of hunger for acceptance, for love, still searching for any reason at all to go on, I fell into a relationship with a woman. I got the first notion of what it might feel like to be loved. It shattered my heart and my newly found refuge, the AA group at that time, ostracized me for that earth-moving experience. Just as alcohol was the perfect cure for my self-loathing, so was this woman a source of the unscathed (sinless touch in the desert of the untouchables) or so it seemed. Just like my relationship with alcohol, I tried over and over to relive that brief relief. It was never forthcoming but rather, answered as hammer slams upon the chisel in the fracture of my soul.

In my ceaseless quest for who I am and why I am, I entwined myself with a great spiritual leader. That is where, ever so gingerly, I opened to an essence that had been screaming unheard for recognition, I can recall now, all the way back to when I was five years old. From this person I was taught the greatest gift of all. It is the gift of giving.

I know people who will answer the phone at two am. Get in their car and drive out in the dark to pull a stranger from the gutter. I know people who will listen to a stranger's sorrow for five hours on a Sunday afternoon. I know people who do random acts of love and no one, not even each other, knows their names. I know people who practice unconditional love. It's not the love for a mother or daughter, or father, or son, or lover, or power, or money. It's the love that saves lives without merit, reward, payment, or even acknowledgement. What AA appears to be from the outside and what it is are two very different pictures.

When, after twenty years, my spiritual leader perished I spun into such a desolate grief, I turned in a desperate attempt to ease my loss, once again to the closest thing I had conceived as a mother's love. I turned again to a woman and I very nearly perished myself. I learned, with razor-sharp clarity ~ the only refuge to life is God. The only purpose is to be of service. If I want love then I must *be* love.

It is not the wonder of nature that is the beginning and the end. It is the realization of what harmony causes it to flourish and what confusion causes it to disintegrate that opens life to its awesome potential.

It is not my job to be a girlfriend, a wife, or a mother. Because my heart is shattered, it is my job to mend a shattered heart. It is my job to tell you to wear your problems on your sleeve. It is how we heal. It is my job to listen.

After thirty-three years the rage still rises in my throat. My heart still screams at the false accusations. Because of that I know my job is not done. Because of those screams my mission is clear. It takes a heart to reach a heart. I've found mine. Here it is.

It is not the rabbit that materializes out of a magician's hat that is of consequence. It is the movement that produces an awe that gives completion to the intention, to entertain and be entertained. That is the fulfillment.

Love is not found outside oneself but rather, billows from deep within illuminating a ferocious wood to reveal a quiet place to dismantle the armor and cleanse the wounds. When that happens nothing . . . nothing else matters.

If it weren't for the pain I never would have done one thing. I would have done nothing at all.

I've read innumerable books that told me in innumerable ways of the peace-of-mind attainable. My question was always; how did you get there? Everyone has a story. Every seeker who has found this luminous warmth of peace didn't just wake up peaceful one day. Knowledge that peace exists is not peace. The rutted road that emerges there is not an easy road to take. It is unmarked most of the way. Every time I have gone off into the misery of deceptive consummation a piece of my "self" is chopped free and I have sought with a deeper earnest, my quest for peace of mind.

It all takes place in plain view of life at the speed of piling day upon day. Each agony is met with release. Each despair is met with hope. Each bit of enduring rage is met with a deeper love. Each broken dream is met with a better plan.

Life unfolds. It unfolds without permission. To find wings is not a neat and tidy journey. Many, many times I've landed smack on my head. Mine is a stone-cold life on fire with the intention of finding what is true.

In the ocean of peace-of-mind, quiet is the heart inside of me stripped and cleared of every one of its imposed names. I have found an emptiness that is full, even bursting over the rim. I have found God. I have found a compassion for whoever else is in mad pursuit of such indescribable freedom. I have found love that is true.

SED

DEDICATION

This book is dedicated to all the women who have come into my life and drawn me forward, out of myself, that I might have the greatest of all opportunities. To be a light radiating, as is its nature, from the center out illuminating the beauty that diminishes every shadow that creates a measure in any form that assumes a limit to the beneficence of femininity.

Thank you to Mrs. "D", Sr. Pat, Mary Jane, Cheryl, Cathy, Kay, Elaine, Alice, Michele, Marcia, Nina, Carole, Toni, Patty, Jean, Carolyn, Marilyn, and all the un-named woman who have shown me who I am, but more importantly, who I am not.

IT IS ONLY a midwife of the most divinely inspired kind who can free such a child from this jailed breast. From un-reconciled squalor, this one has the power to take on another's world by complete acceptance and steadfast resistance, unto and beyond the stark-raving-mad disrobing of every veneer from cloth to ugly secret. An ocean of lies strewn about and covered in silk weaves so magnificent that never a question of its validity would have been raised had not my neck been bared on the block.

She died. That is it. Now it is me whom must live. Let me take a moment to tell of the rising temperature necessary for the boiling blood that led directly to the mortal freedom from the first footprint of mortal breath; my reaping of my soul.

None of the on-goings is easily written. For the ocean released from the dam might leave a land barren. What takes *any* person to the willing end of circumstance but the clear realization that confession is restitution, freedom for all the agony of which one has kept the sword drawn, in constant readiness for oneself to be put to death. There is a certain release from dread to the very end that I let it be released.

If the possibility of sin is actual, the greatest sin a family might commit on one member is to decide who that member is before that pitiful victim gets a chance to even wet their feet in the marsh of their own soul-flower sprouting.

When Delaney Died

It all came down to her, just short of
losing her mind, being talked about behind
closed doors. No one knew how to handle it so
some big-shots moved in easily while we stood
around shaking our hands and making accusations
that were as useful as kindling on a fire the morning after.
She spent the best part of her life gathering scraps of
people and mending them back together. She reassembled
whole families. We were all pieces made whole in one way
or another by the dexterity of her tuff love.
Even the big-shots had to admit to the divinity of her
manipulation in their measly saved lives.

A bunch of x-drunks who forgot where they came from, forgot
it wasn't their brainstorms that turned their lives around into
something worth living, forgot the width of the entry to her
open door, forgot,—forgot, sneered at her.
They refused to turn the speaker up when she couldn't
hear at her final board meeting and
when she died they closed in on her legacy like
a drain sweeps every scrap into its' black hole.
They painted over all of her, with her money. Changed
the interpretation of her estate to fit their needs but
kept her name alive for what might fall to their pockets from
hearts that found her absence swimming in a river of tears.

That's it.
A giant spirit is released without
a bang, without a parade, without a voice.
There is no need.
Her mission is too complete to be completely undone.

10/28/02
SED

I HAD BEEN on the board of trustees for a year. Before that honored position, I was a guest to the semi-annual meetings for about five years. I didn't get there like the others. Everyone was someone. Doctors, lawyers, professors, men who actually owned medical centers with letters running in paragraphs after their names, and me, Susan were the decision makers. My credentials were sobriety and a gratitude that showed so true it was clear I was loyal enough to give my life. To me, there was no other reason to live than to serve Mrs. D and I'd do anything and be anywhere she wanted me to do or show. I wanted to be there. I felt both honored and humbled. When I sat in the great hall as a student barely beyond the fog of my last drink, these board members dazzled me. Now I knew I was no more than any of the students and the board members were never more than me. If I could be on the board so could any one of those who wanted to. The greatest gift Mrs. D gave everyone of us was love; understanding, as she said, even as she disagreed.

Mrs. D was the first person who did not tell me who I am but rather, waited for me to tell her. Mrs. D was peace personified. That is what I wanted; what took me twenty years to name. The coupling of freedom to test being me and the opportunity to gain peace on that path of my soul journey toward ultimate, fearless manifestation made me hers with complete abandonment of motive beyond the possibility of such phenomenal actualizations.

I was asked to be a board member and I agreed to whatever end. There was a prevalence of the wisdom to foresee that was as tall and obvious as a great field of sun flowers raising their faces in miraculously majestic unison with the rising sun. That was clear to me. Mrs. D. proved that again and again in the twenty years I remained in her circle. And after all, it was Mrs. D who first loved me and maintained that love in spite of my tests of its validity.

Little did I know or have the ability to conceive what cataclysmic avalanche of events was to befall my years to come. Spiritual freedom is not free.

Improved Illusion

Reality doesn't change.
It is perception that tweaks the hologram.

The backbone of disillusionment is
the key to the rite of passage out

of each inevitable frame of the mind
there is always an improved illusion.

Fear is no excuse for
not moving there.

THE CONFUSIONS

AT THE AGE of 30 I took a trip to California to visit a brother who, ten years prior, had decided to settle there to escape the insanity of our family. I was twelve years into sobriety which meant I had twelve years of healing under my belt. I wasn't free from self loathing but I had come to a level of forgiveness that allowed me to have relationships with each member of our family although obvious cracks broke any consistency and shrapnel lay still with dried blood caked on the many rusty, sharp edges.

We did all the safe, restive things. He worked the whole week I visited. I went into San Francisco, each day alone. It was just like childhood; he hiding in his work, me running to the cliffs of my reach. His wife was just the charm to compliment his expert ability at over-compensating. She did generally nothing but expect more and he did everything to fulfill her endless needs. I felt so sorry for him. One day I stayed at their house and did all the laundry. That night when he came home to cook dinner for his hungry wife and me the smile I witnessed on his face; the satisfaction he radiated thinking she folded all those neat piles just as soon faded to a heart-felt guilty-gratitude to me for having done the loads. As selfish as I remained, I could not imagine not jumping on the opportunity to afford a man who gives so much, this sweat-less reciprocation.

During one of our endless, embellishing conversations about our common be-comings he chanced to ask me if I ever considered marriage. I told him never. Especially since I learned in 11th grade there is a 75% chance a girl will marry a man like her father. I'll not live mom's life I told him. S expanded on the wonders of how relationships help us to grow up. He told a story of what a fool our uncle made of himself being 50 and chasing girls of 20. I told him I was living with a woman. He stared for only a moment then said; *I'm glad you told me that. At least I know you are happy. I can see how you'd be confused.*

A brilliant mind must be able to realize the absurdity of cording happiness to a relationship.

Two years later R informed me my brother and she conceived their first child the weekend of my departure. I supposed S might have been afraid of his own confusion and had the remedy so many I have met use to squash the unremitting question; what is happiness, while the materialization of such a quest remains hidden under the piles of busy distractions we all create and the confusion that persists for our inherent, arrogant belief that we know how to be happy. In the mean time we get moments of happiness while the joy of living completely eludes us and keeps us searching and missing the mark at once.

Six Years to become a Monster

You'll go blind or
become a monster with a walleye.
I sit in the waiting room another waiting room
mothers icy delivery of time consumption.
What do you see? What do you see? What do you see?
Always the same question same white coat
same placid expression same icy hand on my forehead
directing my eyes.
Hate them. They scare me.
Treat me like a number talk to me like a timid kitten big people
decide what I need.

Shivering angst lies silent.
Unspoken perhaps won't be.
The only good of me courage.
Finger nick. I bleed O positive. I'm human.

Sit in a waiting room another waiting room.
Icy mother delivers me to another white coat.
Toys, candy are not reprieves.

On a day of bliss
I am driven to the cinder institution.
After one icy touch after another after another
my pee filled bladder arrives at its room.
There lies my roommate.
See her eye patches? She's not afraid.
She is silent. She is silent.

Sit in my waiting room another waiting room.
Alone
icy mother goes.
I wait
Shivering angst blossoms cold despair.

Cold room. Cold attendant following the
lines on the cold sheet, notes me.
I'm a thing a number not a little girl.

Cold hands take me for a cold, dizzying ride to
a cold room with cold lights and big, cold people with
cold, blue ice cubes covering their heads—
so cold they cover their mouths with facemasks so
I can't see their breath.
Cold hands force my head firm and straight, gag
me with a cold, black, rubber mitt that breathes
dead stench into my mouth.
I don't breath. Then I do.

It's cold and dark. I am alone. I cry.
Where is icy mother?

Can't see. Eyes are covered.
Can't roll. Strap on my back.
I reach up scream.
Thick spiders web no more than twelve inches above my body.
I don't move for fear of that spider.
I cry.
Nurse says shut-up or I'll give you a needle.
I shut-up.

Night becomes day.
The spider never appears.
Miraculously, the web disappears.
Patches come off.
I am released. Go home with icy mother.
Doctor says I am very brave. I am silent. I am silent.

Home brings boiling compresses from icy mother.
Tells me I'll go blind or
become a monster with a walleye.

At school the whole class stands, says
a prayer of thanks for safe return.
Each day boiling compresses with ominous foretelling of
the monster that can be.

Icy mother straps a
black patch over my good eye to make the bad eye good.
Sends me out to play. Afraid, I don't want to go.
Balking is useless.
Ice pushes me out the door.

Peers turn icy!
I am a Cyclops!
No!
I am six!
Too late to save mother!
I bury the patch knowing the price is a beating.
No matter
I'm already a monster!

MEMORY

WHEN I WAS 6 years old everything seemed like my whole life. The sum of my experience was not vast enough for me to hide from yet. Everything was raw experience. There was no option but to run straight into the obvious and take it for what it was no matter how much it made me wretch.

All the little girls in the neighborhood ran away from me. They hid. I searched but I knew I would never find them. They were peering from behind some curtain, whispering to each other. I knew what they whispered because sometimes they'd shout it. I was a queer. I wore a black patch over one eye. I was terrifying to them. Inside me there was this pulling sensation like a rip-tide always trying to drag me into its black ocean. I ran home to hide my horror. I went inside to watch T.V. but mother would catch me right away. She'd tell me; *no T.V.! You need to use your eye. Do you want to go blind or be a wall-eye?! Go out and play!* I was shoved out the door. The slam sound is retrievable still. Thank God I had brothers. They were blind to my patch and they played games that were more fun anyway.

Next door they were making a huge town in the sand, far in the back of the neighbor's property, with Tonka Toys. I was always welcome there. We built houses, stores, corrals, fire stations, the whole kit and caboodle.

It took days to complete. When there was virtually no more we could build we'd have an air raid, blow it to smithereens and start over.

There was a problem with this reprieve. Mother did not want me playing with the boys. From the middle of construction on newly smoothed earth, I'd hear my name. S would just look at me. *Better go,* he'd say. I'd stall for awhile. No use rushing to the inevitable. I'd trudge home. She'd be there, her back to me when I arrived.

Where were you?
Next door at M's.
I told you I don't want you over there.

We're just playing with the trucks. S is there. This isn't about S. It's about you. Girls don't play with boys and where is your patch?

I don't know.

The lightning would flash right then. Stark, white, and stinging, the smack never came when I was ready so it always caught me off guard.

Go to your room!

Up I'd go to my hot isolation. It was a mix of unfathomable frustration, confusion, and desperation for being me. In those days there were no computers, iPods, cell phones, or electronic games. No one had a T.V. in their room. If I put a record on it was not to be heard by any ear pressed to the outer door-side. No doors were to be closed. So to be sent to my room was a real time-out, not as that remedy is implemented today. I'd be up there so long, I'd think mother just forgot about me there. The next time I'd hear my name would be when it was time to eat. It could be 30 minutes or 4 hours. I'd hear her calling out the door.

My mother tried several methods to make me lady-like. She'd call the neighborhood mothers and have them send their little girls to my backdoor. I'd be somewhere in the house wearing my eye patch and the doorbell would ring.

Susan, someone is here for you.

I'd slither to the door. There they were. That pulling sensation would start and a ball of pressure like a balloon over-filling so much its red would turn pale-pink then white just before bursting into shreds would be expanding at the base of my throat adding to the undertow. This little gang was a reflection of my self-hatred. I hated them.

I glared at them with my one eye. As if I was a fancy thing, the one named Kerry would start in this baklava voice; *Hi Susan.* I loathed the sound of my name being said. It embarrassed me to hear it. *Do you want to come out and play?*

No.

Susan, go out and play with them.

No.

Get . . . Out. mother would growl under her breath so only I could hear.

Each step, heels dug, I'd follow them down to their lawn. First we'd make leaf houses. The leaves were raked into squared off rooms with doorways. It was fun. When the houses were all done I'd want to wreck them and start over. That was an appalling idea to them. I was like a bear among doe's. They wanted to save them. Go inside and eat cookies and watch dark shadows on T.V.. Dark shadows was a soap opera about this guy who laid in a coffin but wasn't buried because he was really alive and everyone in the show kept waiting for him to make his move. This choice of activities was worse than solitary confinement to me. At least in my room I could conjure up secret games and fart when I felt the urge.

I didn't stay long in their house. I'd leave. On my way out I'd destroy the leaf houses because I knew they only saved them because they didn't understand the only fun part about them was in the construction phase when all the minds ran free and wild together in a magical lose of what is, in the process of the free-flow of creating.

When I got home mother asked; *Where were you?*

At Kathy's. I'd say without fear and with a bit of pride because I was doing what was right.

She'd say, without any change of expression;

Where is your patch?

I'd dig it out of my pocket all folded up in a knot and hold it out proud. I didn't lose it. Her face would scowl in the ugly-eyebrow-knit and her ugly mouth would tighten just before the white light flashed.

Put it on! You're gonna go blind or become a wall-eye!

I was 6 years old. I had had 2 eye operations by then to correct my lazy eye. I hated the big people who talked in baby voices and stuck me with needles and gagged me with rancid black rubber masks that left its rancid-rubber smell in my throat for days after their attack on me. I hated mother for not protecting me from them.

It was only once in a while I'd get to go watch dark shadows. Usually the game I was called out to play was hide and seek. I was always voted the monster because I had only one eye. I never could find them. Once in awhile I'd spot them peeking out an upstairs window from their house. I'd go home to hear; *get out!*

I'd say; *I already went out.*

It's too early. I'll call you for dinner.

I'd go out in the driveway and hang out with my brother P, in plain view so I wouldn't get in trouble. I was often accused of playing with P. I never understood the accusation. I was playing with P. What was wrong with it neither one of us could figure out. So, P would go his way and I would go back to being alone. I hated being the neighborhood monster, and the dirty thing that lived in our house.

When father came home from work the relief was, my self-loathing became abject fear. Father was always ferocious when he got home. After a few drinks he was un-caged, feral, and ferocious. All I had was my brothers. We clung to our common link to survival. We had each other. That is all. When I was torn with a grave inquiry I never once understood, from their bond and yanked into separation I was only more convinced of my horrific existence as something born other than human, a thing lethally poisonous to my brothers, and something monstrously queer to the little girls in the neighborhood. I'd rather fear my father than consider what I was.

SHACKLES

Without reservation the sky exhumes emotion—
reveals explosive depth.
I, in awe of its insistence see
trees let leaves turn faces to its tears
bow to its fury and

Armed in human shackles I wonder
why such rules of concealment we cast.
Emotion like dragon's breath breathed
from a babies mouth—
fear burns from flaming nostrils in silence
within each
the volcano erupts like
the eye of a storm.

GRADE SCHOOL

When I entered grammar school my eye problem guaranteed me a seat in the slow reading group. We were 6 or 7 in all. We were placed in a circle in the front, corner of the room, separated from the rest of the class. While they read independently from the grade level reader, we sat with Sr. Bridgette reading aloud from a simpler text. That pulling sensation was ever inside me. I was terrified of Sr. Bridgette. She was enshrouded with a black habit that revealed only her two eyes, her pointy nose, and her thin lipped mouth. Her eyes were highlighted with big black eyebrows and her mouth tended to match with a sparse mustache of the same shade. Her black garb fell perfectly in overlapping panels of starched, impenetrable material to just above the floor where two rounded black shoes exposed no more than the toe coming and the heel going in a well polished leather that covered what I couldn't imagine. She wore a set of black rosary beads that lay in the folds of her mysterious cover. They hung from her waist to the edge of her habit. Those rosary beads were very cool to me. I always wanted to touch those untouchables. They never made a sound like ordinary beads would. They were blessed; silently sinless.

My grade school years are most recalled by memories of my teachers. The first and second grade is a blur of dimly lit hallways. We learned to be orderly. Stand, sit, and walk in lines either by height or alphabetical placement. We learned not to talk unless called on. No giggling. No glancing left or right. No chewing gum or eating candy in school. We learned to stand straight without leaning on the wall when in the line for the lavatory. Be quick and wash our hands. Everything was a sin. Heaven seemed an impossible goal that was always worth striving for, ever harder, with each new edge to every old rule.

Those were the days nuns were allowed and expected to use physical force to mold us into saved Christians. God knows we were nearly impossible to save, bunches of scalawags and heathens that we were. One day, after a hefty snow fall we all had waited for, we had a little too much wild release in the schoolyard. A great snowball fight broke out. Those clumped balls careened in chaotic laughter right up until the bell rang. By that time the whole lot of us was wet and red-faced, tussled and completely undone for the level of presentation required to take classes in such a refined, Godly establishment. We lined up and marched in all wild-eyed and bushy tailed. When we got into the classroom we were all stood in a straight line across the front of the room. Each of us was given a smacking across the back of our still red knuckles with the wooden ruler. It was like a gnat bite compared to my whippings at home. I know that happened in fourth grade because it was Sr. Leo who gave us the ruler. I don't know how she knew who the culprits were. I suspect she scared us into confessing by convincing us God knew who we were and it made the sin ever graver to not only commit it but to then lie about it. We turned ourselves in. Better to be punished by Sr. Leo than by God who wouldn't be so kind. No one wanted to be doomed to the fiery hell of such wrath.

In third grade I had Mrs. Hayes. We learned "the times table". Whenever the class got too noisy she banged a police stick on the side of her big wooden desk and yelled; *Auwlrighty! . . . tonight you will do the two, three, and, four times table ten times each!* That was the punishment we received over and over using different denominations each times. It was a great learning tool and better than the fires of hell.

In the third grade I gave out a lot of bloody lips and noses. Boys always wanted to fight me. I was still equal enough in size to knock them all down. The good thing about being a girl was I didn't get in trouble for beating them up. If the table was turned any one of them would be in the principal's office.

When I was in the third grade my parents told us we would get fifty cents for each "A" on our report card. That semester I got sixteen "A's"! My excitement dashed like a bucket of water on a candlestick when an eight dollar promise paid out two dollars because I didn't need all that money. It was always confusing to try to figure out the deduction of reasoning especially when it should not evoke any feeling. It should just be accepted. I learned to act grateful and to not question. I also remember third grade being my Guinness book of world records for unsigned conduct slips. I had 42 hidden in my top drawer. Mrs. Hayes never followed up on them. At the end of the year I ripped them up. Why push my luck I thought.

It was when I was in third grade that my mother gave birth to her fourth son. The family was filled with joy. After much talk of getting me a sister, my mother beamed at her new baby and said to me; *What do you think? I always wanted little boys.* I said; *me too.* I learned to feed, rock, and change diapers. At eight years old I preferred Tonka Toys and cowboy pistols to dolls but this was beyond all wonder. I loved PJ. I brought his picture to school and passed it all around the class. I was very proud.

Fourth grade was the end of the primary grades. I was still constrained in the slow reading group. I knew I could read better than I was told. The teachers were all unmovable on their outdated determination. I was no less determined to prove my ability to read. I was told the prerequisite to move into the general reading population was to successfully complete the phonics book and a certain level of speed reading assignments. We were allowed to pick and move on our own pace. I completed two phonics books. I finished and passed all the speed reading tests. I showed all my results to Sr. Leo, my second grade teacher who also taught fourth grade. She was unwavering in her educated conclusion. I was not going to move up. She didn't ever look at me. I still recall the shadows in the light crossing through her mustache. She looked down, at my results. Then she said; *very good.* I asked again and again if I could try the higher reading group. She was always sure I'd fail. She said; *No.* It was always impossible to figure out the deduction of reasoning. I was certain of one thing though. I couldn't trust it.

It was Mrs. Penotti, my other fourth grade teacher, who allowed me a little bit of special treatment when I returned to school after my tonsillectomy. She had the most rancid breath I ever smelled. We all wondered if she ate dog-doo. She was always sucking on mints. I guess she knew it stunk too. The mints didn't help. They enhanced the garlic-dog-doo-heated-re-breath, kind of gave it a little oomph for depth pronunciation. When I came back she gave me a whole bag of her mints. My first appalling thought was she is trying to give me her bad breath! The rule was, if you were caught eating candy in class you had to come the next day with a piece of candy for everyone. I didn't have to share my candy because I had had my tonsils out. Embarrassed and confused, I took the candy because I didn't know how not to. But, I couldn't take it all for myself. I asked if I could pass the bag around and give everyone one. I wouldn't feel right if I hogged the whole thing. That would be despicable of me. And, if I was going to get bad breath everyone might as well share that too. One thing I was well taught, in a large family and by every nun who got the chance to save my selfish soul, was to share. She made a big deal of my generosity. I didn't see it as generosity. I saw it as something I could handle in no other way. I was always trying to get my thinking around the motivations of other people's thinking. I never could.

The only other outstanding teacher in grammar school was my sixth grade teacher, Mr. Puleo. He made Danny Finnerty sit in a closed closet all morning many times. Other times he'd make him stay in the push-up position for five minutes. At times there would be four or five of us standing face to the blackboard with our noses pressed in little circles he drew. I don't remember what the other kids did wrong. I was always punished for not answering his questions. I was more terrified of him than I was of my father. When I was at his disposal I was in his foreign land. With my father, I had my room to run to.

I was taught, with the back of my father's fist not only to *not* speak but, to *not* move any muscle on my face when my father spoke. Mr. Puleo brought out that reaction in full force in me. I so inflamed him for my stone-statue-like reaction to his loud inquiries that he separated me and my desk from the entire class. He treated me like a freak. I felt like a freak in his class. I was his example of what happens when one practices mutiny. I could neither defend myself nor absolve myself by speaking. I was completely entangled in my reaction which caused his reaction which in turn caused my reaction. We were at irreconcilable, unexplainable odds. Because of my age, I was the one who was punished for the communication blockade. His face often turned scarlet while his neck veins bulged trying to get a response from me, while I would be sinking deeper and deeper into a profound and utterly terrified silence. I was often sent to the principal's office. It was a glorious relief. I was safe there. I was there so often during that year I was sent to run the mimeograph machine with another bad kid named Kevin. I never asked him what he did and he never asked me. We both liked being there.

One day Mr. Puleo told me I was the ugliest girl he ever saw. I just stared at him. I always knew I was ugly. He said it, out loud in front of the whole class. They were all looking at my ugliness. He told me I didn't need my glasses. Then got the class to laugh at how I was faking my eye problems to get attention. He ordered me to take off my glasses. I just stared at him, frozen, not even breathing. He screamed; *I despise you! Go to the office!* I got up shaking, slinked to the door and down the dimly lit hallway in mortified relief. After school that day I went home and asked my mother; *what does despise mean?*

She said; *what?! Where did you hear that?! Don't ever say it again! It's a bad word.*

What does it mean? I persisted.

It means someone hates you. Who said it?

Mr. Puleo said he despises me.

He did not! He would never say that! Don't ever let me hear you say that again! That was the end of that.

In just that way, reinvented in one thousand different manifestations, the entangling pressure of denial turned doorways to the freedom-born-of-truth into a map-less maze of catacombs. Someone I didn't even know, someone who couldn't possibly know me *despised* me. I am *so* horrifying that I am despicable, was my conclusion.

I tried my best to get on good terms with Mr. Puleo. I had no side. I learned to deny the truth. He showed us his canker sores in class. He invited us to pool parties at his house that we were required to attend and wear bathing suits at. He supplied us with beer and, to a select few, weed. He lined up the desks in class into two sides; the ones who answer questions and the ones who didn't. The winners are on the answering side. I crossed back and forth a few times the remainder of that year. We were ten years old, ready for a new kind of molding. Mr. Puleo served his purpose in turning that wheel. I despised him.

Final Agreement

I didn't get it then.
All I had to do was be pretty.
Pretty mean.
I thought those words went together like
cartwheels or grandmother.
As far as I knew they were getting what they asked for.
Still, I sat, hours in the corner of my sweltering room, punished.

I buried that eye-patch so many times,
I can't believe the yard isn't full of eye-patch weeds.
I told the neighborhood kids I didn't need it anymore.
At dinner time I got the spoon before my meal.
It's much worse eating it cold.
I know.

As soon as that patch hid my eye again
those kids ran away, again.
Eventually I graduated to glasses and braces.
I was relegated to the ugly crowd.
I did what they wanted.
I was pretty
mean.
When I found a drink to oil the savage
all the rage ravaged me.
Pretty is relative and mean looks insane

They caged me to see if I was hopelessly feral.
It was a chance to quiet my growl and lick my wounds.
Thirty years later I do cartwheels and feel grateful because grandmother
is alive so I can tell her pretty is a trap and mean is a way to survive and
she agrees.

FAMILY

My older brother, S disappeared from family life by the time grammar school started. Perhaps his way of dealing was better than mine. I'll never know. I can only say I'm not unhappy at all with the way things turned out for me. I don't know how life is for him. We both survived. He virtually locked himself in his room for the next twelve years. Oh, I'd see him. We were in high school during overlapping years. He was given the thankless chore of watching after me. I received quite a few lectures for my radical behavior and a few good punches if I answered him back. S was a very good brother. He saved me from some situations my poor judgment would have gotten me into grave trouble with had I been left to my own thinking.

As children growing up, I grew up with C and P. Being brought up in a neighborhood under constant construction, we played in dugout foundations, sliding down basement sized dirt mountains on flattened refrigerator boxes. We were like monkeys climbing all through the skeleton frames of houses to be. We whipped dirt bombs and acorns at each other until someone got hit hard enough to cry. We played keep-away, kick-the-can, football, cops on motorcycles, Sundance kid, and monster.

Monster was a game in which C was always the monster. We played in the basement after dark with the lights turned off. The only rule was you had to switch bases. There were two bases. One was at the bottom of the cellar stairs. The other one was at the back door. C hid out in the dark between the two bases. There was a lot of screaming and loud laughter. With 5 or 6 kids playing you could get to the other side without getting tagged by the monster. Everyone who got tagged sat under the ping-pong table and waited until there were a few captives. When there were enough the lights were turned on and one by one everyone would hold each captive down while C tickled the heck out of them. Then the lights went out and we started over. This raucous game was only played when my father was out of town. Otherwise none of us would be alive today to tell about it.

One night while highly aroused and in the fit of the game someone shouted; *listen!* A sweeping silence befell the din. Sure enough we heard a scratching.

Someone yelled; *it's just a leaf!*

Someone else yelled; *no! Listen!*

When suddenly a head, all misshapen, shot up in the cellar window everyone blasted into screams and trampled toward the stairs. The multiple shrills rose up with the clobbering little feet into the kitchen and flooded into the den. The back door flew open and slammed against the back closet, burst wide by a swiftly moving bent over animal running right toward the undiminished over-stimulated, mind-blasted group. Right out front was little P. The stark terror on his face, the stiffened position of his completely outstretched arms, the ear deafening shrill of his scream brought us all to bear on the monster. He was falling backwards and someone started to yell. *It's mom! It's Mom! P, its Mom!* To which P fell to the floor in tears. Mother ripped the stocking off her head laughing and grabbed P to calm him down. That fun and games trick worked very well once. Mother had endless ideas for scaring us when father was away. Father was generally away two weeks out of each month. Mother's biggest threat was Father.

It wasn't until 40 years later, during conversations with grandma R., that I could get real clarity on the roundness of childhood. Growing up is not a linear experience but rather, a round experience that molds into an adult ball of all that happens that, hopefully, can continue to roll with life. It is neither all good nor all bad. Hopefully, what the ball is embedded with is the strength to survive each day that comes to be at hand. After all, if our feet keep hitting the ground that is all we really have. As much as my mother found pleasure out of scaring the living daylights out of us, whether it was as a stocking-headed monster or a description of the man who was going to come with his skinning machine and skin our hands to the bloody bones if we were caught lying, she also found great pleasure in educating us in the arts. She took us to places of high society, places of beauty, awe, and human renowned brilliance. We experienced New York.

A VERY GOOD JEWELER

And this you will feel:
nice, very nice, like an ice cream cone, vanilla
sprinkled with chocolate jimmies:
Something close to black and white because
this is what it is black and white.

And this you will do:
smile, a welcoming smile, like a crackling fireplace:
warm, inviting and untouchable because
this is what you are,
warm, inviting and untouchable.

And this you will be:
Givenchy, Ralph Lauren, Broadway—
something very upscale, metropolitan like
clicking Frye-boots prance past fallen rags lying
on the dirty sidewalk in the vapor of urine.

And this you will see:
nothing, nothing besides the polished shine of
your diamond roots.

And this you will say:
nothing, nothing about the sin—
the sin of being you.

And this you will know:
the rightness, the rightness of the beatings because,
it is black and white and
this is all that it is—
you will never be the right color,
never clear, but cut,
chiseled to a gem that refracts
a very good jeweler.

I THINK BACK to those times when my mother took the lot of us into the big city and I think my mother was a brave woman. She took the first 4 of us into New York City a lot. We were little kids, the youngest being perhaps 5 years old. There was no shortage of money so my mother had the financial go ahead to raise us into the adults she herself dreamed of being. We were to become perfect. We experienced the spectacle of "The Nutcracker", the gangs of "West Side Story", the tragedy of "The Man of La Mancha", and the comedy of "Annie Get Your Gun."

I remember the enormity of Lincoln Center the cold winter night I lost my hat. While exiting the theatre, descending the grand, bending staircase amid droves of theatre goers my mother said; "Susan, there is your hat!" We were edging down along the balcony and there it sat nestled in the rounded, wood swirl at the bottom of the great banister. Someone found it and placed it in the perfect outcrop. It was a colorful, French-knit cap. It was like spotting a cardinal in a pine tree.

My mother took us to Rockefeller Center to see the tree and the skaters every year. We walked the avenue of windows to see the moving decorations in Macy's, Saks Fifth Avenue, and all the store fronts that lined Fifth Avenue during the holiday season. We went to FAO Schwartz to see unimagined toys and stuffed animals too big to fit in the car let alone to dream of taking to our bedrooms. Every year we trekked to St. Patrick's Cathedral and sauntered with the throngs of people to see the crèche. Sometimes we'd get to light a candle. But since there was no one who had died, there was no one to pray for. We went to the Museum of Modern Art and took tours of tombs, jewelry, pottery, hieroglyphics, and the brilliant works of artists whose names I never could rightly pronounce. We went to the Museum of Natural History to see many different exhibits. When we came to the room where the most dangerous mammal of all time was kept we rushed in. When we couldn't locate the display my mother pointed it out. It was a mirror purposely distorted to make the onlooker appear bigger than he actually was.

When my father was present we went to big restaurants. We looked out over Central Park South from The Top of The Park. We ate in the décor of forestry at Tavern on the Green. We experienced gorging at Momma Leonie's. And we expanded our acquired taste buds at Sardis. We learned to put our napkins on our laps. We learned to sit straight, the proper holding of utensils, the quality of being low-spoken, and the dignity of sitting still. We learned how to act like the rich and famous without fortune or fame. My mother told us we could go anywhere if we knew how to act right. To nail all that learning home my mother only needed to dig apposing bright red fingernails into one of our pink thighs to bring us back to attention. My father only needed to look at us. If he raised his eyebrows you were sparring with death. We learned how to act *while* in public. We learned to dress like gentlemen and a lady.

The un-comfort-ability of patent-leather shoes, slippery on grit, a ruffled dress, and a coat that wasn't warm enough was part of the embellishment of femininity. I swayed between surrender to my lot and loathing for my unique discomfort. It felt pathetically ridiculous and absolutely unfair that I had to be made so helpless and immobile in a totally inadequate code-of-dress while my brothers wore warm pants, shoes with rubber treads, and pea coats. My family was my whole world. Anything that set me apart separated me from that world. I hated not fitting in so I could run with the clan. No one was helping me to see any benefit to what was a complete dilemma to me. My dilemma was the ostracized state of being a girl. In my whole world, that was the unending irreconcilable difference. I was like a puzzle piece that got dropped in the wrong box just before sealing it to ship to the store.

A Fat Yellow Flower

How do you think it feels
to be the dandelion?
Every time you stick your head out
someone grabs you by the neck and
rips you out of the ground as if
you can stop your roots from sucking
life out of mother earth.
From your core root you can't figure out
why it's not ok to be
a fat yellow flower
in the middle of a gazillion green blades.
So,
no matter how many times
you get torn by your neck from your stem
you just keep sprouting back.

4/24/08

Every year we spent the month of July at the Jersey Shore. At the age of 5 or 6 my mother figured out a way to get me into a bikini. I had been, up to that point, wearing a yellow and white striped boy's bathing suit and fitting, happily innocent, right in.

One boiling beach day, while my brothers and a group of little boys and myself were rolling in the sand at the water's edge she yelled, hey everyone! We all looked at her in anticipation of perhaps an Italian ice treat from the daily ice cream man. "You can see Susan's boobies! She has no top on!" I'm sure from the reaction it didn't occur to anyone I was a girl running topless and full of sand just like every boy on the beach. Everyone was pointing and laughing. I ran to my towel and waited in desperation for the attention to fade back into the sandy mess it arose from. I wore a bikini from that day forward. That July I kept myself separate from everyone as much as possible. It was the most comfortable choice.

My father worked Tuesday, Wednesday, and Thursday of each of the weeks we spent at the shore. He came down to the shore Thursday night and stayed until Monday morning when he drove back up to work in New York and sleep in our house in Bergen County.

My parents were hell raisers. They were young and beautiful. They were graced with the benefit of good health, money, and vivaciousness. They partied hard and were great entertainers. On weekends there were lots of steamers, corn on the cob, grilled beef, chicken, fish, and most of all there was lots of booze. They knew a lot of people who vacationed with their kids during the same month. We watched listened and learned from those raucous, sloppy adults until the wee hours of the morning when they would finally stumble on the stones between the houses back to their own rentals. Occasionally we'd come down and find one passed out on the couch or the floor souring the fresh salt-air-breeze of the morning.

We'd be trudging down to eat cheerios and find out what our morning chores were. We each got a daily chore on a month-of-July calendar that rotated equally across the five weeks of the month; Hose the cars. Rake the rocks. Wash the dishes. Dry the dishes. Vacuum. Clean the bathrooms. Sweep the patio.

We were not quiet by nature but when there was a big sunburned, sweaty, smelly man snoring in our daily short lived cartoon space we dropped a couple of pots, by accident of course, and started the vacuum early. Sure enough my father would come bounding out of his room in his jockey's and slug whoever was vacuuming with his clenched fist while he yanked the machine into silence and blurted; "Not before 8!" Whoever got punched was crying so we'd all get thrown out. This was complicated. Things just don't work like a clock. You'd think we'd be free to head for the beach but it wasn't that simple. We were still in our pajamas. We weren't allowed to leave them anywhere or there would be another beating coming our way. We had to leave them in our drawers, folded. So, we couldn't just pull our bathing suits off the line and change in the outdoor shower. Though my brother C would hide his throw-offs behind the chairs in the cupboard under the house. He'd inevitably get caught and whipped. The whippings didn't seem to stop us from trying to get away with mischievousness. We just got more inventive with our strategies at doing whatever we thought up. The other dangers of just leaving for the beach were we had to do our chores every day before we disappeared and we weren't allowed to leave without permission. Everything was checked before we were set free. Any way we moved in error brought on punishment determined by the parent who was giving punishments out at that moment. We had to wait. It was a recurring morning start to be stopped. But it made us *want* to go to the beach. The beach was a hell of its own. Once we emerged over the dune we were to remain between that desert-hot mound and the ocean from 9am until 3pm with a 45 minute lunch break. We were allowed to cool our feet while we made, ate and cleaned up every crumb of what we could chow down. We were being timed. My mother would be back to pull out one of my father's belts and beat us if we broke into playing and laughter that took us overtime. She'd sneak in and be upon us before we could run out the back or front door to a short lived escape. Any escape was worth trying. She made sure we didn't get one.

As for the occasional overnight crasher, as soon as that grizzly bear rumbled out the front door, supposedly saving face, my father would unlatch the back door. "Let's go!" He'd growl like we were convicts who should be fed mud for their wrong doings. "If your chores are done, get your suits on. Get what you want for the beach. Whatever you bring you are carrying home so don't take too much or you'll be making two trips later." It was a joyful and lively rental we filled.

Sometimes after lunch we'd see that burnt bear up at the beach. My father and him would be tossing a football back and forth, laughing about how much fun they had the night before and warming up for the night ahead.

Everyone visited us at the shore. Grandparents, aunts, uncles, cousins, and friends were all invited at different times. The one time I was allowed to invite a friend we fought the whole week she was there. The other friend I had when we were on vacation was my cousin. She and my aunt and uncle often rented at the same time. Her father and my father drank together into complete idiocy. They had a lot of fun. My mother and aunt weren't far behind but they upheld a woman's composure.

One night while the adults were doing hand-stands in the living room me and my brothers were up on the roof throwing packs of firecrackers on the windshields of passing cars. We threw those sparking mini hand grenades until we got a bull's-eye. Then we were down the steps and out the back door running between houses for a couple of blocks only stopping to laugh hysterically when we were good and safe. We were well groomed hell raisers. My parents were doing a great job of making us well rounded.

There was a cottage a couple of blocks down that had a detached garage with an unlocked door and a refrigerator filled to the brim with cases of beer. Some older kids found it and the information of such a treasure zipped through the alleyways like a racing river in spring. We'd slink in and snatch a six pack then race through backyards to the beach. We sat under the lifeguards' overturned boat. There were usually three of us. C, Scot Lance, and I got loose on 2 beers each. We were ten years old. Scot was a friend of mine who became my brother's friend as we got older mostly because my mother had forbidden me to play with him or C for that matter. If I wasn't breaking rules running with them I was with my other brother P and his friend PR riding bikes or playing some sand game in the cool evening dunes. If neither of them were around and my cousin N was down, I'd go out with her. But, she was five years older than me so I couldn't always go with her. She had a friend named Beverly who sometimes babysat for us when my parents went out. N and Beverly liked the lifeguards. N told me one night that Beverly was very excited because the lifeguard gave her five fingers. I was sworn to secrecy. I had no idea what she was talking about. I only was sure N envied her friend and when I understood I would envy her too.

The endless memories can go on endlessly. Time doesn't wait. Childhood happens like the engaging of one drum after another until so many drums are pounding at once it is either the sound of music bringing the listener into its inevitable crescendo forming a clarity of rhythm that can be tapped to or it becomes a tumultuous rampage of bangs that drives that listener into a deafening chaos of sound that leaves them on a battlefield completely disoriented and so incapable of defense. I bring you, momentarily, to the other side of a year.

Five Brothers (A Tribute)

Before I can see over a countertop
Knee deep in grass
I wish the sun to cut my shadow differently.
All I want to wear is the robes of Princes. But not one fits.

One covers a brick mansion with rooms I never will see.
This tree of knowledge imparts generously his wisdom to me.
Always a warm hand, like a father's touch, he protects me.

One covers a silent impression, secret to a woman's eye but
impossible to conceal like
trying to contain an ocean in the depth of a sea.
A tempest, muted, bestows bunches of roses thrown across
a light breeze. Red bursts hot in waves of emotional wheat.

One drapes a giant who is driven like
a train a railroad cannot contain, who carries my dream.
Breathes my air as easy as a gush swells a swollen stream.

One warms a bear who is like smoke from a mountainside.
He is undeniable amongst the trees. Keeps a well stoked
flame licking the dark out of night.
Lets me sleep when
there is no time to sleep.

One decorates the likes of a monsoon breeze.
This prince is the tensor lamp on my shrouded spirit.
A man with the fire of a utopian, the palm of
a philanthropist in the cloak of novice dream.

The counter shrinks short or I grow tall.
The grass is below my knees.
I see.
I've no desire to wear the robe of anyone of these.
Smoke rises from the glass top lake. The reflection

is unveiled. Heaven's plan is cast before my feet.
I drop to my knees, shamelessly concede
I have, from each, born of their bonded reverie,
a gold-star-tipped garner tied loose to me.
Princes they are!
And Five!
My God
My God
You must treasure me!

When I turned eleven years old something wonderful happened. My mother had another baby. That made six of us. I'll never forget my father coming in my room in the hours before dawn when those final two babies were born. He leaned over my bed. In a warm whisper he'd say; "Sue, guess what it is?" With the hope it was what he wanted I'd say; "A girl?" And my father whispered again: "Another boy." Neither of us knowing we were both relieved, I asked what the baby's name was. On this last one my mother couldn't decide so my newest brother had my mother's name to start.

I never had a room to myself. My older brother was the only one with enough qualification to get that. Born on my father's birthday, this baby was the apple of my father's eye and my mother's baby boy. J was my last roommate while I lived in my parents' house. We were roommates until I left for college. I was expected to take care of him like he was the king's gold. I wanted to.

The family gathered around when the new baby came home. We all wanted to hold him. Taking care of the baby was the first chore I actually wanted *and* got dibs to. J was born in March so when July came along he was just 4 months old. My mother reasoned: In all the years, so far, that we had spent July at the jersey shore, I never made one friend. It never became un-appalling to my mother that I only wanted to hang out with my brothers. She insisted there was something terribly wrong with me for wanting to always be with them and to have utterly no interest in making friends with the girls. It was clear to me. I hated girls. I loved the boys. How would she know how much fun they were?

I was too old to be allowed to keep spending time with them. It could only mean badness when girls hang out with boys. I always wondered what the heck she was talking about. We all loved each other, protected each other, and had fun together. I couldn't understand why I wasn't permitted to go where they went. I knew where they went. It was no more dangerous for them than it was for me. I was deeply gouged by this forced separation. I had a resentment like an abscessed tooth against my mother for her ungrounded conclusion that I had some inherent fault of mind for my insistence to choose my brothers and their friends as my comrades.

I was sorely tired of being ridiculed, grounded, and punished by some form of embarrassment for wanting this choice of relationships. When the remedy became, you will be the babysitter for the two babies, PJ who was 5, and J who was four months, I had no re-course but to babysit. So, my parents and my first four brothers went out, partied and did what they do and I stayed home and watched the little ones.

In the morning, after my chores were done, I was to prep the little ones for the beach and take them up there at 9am. My mother usually showed up an hour or two later. My favorite brother usually came with me. I don't know if he felt sorry for me or just loved me the way the rest of them didn't, but, he always was there to help me. He always supported me in my quandary. He always listened to my side. He always ran for me. He was the one who would just sit home with me when I'd be left alone and everyone else would take their freedom to the end of its rope. He'd say to me, when no one heard him; "I'll stay with you Sue." I wouldn't say anything in reply. He knew how deep in my heart he sat and I guess that mattered to him. I Thanked God whoever or whatever that horrible thing was, that I wasn't completely alone no matter how my mother tried to make it that way for me. My brother P and I had a closeness my mother could not rip apart no matter how she tried. That was because P wouldn't allow it. If he hadn't stood strong I would have let the undertow pull me away from him like it had from the others, hoping I wouldn't have to hold my neck above water for too much longer. P was my one string to the possibility I was sane. One more thread snap and the chasm of Black Ocean where I dreamed of the release of drowning would have taken me and swept me into its reality before I met with my teenage years

For P's friendship he was assigned to carry the umbrella and crib to contain and cover the baby. He dutifully carried out his role. He hung around until my mother showed up. Then he ran over the dune and disappeared to play with his friend of the same name, PR. If P slept over PR's house C was assigned to carry the baby supplies to the beach. I'd walk up alone and find where he left everything in an easily identifiable pile and set it up on my own. C would do the chore unseen and never heard from.

My older brother S was there but I only know that from seeing family pictures. He was like the family ghost. A shadowy thing that would lead a game of beach football until someone got hurt and was screaming then he'd fade into the landscape. I can't tell you what he did. I can only say he didn't do it with us. I perceived him to have a general loathing for all of us. We were like the cave dwellers he had to live with long enough to be fed until he got big enough to leave. He was unnoticeable. Everyone paid him no mind, everyone except grandpa J but, I'll tell you about that later.

When my mother came to the beach she was covered in sun block and a big brimmed hat. She wore gigantic sunglasses. I always remember her glopping on lipstick then pursing her lips to make the high-cheek-bone look. She came with her chair, towel, and bag of goodies. She was a beautiful woman. As she approached I took a pausing glance as I made my conclusion: Beautiful women are mean. In the bag were cool fruit, water, lotions, magazines, a newspaper, and her book. I would get relief from watching my brothers but I wasn't free to leave. My mother came to the beach to *not* be disturbed. She wanted no talking to her. She wanted to read her book. My father was much the same when he arrived though he'd take us for a swim on his back in the ocean and have a catch with the football, baseball, or Frisbee. We all liked going for walks. Sometimes I'd get to go if someone stayed with the babies. C would show back up skimming the beach on a board, riding waves on his belly or a raft, digging up sand-crabs and slinging them at someone's back, playing cowboys or army in the dunes, or sneaking back to the house to drink cold soda and eat forbidden Oreos. He was always good for getting right to the cliff's edge of disaster. He had a devilish and interminable well of ideas in his boyish mind. He was fun. The problem was the fruition of his ideas, far too often, lead to a very painful beating from the latest tool my parents had found. But I'd go anyway. We'd run off the beach and down the block to play tetherball on a neighbors front gravel until we were called away from it. We were kids in the days when beating your kids was not only not illegal it was condoned. We left the beach early and we got the strap, the spoon, or the paddle. We were beaten until we thought our arm or leg was broken. We stood in line to get it.

We were the last of the baby boomers. We grew up behind the flower children of the Vietnam War, The Grateful Dead, Crosby Stills Nash and Young. Great political upheavals we could not understand took place in front of our footsteps. Behind that we set our opinions based on our experience. It would not be the same for our children. None of us had a clear thought on that. Each of us lived it out.

I clearly remember the day President Kennedy was shot. I was playing across the street with a kid named Kenny who had muscular dystrophy. My mother called us home. She was lying on the couch crying. That was unfathomable. I was five years old. We grew up in a time, as always, of great human change. I can only hope it is not one big circle we are going to keep running back around over and over and over forever.

So, when we were caught off the beach, we were punched or beaten with a hard object until we writhed and screamed in pain. Did we stop running off the beach? No. We always looked to the times we didn't get caught. I recall the year my parents found the boat paddle. I think it was a little unwieldy for them. It didn't hurt as much as some other objects they used. The worst thing my mother found was a black rubber hose. That was an eighteen inch piece of hard black rubber pipe that gave a particularly stinging whap. It left bright red welts on our pink thighs. We were beaten with these weapons until we disposed of them. The paddle and the black hose just disappeared. My parents didn't pursue questioning on such disappearances. They knew we'd never, never tell. One good thing about having brothers is there is no tattle tale. We'd all just sit at that kitchen table being interrogated, knowing who the guilty party was and no one would tell. We all got a turn at being guilty and keeping the secret. It was well worth the unified front, even if we all got punished. It was always worse to be beaten alone. Then you really got it. You'd get one whipping for the crime and a second beating to teach every one watching the lesson.

Long Beach Island is an 18 mile strip of beach land that lies between the Atlantic Ocean and a relatively narrow waterway named Barnegat Bay. Back in the late 1960's and early 1970's the highways that run the length of the island were mere side paths compared to what they are today. The main highway running the island was a rural two way road. There were few traffic lights and no crosswalks. A person could see the bay from the ocean side of the island. If it wasn't for the dunes a person could see the ocean from the bayside.

My parents always rented a house on the beach side. We rented four houses down from the beach on Old Whaling Lane for many years. We were only permitted to go out toward the beach and the rule of staying on the beach for the entire day held with the permit to leave for lunch and come right back unless my mother brought lunch to the beach for us. Then we were not allowed off the beach all day, no breaks. For us kids it was an impossible regimen to follow. It was downright torture. We were supposed to be grateful for our vacation. It was, to us, like being cast naked in the desert for a month and while our pale white skin scorched, blistered and fried into freckled tans we were expected to be happy about it. If my parents wanted a vacation from us, they should have just gone away instead of controlling us as they insisted for that grueling month they kept insanely insisting was pleasurable. I think the only one who got pleasure out of it was my father. He got four days a week in complete solitude from us for an entire month. Years later my mother told how much *she* hated that vacation.

My place as the babysitter was like being assigned open-sun chair duty in the Mohave Desert. When my parents went for a walk or swim I was assigned to watch the babies. J was confined to his crib but PJ was a wild little boy, scampering toward the ocean every chance he got. He was fearless and I was dead if he was seen too far from my reach. In the wink of an eye he'd be no bigger than my thumbnail away from me. Horrified, I'd tear down the beach to grab him when, on occasion, I'd be slammed on the back of my head. Lightning and thunder are shocking delivered with a grown man's fist on a cloudless day on the ocean's edge. I'd lose my footing but I wouldn't fall. I learned to curse without the slightest expression. "Go get him!" my father would mutter. I'd quicken my pace more to get away from him than to corral PJ.

One day, the three of us, C, P, and me decided we were going to cross the forbidden roads and check out the bay. It was the middle of the week. My father was up in N.Y.C. working and my mother was some place. The bay was exciting. A person could go right in up to their waist and not have to expend any energy watching for the inevitable wave that so often sent them swirling, knees hitting the sandy-shell bottom, bathing suit being swooshed with salty seawater-sand. The bay was full of ocean life. We caught as much as we could and put all our little creatures in a big tub filled with salt water. We swooshed the seawater with our hands to make it life like for its new inhabitants. We caught minnows, hermit crabs, eels, horse shoe crabs, and even a small sting ray. The kid next door was bigger than us. He helped us carry our big catch home. We kept it at his house because it was gathered from a forbidden place and the tub, after all, was his. It was really cool to squat around our little terrarium and watch all the sea animals. We were so excited we told our mother. All she was interested in was the fact that we crossed the road to get to the bay. That was the last boat-paddling. We were so beaten with that paddle, we were all filled with a vengeance. As soon as we got a chance that paddle went for a last sighting, floating away in that forbidden bay. We continued to be mischievous kids. We continued to get the daylights beaten out of us. In those days there was no Ritalin or Paxil and there was no calmness in a normal child. We were wild, unruly, and stricken with short attention spans and negligible memory. We learned to sit still. We learned orderliness. We learned to pay attention. We learned to remember. We learned discipline and punishment. We learned wonderment and amazement. We learned penance and atonement. We were brought up in the late 60's and early 70's, the last of the baby-boomer Catholics.

It had always been my fault when rules were broken. For some reason I was supposed to know more. I didn't and that made me somehow deranged from whatever the heck normal was. My mother did not want me playing with my brothers. As far back as I can recall, I was dirty and had the capacity somehow to spoil their inherent Godliness if I got near them. As a result there was a constant pulling sensation in my solar plexus. My mother's insistence of this apparent fact made no sense to me. What it did was fill that black suction vault in my chest with defensive rage. It was heart wrenching. I was beaten and grounded regularly for crossing my mother's line but it never stopped me from continuing to push to hang out with my brothers. I loved them. They were my best friends, my confidents, and my co-conspirators. My mother insisted I find little girls to play with. I was deathly afraid of that prospect. My experience with girls was, they gang up, whisper and run away laughing. They were not going to get a chance. My mother would walk over to a strange group of girls on the beach and ask them to come talk to me. I'd be mortified. One time she gave them our address. In the late afternoon there was a ring at the front door and she called me downstairs. I came down the stairs and there they were. I was horrified! My mother told me to *get out*, berating me right in front of them. I sunk into despair. Then she said; *if you won't go out then go to your room*. As I climbed the stairs to solitude I heard her apologizing to the little girls and telling them I was a weirdo. Then she clomped up the stairs and laid into me about how I must have some kind of a mental problem, how I was a freak, and how I was not going to spend my life hanging out with my brothers so I better make some friends. My mother told me *boys don't want to be friends with girls. They don't want you with them.* With sly eyes I looked straight at her and knew she was a liar. My brothers never acted like that, especially P. P would do anything for me. He even sat home with me nights when everyone went out and I was assigned to babysit which happened almost every night, at least every weekend night. I still hear the echo of his voice. He'd say, in a low whisper; *I'll stay with you Sue.* Thank God for P.

DAUGHTER

They worried. Looked at me with that
off-center look, trying not to be
so obvious. They had no idea when they
opened the gate I'd run out into
that yellow field. Keep going until
I was a dot they'd never reach. They
never figured I'd throw away my
clothes, lose my virginity to the unspeakable.
They never imagined I'd home under
a highway bridge. Girl becomes Troll.
Lost language bled between ovulations.
I became the unidentifiable object living
in their house, casting beams of light on
missed cobwebs, unlocking closets of decay,
hanging mirrors of conspicuous horror.
When I finally scared myself enough, even
the snuff of weeds, tables of pills, oceans of
brandy couldn't reach deep enough to drown my
heart in the vomit. I let them leash me. Send me
out of sight. Save their name from attachment to
a story like suicide.
They sent me to a place that was a holding chamber
to acclimate me to a life outside of Hell.
Twenty-five years later they worry. Look at me with
that off-center look, trying not to be so obvious.
Still unidentifiable to them, I just play the part,
the daughter they can't see who escaped the cobwebs,
the closets and faced the horror in the mirror.

That became my vacation; babysitting. My mother reasoned, since you refuse to make friends and you're *not* going out with your brothers you can babysit. My responsibility quadrupled with the birth of J. So when my parents and whatever friends of theirs were down at the time went out to some sandy-beach club to get sloshed and my brothers ran off somewhere in the looming summer dusk, I sat home with little PJ and J and sometimes P and watched T.V. until I discovered something much better to do.

My parents were big into screwdrivers. There were always a couple half gallons of Wolfschmidt vodka on the counter-top and quarts of orange juice in the refrigerator. When everyone went out I found that mixing me one of these concoctions was better than any movie, or any game. It wasn't long after discovering this treasure trove of serenity that I waited in excited anticipation for everyone to get out. I started to drink whenever they went out. It greatly enhanced my imprisonment at the shore. I looked forward to my imposed isolation. This enhancement was to become untouchable. A refuge for the heart is never easily torn down or ripped away. I had discovered one.

The morning after my parent's night out howling, my mother was in the bathroom puking and my father was a raging bull. While these mornings had once been a black-cloud-thunderstorm I now, didn't care. I now had a reward worth waiting for. With each speculation of them going out an excited tingle ran in place of the incessant pull in my chest. I didn't need anyone.

There is only one time I recall vomiting the morning after from my drinking. My mother pounded up the stairs and asked; *what are you doing? I said; I'm throwing up. She said; you are disgusting, and went back down stairs.* She never said another word. My mother never wanted to be inconvenienced. I had always been a very inconvenient child. She had no time for whatever was going on with me. I was twelve years old.

The Whistle

My Grandmother, where my roots cling from to reach for the sky,
doesn't like to read my poetry. She says there is too much night.
Asks me about all the daisies that bloomed, the sun that shined
on their faces, the little blonde doll who played in them in a
frilly dress at Easter.
I run through my doll collection. Try to remember
which one she is referring to.
The echo of her melodious whistle annunciates her thrill of
spending her time toiling to fill our table with a cornucopia from
garden to livestock to bakery—Hot, cold or perfectly tepid.
The scrub-up of all those pots, pans, dishes, glasses and mugs
never gives rise to a change in the tone of her whistle.
Being first generation of her first offspring, I should pick up
where her tune drops off. Problem is
I can't remember the doll.
I remember my favorite high-lace farm boots with the deep
tread I only get to wear when I visit my grandparents' farm.
I remember holding the wheel to the tractor that vibrates like
a tire on a loose axle while my grandfather spreads manure and
dodging hay bales he kicks at whoever is stacking in the wagon.
I still hear his giggle when he squares me on the back with one, his
shoulders shaking up and down. I remember icy, crisp, moonlit
nights firing up through mountain chutes, deafening the forest with
snowmobile engines. I remember diving tackles in hay pretending to
play big league football and finding whole litters of downy furred,
still blind kittens snuggled between barn floors.
The farm is my childhood sweet-grass. I just don't remember the
doll and I never whistle when I work in the kitchen.

9/19/02
SED

BEFORE I GET too far, there is another whole aspect of this time in my life I cannot leave out. This was the best of childhood so voted unanimously by all. S claims it saved his life. P claims grandpa J imparted to him every bit of integrity he has. C agrees it was our childhood sweet-grass. PJ and J were a bit too young to fully understand the immensity of its importance in our rounding into adults.

My father's parents, my grandparents owned a two-hundred-sixty-eight acre farm in upstate New York. On that farm, my grandfather taught us, each in our own way, we could do anything. That was the perfect dichotomy of what we were taught at home which was we were a lot of dopes. My grandfather could build or fix anything. When we were with him we built or fixed whatever it was he was building or fixing with him. We worked like leathered farm hands. When we worked we were rewarded with huge, hot, delicious meals with more fixings than we could swallow. My grandmother was an un-tiring, un-endingly jovial, feverish cook. The house was always wafting with delicious aromas. When she wasn't cooking a meal there was always something simmering on the stove.

During the summer when we were all out in the frying sun of a freshly hayed field loading those bales of hay onto the back of the perfectly running jalopy hay-truck my grandfather kept in smooth running order, my grandmother would be the one inching up and down the rows as we picked-up, tossed, stacked, and picked-up those hundreds of bales waiting for us. When the truck was filled to its max, we'd all hop on the back and head for the barn to unload and stack it there for the winter supply. The bales had to be stacked tight so a person could walk across it without slipping a foot in a crack while stacking the next level up. In the end it was two full floors of hay. I was never a stacker. That job fell to my grandfather or the next biggest man available.

Every day at noon we'd all head down to the front porch of the house for a choice of favorite cola for the kids and beer for the men. We'd eat fresh, hot baked bread with butter, kielbasa with sauerkraut, homemade pickles or sandwiches made with fresh cold cuts and cheese. There were corn chips or potato chips. There was a variety of salads. We ate until we were stuffed. Then we rested for awhile before heading out for the second half of our work day in the field. It was a time of great bonding, love, and family togetherness.

Grandma had a way of making me want to help her. I took pride in helping her serve everyone. It was so different than the way I felt being forced to serve for my mother at home. The same process can appear so different in a different world. The farm was our other world. Grandma always called me Suzie. I loved that. She was always whistling. I practiced my whistling in private. I couldn't whistle like grandma, not yet, I thought, anyway. Grandma loved everyone, even me. I was never separated. With grandma I was one of the kids. I loved that inclusion. During those lunches as one we laughed, talked, and waved to the occasional passing car. The people in the car always waved back.

I recall one lunch C said; *Sue, watch this!* He made a cup of water with his hands and held them out. A humming bird flew over and hovered right at his hands brink and drank from his little well. Another time two chipmunks ran right up one of his arms, across his shoulders, behind his head and right down his other arm as he sat in the grass. C said; *did you see that?!* P and I said; *yeah! That must be why you got the name Chip.* C was always bringing creatures home. He could go out and find dozens of salamanders. One time he caught forty frogs. Little did we know he was taking them home to NJ to feed them to the eleven snakes he had previously found and brought home. He later let the snakes go because he ran out of frogs to feed them. When a neighbor three houses down found a three foot garter snake in his garage it was said to be ten feet long and C was accused of endangering the neighborhood with poisonous snakes.

We played as hard as we worked. The missing division between my brothers and me made the farm a place of perfect refuge. I loved going there especially if my parents weren't there. When they were absent, there was no pulling sensation at all. I felt like the world was right and I was right in it. My grandmother kept cool farm boots and gloves for each of us. I loved wearing that cool stuff. There was no dress code I had to follow alone. I was unquestioningly allowed to run with the boys.

Another special thing my grandmother had was a certain bottom drawer filled with Russel Stover candies. We would sit together in a semi-circle and press our thumbs into the bottom of every single one of them to find all of the caramels. Then we'd wipe them all out. Grandma would tell us not to do it but, we never stopped and we always found a fresh box in that drawer when we went back.

Grandma took us into town and we'd each get a cowboy pistol and holster. Oh, how we loved to play Butch Cassidy and The Sundance Kid. There were plenty of mountains, shallow caves, outcrop rocks, woods, and dirt paths to tramp and slither around on. We had the barn and all of its hidden coves and chutes. Our childlike imaginations ran rampant up there and grandma never put a dent in it. She just let us rip. My grandfather let us shoot cans with his 22 rifle. We drove the tractor, the farm truck, the snowmobiles, and a mini bike up in the fields.

One day my grandfather had us all climb into the back of his pickup truck. He loved doing that. He'd zoom up the bumpy, dirt roads leaving a cloud of dust in the air while we'd hang on for dear life. We could hear him giggling, getting a kick out of us hitting the deck in the back all laughing and occasionally shrieking. He was taking us blackberry picking. He loved grandmother's blackberry preserves. Grandma gave each of us an empty, gallon milk container with the top cut off. We bounded off to a property that was bursting with those sweet berries. Grandpa zipped off the road into the ruff, bump embedded field far enough to conceal the truck. We all jumped out and picked as fast as we could. We were trespassing. In no more than ten minutes we had enough for days of cereal bowls topped with berries and jars of left-over's to be cooked and sealed into preserves. It was very exciting. I loved everyone doing things together.

The next morning grandpa and S were the first ones to adorn their cereal with those scrumptious berries. They were quickly followed by P. Soon after the first mouth full S spotted a worm wiggling out of one of the berries, then another, and another. He screamed; *there are worms in the berries!* Everyone freaked out. Grandpa did that shoulder giggle he did and said; *aawwh, it's just a little protein. They won't hurt you.* Grandpa ate three bowls of cereal that morning. It was better than wasting all that food. We all skipped the berries. There was plenty of other breakfast fare to choose from. While we ate we were washed in the God-like image of grandpa accepting yet another incredible undertaking. He ate ALL those worms like they tasted delicious. And there was never to be any after affect on his herculean physique.

His Glove

When we were little, my grandfather
used to burn fields. We all formed a
circle around the fire so it wouldn't spread.
All the hair on our arms was singed into
white filament curls even though the flames
never rose above our ankles because it was
only grass he burned.
Somehow it made the crop richer.
He was always making things richer.
He sprayed cow manure on everything, even
grandma's vegetable garden. We all grew
up strong and everything always plumped green.

By far the richest fertilizers he spread were
his tireless work ethic, his steely honesty, his
iron cased integrity and his belief;
We could do anything.
Grandpa enriched us with these by giving
his heart that surrounded each of us like
the hand of his glove.

10/9/02
SED

No MAN HAS ever come close to the admiration I have for grandpa J. If the definition of integrity could be personified it would be grandpa J. Grandpa had a saying; *"Hard work was never easy."* We all still say it today, some forty years later. He was a man that made you want to work and work hard. He and grandma were a perfect team. She ran the house and he ran the farm. Their overlapping roles made for a virtual absence of resentment for having to do anything. Everyone was on the team.

One time when I was up there in the deep freeze of winter at 6am I was called to go out to the barn with grandpa. It was about—5 degrees. The snow banks were piled ten feet high along the sides of the road. The stream was frozen solid. The barn was a warm 25 degrees. The heat emission from sixty-three cows was the source of difference from the inside and the outside air. All of the intermingled breaths put a constant low billowing warm vapor into the air. The chains rustled and a couple of low moans rumbled down the long rows of shuffling hooves when the few bare light bulbs sparked illumination against the long shadows yet an hour before dawn. Grandpa had a Bunsen burner and we went out to defrost the pipes so the water troughs could fill. Those cows all stood over their little steel bowls. They knew what was coming. Their hooves chafed at the cement floor. They couldn't wait. I was always so hungry when I did the morning chores before breakfast with grandpa but it was well worth the hunger pangs. I loved that he let me do these fix-it projects with him. It made me feel important and smart and useful. He always made me feel proud too.

By the time we got the water running I was frozen and starving. Grandpa always made you feel like a champ. I loved the feeling of cold hunger. It was value.

After breakfast I shoveled the manure out from under those sixty-three cows. Inevitably as I was scraping the barn floor clean a cow would raise its tail right over my head and release a fresh, sweet pod right on the hoe. If the steamy pile splashed me as it splattered the floor I didn't care. Grandpa always came in for lunch splattered with cow poop. If there was anyone I wanted to be like, anyone who I admired, it was grandpa.

There was no division between boys and girls. The same expectation spread across all of us. The hardest workers on the land were "The Green

Girls." They were a corn fed crop of farm girls stronger than any boy who dared to test their strength. They never whimpered. They worked harder than anyone grandpa ever met. He held a rock hard respect for them for that. That was quite a mark to hold. They were bigger than any of us. We were scared of them. They always came on nice but as soon as they got us alone they'd tickle us until we cried. The Greens had a dairy farm. Grandma bought milk and eggs from them. They had a huge, smelly chicken coop. They also had rabbits and pigs. I remember there were no carpets in their house, nor were there any finished walls. The inside was just a slice cleaner than the chicken coop. There were hundreds of egg crates stacked all over the living room and kitchen. They were very good friends of my grandparents. The girls were my grandfather's best hired help.

One day one of my brothers and I went to the Greens farm with grandpa. It was the sub zero dead of winter and their truck wouldn't start. The wind was cutting like a razor to add to the unbearable icy air. Grandpa worked on that engine for over an hour without gloves on. I'll never forget his hands. They were like big rocks with fingers. I don't know how he could move them. When he scraped his knuckles the blood would freeze as it hit the surface of his leather-glove like skin. It was too cold for them to bleed. Everyone stood around hopping up off their toes to keep their feet from getting frostbite, banging their mittens against opposite arms to force heat into their hands and switching back and forth from standing rigged and shivering. The way he worked it was as if it wasn't even cold out. Everyone was at the ready, waiting to be of help.

When grandpa asked you to do something you were glad he asked. It made you feel proud that he trusted you could do it. And it didn't matter what it was. It could be, get me the Phillips-head, and you jumped for it. You were, for that moment, a hero because you could do it. Everything was noteworthy to grandpa. No one was better than anyone else except, all lazy people were not to have any energy wasted on them. The rest of us got his praise which we all savored. Grandpa got that truck running. I wanted hands like grandpa.

In the spring we opened clogged waterways, tilled the garden, and spring cleaned. One particularly burdensome job grandpa gave us was to pick the rocks up out of the field. He'd park his front end loader tractor out in a spot in the field, drop the bucket on the ground and tell us to fill it with all the rocks we could find. It was an endless and un-gratifying job. You couldn't see any difference after hours of filling buckets grandpa would carry away, dump and return empty to fill again. C usually disappeared, if not immediately, very soon after. Grandpa always knew when the bucket was full. He probably saw us starting to stray. We would never tell him the bucket is full. He'd show up right on time, empty it and move us to a new location. The one fun part was we'd get to climb onto the top of the bucket of rocks and grandpa would raise it all the way up and give us a ride to the dumping spot, which was usually one of the endless holes he wanted to fill. Then we'd bump and bounce up to our new picking area. Grandpa never said anything to anyone who disappeared from any job. At dinner time is when he got his word in. To the ones who worked he'd tell what a good job they did. Grandma would go along with the praise. He'd ask them if they wanted seconds because they must be hungry after all that good hard work. Grandpa would serve the seconds to their plate. To the ones who disappeared he'd say nothing. On the occasions I didn't work with grandpa, I hated the second serving part of dinner. I once asked C if it bothered him. He said he didn't care. He said he'd rather flip rocks to find salamanders than flip them, endlessly, into a bucket just for a little praise.

Summer brought back haying season. The fall brought school. The only one who spent virtually every weekend of his growing years at the farm with grandpa and grandma was S. He still swears to its immeasurable importance in his success. The rest of the first four of us, or the first family as my two younger brothers came to refer to us as, were much less fortunate for having missed what S got.

In the fall was wood chopping. The big event was Thanksgiving. Our big family, my aunt, uncle, and cousin, my other grandparents, and my great grandparents, along with some burly hunters who slept on cots in the basement came together at the farm for Thanksgiving. Everyone in the family took a part in the gathering, chopping, loading, hauling, and stacking of the winter's wood supply. It was a lot of fun having everyone out in the cold muddy field working together. Those days were grand.

On thanksgiving in 1969, PJ was three years old. We drove up Thanksgiving morning, seven of us, in the station wagon. It was the year of Woodstock. It was the year of the blizzard. Usually it took two and one half to three hours to get to the farm. That Thanksgiving it took us twelve hours. There were twenty car pile-ups, one slamming into the next into the next, all the way up the NY State Throughway. It was a blinding snow storm. The roads were a sheet of ice. Once my father committed himself there was no turning back. At one point we sat stranded with the thousands of other cars, for three hours. My mother occupied us with map games like "name the capitol" or guessing games like "animal, vegetable, or mineral." She fed us raw Thomas's English muffins.

The farm was about four miles in on a dirt road. My father had gotten off the highway to call grandpa. Grandpa told him, don't take Goddard Pass, a dangerous and beautiful road grandpa nicknamed after a road he traveled in Switzerland. Grandpa advised us to take the low roads and call him when we got to Downsville, a town about a thirty minute drive from the house in good weather. My father dutifully followed direction.

It was all timing. At the call grandpa left the house and drove to the end of his road. He plowed his way down to the bottom and was waiting there to plow a path for us back up to the house. There he was like a lighthouse in a fog swallowed, rock jutted inlet. We would get home safe. S jumped right in the truck with him. Grandpa had a steel door laid in the back of his pick-up and chains on the tires. Nothing was going to stop his plow. The path grandpa broke on his way down was completely obliterated. He plowed the way open in front of us.

We were the arrival of a huge caravan into a quietly waiting, fire warmed abode on a bristling cold, fiercely snowing, blustery night. We were excitedly welcomed. We made it. We had missed Thanksgiving but grandma had removed that splendid cornucopia to present it just as superbly on the following day. Instead, the table was filled with salads, hot, fresh bread, fresh cold cuts, and some hot cheese and vegetable platters including a fresh made, steaming lasagna. Everyone ate. While we ate grandpa disappeared and very soon, out on the front lawn, was heard the sound of snowmobiles warming up.

The snow had stopped. The sky was miraculously cleared to a million winking lights you could only spy from the black dome of the farm. The moon knifed long streaks of its sun-reflection through the trees and painted swathes of luminescence across the open fields of pristine, sparkling, unscathed mantels falling away and rising again into unbroken glens and monstrous hills all rolled smooth as frosted-milk-glass over the craggy earth that hid beneath. It was spectacular. Everyone was together in great joy for the momentous event of the evening after a most treacherous day on the road. It was eleven o'clock at night and with full bellies; we took turns cutting trails, flailing snow in billowing fluffs out from under the whirling tread as we held the throttle full open ripping out across the field, up the side of the mountain, across the top, down the chute airborne for a few feet before re-gripping the freshly laid white velvet and ripping scar upon scar deep into that unblemished space. The treasure of sublime silence was instantly lost. We were wild.

When my father and uncle got together they were madmen. We could hear them, way up on the top field, their voices rising up over the engines. My mother's mother lived in Jersey City. She had taken the bus from The Port Authority the preceding day. She was as enthralled with the events as each one of us was. My father tore up to a stop in front of us and yelled; *Ma! Hop on!* His own mother would have declined. I declined. Their minds were too washed in the hard stuff to still manage enough sanity to deem them trustworthy of their own well being let alone anyone else's. Grandma R got on. Off they flew to the top of the mountain, through the chute jump. My father ripped to the left, flipped the snowmobile and sent grandma sailing into the snow. They returned at a slower pace. Grandma got off a little bit dazed and completely thrilled. She had the experience of her life. She got a big shiner with a bump on her forehead. She loved it. None of us could believe it. She never could tell the people she worked with how she got that black eye. She said they'd never believe it. She could hardly believe it wasn't some fantastic dream come true. She spoke of that night for the rest of her days. We speak of it at family gatherings still.

The farm was every person's release. The men drank themselves into idiocy. The women did their share of partying too. The children were allowed looseness as well. There was no harm at the farm. The only rules were, no riding the snowmobiles on the huge, frozen pond grandpa had dug out. And no riding them on the roads. The silo was off limits and, when my parents were there I had to sleep on the far end of the house in an icy room called the back room. If there was a baby, he was my roommate. If my cousin was there she was my roommate. When my parents weren't there grandma saw no harm in letting me sleep up in the attic-dorm with my brothers. It was scary alone in the back room even with the baby. If my cousin wasn't there I had nightmares of the cows breaking in through the windows and isolating me, trying to get on the bed and trample me. I begged to go up in the attic but, if I cried too much I got whacked so I didn't push it. I just shut up and hated it.

Grandma M was an incredible woman. She was generous, always jovial, loving, reasonable, and very strict. It appeared she had an endless supply of energy and ideas to make everyone feel at home, satiated, and comfortable. When my mother was there I was expected to be by grandma's side helping with cooking, set up, and clean up. I wasn't allowed to play in the other room, watch football, or scoot out in the snow as my brothers were doing. Even my cousin didn't have to do anything. I felt like Cinderella though at the time I didn't know the story. I hated being my mother's daughter. There was no good place to be when she was around. I began to hide. I wanted to be unnoticed, forgotten would be great. I was as selfish as any other child my age and I was surrounded by them as siblings. I felt I was the one pointed out to have no rights to the inherent selfishness the rest of them relaxed in ignorance of. I had no understanding of grandma's immeasurable, unswerving good cheer. I was filled with resentment. I didn't want her job. I just wanted to play. It is interesting though, when I was alone with grandma, I did everything I could for her and I wanted to. It was when my mother was directing me that I became so inflamed. No family party was ever a party to me. It was a time to be on duty, to be the maid without hire.

None the less, the farm was everyone's childhood sweet-grass. In a childhood world hidden behind closed doors with mouths well trained to stay shut with the adage "don't wear your problems on your sleeve," with the dire implication that you shouldn't feel like you do, the physical emancipation allowed in that civilized wilderness exploded in an insane display of human frustration released. A spiritual hunger was met there, head on, and quenched forthright with the earth, the air, and the distance set between escape and reality. Each of us children met with that release. Each of us children returned to the reality of our life under the same two parents.

Like the palmer method, events sprawl out into circles of overlapping seasons that make up the characters in sentences of overlapping lives.

These early family memories are a conglomeration of events that coil over the course of the same several years. If years are laid flat like round dials on top of each other, everything that happens after everything else can happen before. It's all just one childhood.

Fly Trap

How do I know where to paste the landing pad
for the fly buzzing in my corner-less brain when
the womb from which I come displays love
by issuing orders of silence and disappearance?

How do I stop the buzzing sound when
the man who loves my mother comes home
after midnight drunk and fucked by some
she-hound who remains in my visual nightmare?

How do I sleep when the fly is joined by six more buzzing flies?
The crash of his college cup hitting a mirror in their
room makes the quiet of night a black dream.
A fitting introduction to proclaim his resolve
how he will never leave his castle.

How do I make sense of one hundred eyes making sense?
I'm told my hips are just right for babies. I wonder
why that's important. Why I'd want to create a life
with the expectation of sharing my bed
with someone generous enough to share his bed with someone else.

How do I stop the fly from banging to get out the window
blown in my brain where those I don't want looking in
look in and see the lust of love I've discovered,
the one that leaves me frozen and steaming together?
Wasted words, actions, time . . .
driven into a meaningful heart.
Kissed, fucked . . .
disguised as something important something that will
grease the fly
leaves me sitting on my ass in mud, dazed by the
eggs the fly laid and
the maggots that fill my brain with
one hundred baby buzzing flies.

THE MAKING OF character is framed like a house. Every piece of wood, if true, nails into a foundation that erects around a center fireplace that generates warmth for its world surround. When the structure is completed its integrity can be ascertained by what smoke rises out in accordance with the season.

While the family was a fine specimen to observe through the blind eye, its ritualistic attendance at church and well executed manners in public were not the smoke of a well centered hearth. They were rather, the post traumatic stress syndrome of a steady ground work of force and fear.

As my mother's one hardship I could have at least been pretty and somewhat useful. Unfortunately I was ugly and obstinate. I fought tooth and nail to be one of the children. My mother fought tooth and nail to keep me separated.

She reminded me often of how lucky I was that she had saved me from becoming a wall-eye. Now it was my hair that was a mangle-monster tangle. Determined to get some kind of beauty out of me, it was our ritual that I sat in front of her each night as she ripped a brush through my rat-nest-hair, as she called it, always threatening to chop it all off and let me fall dismally into the abyss of the once and for all hideous. I tried not to but, sometimes I cried because it hurt when she ripped the hair at the base of my neck. My head would whiplash back when she'd get a good tug and she'd yell at me for being dramatic. My mother rolled up my hair tight in plastic-rollers after dragging all of what she referred to as *the mats* out. The rollers were covered with little rubber spikes that held my hair in place around them, then each roller had a swinging arm that clipped the wrap in place. My whole head had the feel of having my hair pulled out. When I lay my head on my pillow the indenting of the little rubber roller spikes added to my nightmare. The next morning, before school, we'd have our little ritual of tearing out the rollers and brushing my unruly hair into something I suppose my mother considered an improvement. It all seemed like another form of torture to me. I cared little about curls and what it involved to get them made me hate the thought of any kind of hair dressing whatsoever.

There were certain attitudes I adopted which are yet to be pulled free from my original framing. As children we had meetings to discuss how to deal with my parents. My brothers had their own experiences to unravel into sense. We couldn't actually help each other. We were all in it together. There was no solution, only a common bond of mutual abhorrence and loathing that somehow made childhood under their roof bearable.

We were not allowed to touch my mother. I clearly recall her saying, *don't touch me!* I never thought that was odd until many, many years later when I mentioned it to someone and they reacted as if it was very odd to act that way toward your own children.

My father was like living with an unfed wolf. When he came home from work, we'd run upstairs before he came in the door. However, if there was a show on T.V. we were enjoying we'd sit him out. No one wanted to have eye contact with him. That would draw his gruesome personality to focus. He turned like a wolf toying its catch by pressing its teeth in its preys' neck ever so slightly harder and harder until blood was drawn, then just tearing into the jugular because nothing could stop the beast once it tasted blood. It started with the question; *what are you watching?* We knew right then, it was all over. We might as well just turn the show off and go upstairs. But we were already engaged. No one could move. If you moved the attention shot onto you. So we all sat frozen while the latest victim was victimized. When he would finally finish insulting whoever the victim was that night we'd all run up the stairs asking the poor kid; *why'd ya look at him?!* And whoever it was would say; *I didn't! He was looking right at me!* It was always a lose-lose deal. It was both relieving and unnerving when he got his martini mixed and drank that icy concoction every night. He'd go upstairs to his room with his drink and his peanuts and be gone for a peaceful interlude. When he re-emerged he'd be as mean as a yellow-jacket whose nest you just stepped on. Thankfully he'd pass out after he and my mother had their private dinner. Generally speaking, we all felt like vagabonds; stupid, useless, and afraid for those accusations which seemed so true from my parents' mouths.

We never saw my parents kiss, touch, or even hold hands. There was no physical demonstration of affection. It was like living in a house of survivors. I didn't expect any indication of affection. I had no idea what it was. How could I? I thought love was being fed and clothed, going to shows, and catholic schools. The only caring touch that took place was the holding of the baby. I guess it was good my mother had so many. We were always told we were lucky we had each other. My brothers were everything to me; they were number one and only in my world of the sinful and the untouchables. They were my only connection to a desire to live. They were my refuge of relief from being me. I constantly questioned my mother as to why I was punished for playing with them. The question was never answered and always intensified my mother's anger that caused her to enforce a more stringent separation. It tore me to shreds. My mother held those shreds out as proof of her obscure accusations of my insanity.

One of the main supports in the framing of my character was that there was something gravely wrong with me. My mother did not want one of her sons to catch it. A supporting beam that ran the same length was a fire-rod that smoldered non-acceptance of that accusation. I would die or find a way out before I settled into my mother's resolve that I was inherently insane. There were some relatives on her side of the family who suffered mental illness. She wasn't going to categorize me with them. She never stopped trying.

The problem for me was I was a child. I had no permitted voice. When I dared to try and reason this beam out of my structure, my mother would mock me. She would insist I was conjuring the whole implication up which was further proof of my paranoid delusions. She insisted I needed to be more dutiful as a girl. Do my woman's work. Expect nothing and give it all. *Stop wearing your problems on your sleeve;* she'd say. *No one cares.* My mother taught me; women don't get love. Stop looking for it. Love is for men. Find a man and love him. Then she'd add a little advice; get one with money. Money makes it easier. Find one that is good looking. Remember he's going to be on top of you every night. You don't want to have to look at any ugly face with stinking breath on top of you every night. God, she made it sound awful. I'd rather die than live a life manifest with such hate.

So determined to make a little lady out of me, as a young child, my mother's mother paid for ballet classes for me. It was a love-hate affair. I was thrust in with the same little urchins who ran and hid on me when they thought I was a one-eyed queer. This caused great anxiety probably for everyone. However, they had each other. I was always the one-man-out so to speak. On the other hand the classes forced us into a somewhat normal exchange. We got along fine during our common endeavor. Our impasse was put to rest during those years together. We were all just little girls growing up. But, I never became friends with them. I was there because I had to be. I'd have nothing to do with them if it weren't for ballet. Everything about ballet gave me a balloon of suction in my solar plexus. I couldn't breathe pirouetting from the line-up solo across the studio floor. I choked to hear my name to come forward and have my turn at each new step we practiced. I froze into a melt during the horrific recitals. Ballet was a six year rock at the mouth of my stomach. When I was finally given the option to quit, I ran for the hills. My grandmother was surprised. She thought I'd find stardom in my feminine aspiration. I didn't want to be a star! I wanted to be accepted. I wanted to fit in, anywhere. It would be like Piggy in "The Lord of the Flies" becoming a star. What was she thinking? My mother wasn't surprised. She knew I'd never amount to anything. She wondered aloud if I intended to play army in the backyard with my brothers for the rest of my life. It seemed like a good idea to me. But, I didn't say that. I'd rather be on a battlefield being shot at with people who accepted me than pirouetting on a stage with people who snickered and sneered when I walked into the dressing room of the studio. I wasn't going to have anything to do with those girls my mother so insisted on. They were kindling on the fire of my personal self loathing.

I did make one friend out of them in those years. We played on the same softball team and we liked to play basketball in the driveway. Our ways quickly parted when we got to high school.

THE BOYS

DURING THESE YEARS I did get an idea of what my mother meant when she said boys don't want to play tonka toys with girls. I had a best friend named Matt for a time. Matt taught me to steal. I didn't like it because I knew it was wrong and it gave me great anxiety to do it. Other than the stealing, we stayed friends and had a lot of fun together until he lit a squirrel's tail on fire. I wasn't there when it happened but everyone knew about it and when I heard him bragging I knew he was someone somehow possessed of abilities that I couldn't accept. I became afraid of him and stopped hanging out with him.

There was another boy in the neighborhood I became friends with. His name was Peter. He was the smartest kid in school. We walked home together most days and we played in the dirt in his back yard or in his rec-room downstairs in his house. Peter helped me get an "A" on a big History project for school. We built an entire clay-African-Village together as I had Sudan as my country to do a project and paper on. It was a lot of fun. One day on the way home from school he prodded me into climbing into some big bushes on the side of the road. He pulled his penis out and wanted me to stick it in my mouth. I was appalled. He insisted. I made him swear he wouldn't pee in my mouth. He promised and I let him stick it in my mouth. It tasted disgusting. I jutted my head back and said; *I can't do what you want me to do.* We got up and walked home. That was the end of that relationship.

There was Michael. Michael had four mini bikes. If I let him fondle my breasts he let me ride two out of four of those bikes as much as I wanted to. The other two were too big for me to handle but, he gave me all the rides I wanted on them. I liked the way he touched me. It was very exciting to be with Michael. He always talked about this other girl who was out of his league. Her name was Rose and she had the biggest breasts in the county. I hoped she stayed out of reach. I'd be thrown to the wayside immediately if she came around. The other girl who had Michael over me was Marissa. She lived around the block. Michael thought she was beautiful. I thought she was ugly. Whenever she was around I didn't even exist. I never liked her. But, I had no choice. She wasn't always around so I got my rides and my secret rendezvous with Michael and I always looked forward to it.

The longest secret relationship I had was with Scot. Scot moved to town when I was in third grade. My best friend at that time was Jeffrey. Jeffrey knew Scot from the city. I met Scot before he moved to New Jersey from when he came to visit Jeffrey. Scot was a blonde-haired, blue-eyed, Czechoslovakian child model. When he hit the schoolyard the girls were dazzled. It never occurred to me to be dazzled. We were friends. Scot never acted, in any way, put off by anything about me, ever. My ugliness didn't offend him. My tomboy ways didn't offend him. His attitude about me didn't change even with all the one-hundred google eyes set upon him. He never pretended anything. He had no interest in all those girls he could choose from. I hated all those girls. Scot, Jeffrey, and I were openly friends. No girl saw it that way. Those nasty wretches cornered me many times. They wanted to know; *how could it be? You and Scot . . . Scot with you?!* It was absurd to them. What was going on, they could not figure it out.

There was pressure from my mother as well. She was sure Scot did not want to be my friend. I finally gave in and introduced Scot to my brother C. They became good friends and I got shuffled to the side for a few years. I did run with them whenever I could but my mother cut that off saying boys and girls don't make friends. They don't want you there. Though they never dumped me or acted like they wanted to as those little witches in the neighborhood had so often done, my mother forbade me to run with them and so, reluctantly, I gave in. I gave in until Scot had more fun hanging out with me than hanging out with C. That took a few years however and, in the meantime, my character continued to be framed.

PARENTS

THE RELATIONSHIP MY parents had was a beam set on the foundation of my frame that laid in the decision; I will never get married. I had a course when I was a junior in high school about marriage and I was told there was a seventy-five percent chance I'd marry someone just like my father. With that information on top of what I saw as a child growing up, that decision dug in like a steel spike in a railroad tie rod. I would never live my mother's life. I would never give any man the power my father had. My mother was brutally and stupidly stuck. I would know better. I'd make sure I never ended up like her. I would die before I lived her life. My mother envisioned me walking in the foot tracks of her own self loathing. As the girl, with five brothers and no sister, it was all on me. I didn't accept it.

My father was a very handsome man. He was financially and socially successful. He was a good athlete. He enjoyed being the golden-boy-star on his high school basketball team. He often shot baskets with us in the driveway, always showing us up with his swoosh-baskets from further than we could shoot. He served his country as a Marine before he went to college and was crowned College King by his peers at that College. My father was quite taken by himself. He was a proud man who had come to expect praise. He had a deep seated beam of character that spoke of being better than others; better by a long shot thanks to his loving mother.

My beautiful mother met her prince charming one summer while he was life-guarding at an upscale public pool. She would never let him get away while he was more smitten by her, by any measure of her adoration for him. Their romance consummated in marriage during the month of August in the year 1955. In June of 1956 my first brother was born.

My father was a man of dignity, honor, and pledges. He pledged to have one wife for life and to raise, with dignity and honor, all children they bore together. From the outside and on the surface, he performed his duties with dignity as a man with honor. He was, in his closed mind, to the steal-support-beam of his frame, a real man; a macho man.

The fact that he traveled a lot was probably how we all survived. Thirty years later, on a boat ride during a family reunion C said, with a feverish wrath in his eyes; *he is a sick bastard. He hated us. I can't imagine ever laying a hand on Cass (C's daughter). She is so helpless and I love her so much. He is a sick, sick bastard.* I never realized his loathing had met my own until that hot summer day in North Carolina together.

Every night my father *did* come home from work it was about 7pm. We would be watching T.V. He busted in the garage door mad as a hornet. The best thing to do was not to have eye contact with him. No one moved, not even my mother. Sometimes he didn't say anything. To everyone's relief he just went straight to the liquor cabinet and got a glass. Then he went to the freezer and pawed a few ice cubes, made himself a martini, grabbed his jar of peanuts and disappeared to his room. The relief of the sound of his bedroom door shutting was palpable. My mother's mother once observed this entrance routine and was appalled that not one person greeted him when he came home after devoting himself by long hours of work so we could reside in such refined luxury. We didn't wear our problems on our sleeves. Neither did we snuggle up to a seemingly docile badger.

When his door was heard opening and his footsteps were heard approaching everybody stiffened. Sometimes he'd just emerge to yell down the stairs to our mother;

B, where are my socks?!

She'd yell back; *look in your drawer!*

I did! he'd snap. *I want the blue pair! Well, they are dirty.*
Pick something else.
Why aren't they clean?
Because I didn't wash them.
Well, I want to wear them!

At that point my mother stopped answering. This ridiculous, unreasonableness was the essence of exchange with my father. None of us had breathed throughout the entire blue-sock discussion. No one made a sound. Soon we'd hear his footsteps go back to his room and the door slam behind them. We snuck glances amongst ourselves. We children took our moments of bonding like food.

It was those revolutionary moments that always dashed from my grip that I'd experience a bond of loathing with my mother. It was a snipped eye contact that begged for relief. But my mother never took a comrade in arms. We were *never* friends. My mother was as alone in her lot as I was in mine. It was a women's lot that no woman would ever help another woman to get free from. It was the great untold; the great unspoken inheritance of being born female; that we were at the discretion; that we could be treated as our man saw fit to treat us and we had to take it with our chins in the air like Hillary Clinton after the entire nation caught her husband getting blow-jobs while sitting at his desk in the white house, running the country. The whole country pressed their lips into bloodless, airtight traps while the great white bubble in the air popped; she is a good woman.

My father was drunk again. We would be like roaches scattering from the sudden light over and over again when we heard the cracking of the floor that gave away his approach.

There were many times when my father wasn't traveling and he didn't come home until very late. Those nights were loud with arguing and threats that eventually went quiet after some door slamming. One night when my father didn't come home my mother got all dressed up. She was a beautiful woman. Many times she sat home in the den and silently cried. I caught her one night and with great trepidation, asked her what was wrong. Children are instantly terrified when they perceive something is wrong with their mother. All of their safety is webbed to their mother. With all the sincerity and fear I had I asked her what was wrong. She barked; *nothing! Go to bed!*

On this night my mother was not going to sit and cry in the chair. We asked her where she was going. There was no babysitter and my mother never went out alone, not dressed like that. She said; *I'm going out. It's none of your business. Go to bed.* She swept out the door in a beautiful rage, slamming the door behind herself. We heard the ignition screech when she turned the key too hard to start the car. The car started with a rev. The tires squealed out in reverse. The car swooshed down the driveway, and she was gone. We all sat in a circle and tried to figure out where she would go like that. But none of what we thought added up. Later that night, perhaps around 11pm, I heard her come home. I was lying in my bed scared. I was glad she came home. About an hour later I was awakened by the front doorbell. My eyes were peeled wide open and drying. My breath was as small as I could make it to keep the noise down. My ears keened. Only the tick of the baseboard broke the silence. Ding-dong . . . ding-dong, the doorbell intermittently rang. Between rings I heard my father's voice not too loud saying; *let me in. Someone let me in.* He had the front door pushed open to the taut chain length. Ding-dong, *come on B. Let me in.* I lied in bed petrified. My body was so stiff with fear it hurt. I thought . . . *It's Dad! We have to let him in! Whose going to take care of us?! Mom won't! I don't want to be left alone with mom! She won't take care of me! She'll get rid of me first chance! . . .* Right there, believing I had to make a choice between mom and dad, even though dad was bad and mean and scary, at least he would take care of me. I did not know who any of my brothers would choose. They all had greater favor with mom. No one was moving and someone had to let dad in. If I did it, it would put me in an even graver relationship with mom. I lied there in agony. No one moved. Dad kept calling and ringing the doorbell. *Why wouldn't anyone go. Shit!* It was up to me . . . I thought maybe, just maybe I can slip downstairs, unlatch the chain, and race back up before my drunken father can see who did it. That was my plan. I tiptoed out of my room, past my parents room, over the creak in the floorboard, down the stairs and, with instantaneous great speed, flipped the chain free and flew, on all fours to go faster, back up the stairs. As my father came in the door he called up the stairs; *thanks Sue.*

Those words sank me into the despairing resolve that spoke of the end of me as far as my mother was concerned. They were two nails in the coffin of any relationship I hoped to pull out of that woman who bore my wretched life.

My father soon came up the stairs. I lied in the dark with my door pushed to only ajar. I wasn't breathing. If he came in I'd pretend I was asleep. But, he didn't come in. When he opened the door to my parents room my mother screamed; *get out of this house!*

He said; *this is my house! If you want someone to leave, you get out!*

The argument got louder and louder. It was the worst fight I had heard so far and there were many and they were always loud and scary. This time was the first time I heard something smash against something else. This time I heard the explosion of a dream that destroyed the precious quality of hope. The fight erupted to a final explosive shattering of a mirror my mother smashed by sending my father's prized college mug sailing across the room intent on smashing his head. After that my mother stormed out of their room and left to someplace in the car. When she returned she slept in my brother's room.

That night, at whatever young age I was, two bolts in my foundation were given a tightening; *I will never have a baby. Babies are traps that keep you locked to a man like this. I will never allow a man to have the power over me that my father has over my mother.* Another bolt was drilled; *I will learn to take care of myself. I'd rather be poor all my life than have all her money and live like this.* I hated both of them for the hopeless despair they knitted in my heart.

MENSES

MY MOTHER'S REPULSION of me heightened when I began to menstruate. There was never a discussion. This was a curse that did not exist but from inside. There was no place in God's horrid universe to even consider tapping the surface even just for recognition; to know on the tip of a pin there was that much normalcy to it. There were pads in the closet and one day she handed me a device that was a white elastic waistband that had two sharp metal clips that hung down; one in front and one in the back. This barbaric type belt was designed to clip onto the ends of the pad extensions in order to hold it in place. The clips dug into the skin but that pad didn't move. The white didn't stay white for long. That gadget along with nearly every pair of underwear I had became grossly stained. Stained panties became an addition to the mortifications that conglomerated to make up me. I didn't dare ask for new ones. There were six of us and I needed to learn to control and take care of myself. Never a word was said or an offer made to help me with this latest embarrassment. In fact, my mother's way of teaching me how to be self sufficient was to embarrass me.

Being the only girl with five brothers and no support from my mother presented me with a dilemma. I was too embarrassed to talk to any of the girls at school. I never heard anyone talk about their period. I had no idea how to dispose of my bloody pads. There was no garbage in the bathroom. There was no way to dispose of them privately. It was solely up to me to devise a system that was personal, efficient, foolproof, and private. So, what I did was keep a plastic bag in my closet. I disposed of my personal waste products neatly, without bother to anyone, as needed. When I got an opportunity, I carried the bag out to the outside garbage and got a fresh bag either to continue this round or for future times of menstruation. It worked well.

One time my mother, who regularly went through my room, found the bag. She was aghast. She came right at me and questioned the soundness of my thinking. She sneered at me insisting there was something wrong with me for me to carry on with this grotesque sanitation technique. Her final claim was that I was a weirdo. I was shaken to discover my idea was so far from normal. I loathed myself for not being able to be normal. In every corner of my mind I couldn't conceive what that might be.

The next Sunday dinner, with the whole family around the table, including my grandparents on my mother's side, my mother told a funny story. She told everyone she found a big bag of jelly donuts in my closet. She told how appalled and dismayed she was over what she had found. She got everyone to laugh at me for my strange collection, and my twisted mind. My head felt like it was going to burst into flames. I smiled because I wasn't allowed a voice. Behind that dead smile, inside my boiling brain, despair and hopelessness were being melded out of the hot-fired steel-rod that ran straight down the center of me.

At the age of twelve many things came to pass. As I already harbored the rage for being the one mistake, the one female, my period was a piece of dry wood thrown in the fire every month. Hormones I wouldn't understand for years, embarrassment, and shame were so great I couldn't stand the sound of my name. I had one friend per year who changed each year throughout grammar school. I never brought anyone home. I never wanted to be home. Anyplace I could find to be outside of home felt safe. I never knew what my mother might blurt out in front of a friend. She never liked one person I ever did take the chance to bring home. I thought there was something wrong with me for choosing every friend I ever chose. They were never right. So, I went to their houses. I snuck to their houses. I stopped telling my mother where I was going. I was always accused of wrong doing. I don't know what ever got her to thinking I was always doing wrong but that nail was slowly hammering home. At some point I stopped trying to be good. It just became an impossibility.

My mother and I had a volatile and abusive relationship. We hated each other with equal measure and we let each other know it. But, I was still a child so I had no defense against her. I was always wrong. She was always right. There was no ally for me.

The closest I came was my brothers. P listened to me and agreed with me but he stayed out of her field of accusation. My older brother S continued to be absent but for an occasional snippet of advise for instance, my mother liked to dump all my drawers so I had to fold all the cloths and put them away. S would tell me; *if each time you wear something you either put it in the wash or fold it and put it away, it will never back up and you'll never get burned for being overwhelmed.* I took his advice. It worked.

During those early teen years C disappeared into his own swell of rage. Years later he told me he was afraid of me at that time. It's no wonder, the way my mother went on about my derangement. His admittance both hurt my heart and opened my understanding of his reactions to me. When I was twelve, PJ was four. He was pure innocence and I welcomed his company. PJ had an idealist love for me that I desperately needed. Little J, my baby brother was one year old. He was my final, enduring roommate in the hell of my time remaining under my parents jurisdiction. I loved J like he was my baby. When J got big enough to climb out of his crib and then his bed, after the lights were out and we were both in our beds, I'd lie there and pretend I was asleep. I'd hear him climb out of his bed and tiptoe across the room. He could just see over the edge of my mattress. I'd hear him whisper; *Sue,* like he didn't want to wake me up if I was sleeping. I could see his blonde head in the dark, just over the edge. *Can I sleep with you?* J was so irresistible. I'd say; *come on J. Get in.* He'd hustle up onto the bed and wiggle right in against me. I'd always move a little bit away from the wall before he jumped in so I'd have a little breathing room once he fell asleep. He was as hot as a potato straight out of the oven. He'd be sweating and I'd be sweating right next to him. After he fell asleep I'd get up against the cold wall to cool off. In a moment he'd be right up against me again. The momentary reprieve from his radiant heat was savored as readily as it was relinquished for his company. As I pressed my back up against the cold wall he wormed in tight up against me and like that I'd fall asleep sandwiched between a hard-cold wall and the only love I had consciously, physically ever felt.

Green Glass

The author reminds me of someone I knew, someone
I didn't care for in a distant past life, one that passed
before I knew who I wasn't.
She used to tell me who I was on a regular basis in
straight-forward, cruel sentences. I believed her because
if she could imagine such a person, I must exist.
I didn't try to change her truth. That was too difficult.
I opted to hide from everyone including myself.
A shadow person with wolverine eyes, no tongue and
ever bristled fur on the nape of my neck, I scurried along the edge.
I hoped I'd scurry right off, not on purpose of course but
by accident so when everyone noticed, I'd be peered at with
a kindness even though it was a pitiful one.
That's not how it went.
The girl went out of my life and then,
my life went out of itself, off a cliff, cut short not by
hitting the bottom of a shear drop but by shattering the
green glass I hid within. I suddenly found myself in a purple
pool of dry wine trying to remember who I was when
I realized I hadn't been anyone, ever.
I took a risk. Climbed out from inside the murky glass,
waded from its' damp stain. Prayed I could figure out my
connection to the name the girl never accused me of, the echo
of which I shrunk from, the one I was Baptized with so I could
begin to walk before my own shadow.
It was then I realized
the only way to begin was first to allow
who I wasn't
to die.

9/16/02
SED

A WELL JUST looks like a small black hole. It doesn't look like you can actually fall into it. But, you can and it's a long drop before you hit the bottom. When you slam that surface it's pitch black. Even looking straight up, the opening is too far away to see the light. The air is damp and cold. It is acutely silent and overwhelmingly lonely.

At the shore I had found the perfect antidote to my entire family. My parents were the procreators of such utter mind-demise.

My father ignorantly divulged some twenty years later that he felt sorry for my older brother S because he could only make girls. S since had had three beautiful, adoring daughters he'd trade his life for. It was a validation, from the lips of my father, of my childhood plight that arrived way over due. It was the unspeakable summary of his attitude about daughters in general. In particular, it was an attitude that fell upon me. I lived under the denied umbrella of that barbaric mind-set. I was his one misfire out of six. No wonder I always felt like I never should have been born. Words don't have to be spoken. Actions speak for every one of those unspoken utterances.

As for my mother, she was quite vocal about her opinion throughout my childhood. Direct words are impossible to misinterpret unless you don't speak the language; I was over emotional. I needed to learn to keep my problems to myself. I was a wall-eye. I had ugly teeth. I was stupid. I was sickly. I was way too troublesome. I expected way too much attention. There was no sense in trying to educate me. I was dirty. My mind must be a garden of weeds. I was designed to get married and have children. I was weird. I walked like a duck. I was totally un-lady-like. I was worthless, and self-pitiful. My mental problems she thought pointed toward needing a frontal lobotomy and finally my mother decided I was a dyke. Whatever I was or was not was beyond my ability to even begin to unravel. What I was, was confused. I was looking for that well where I could jump into oblivion. I was so beyond fixing, all I could think of was dying. The only relieving remedy I had found was the same remedy my father had found. It was the one I had discovered at the shore.

I drank and I got obliterated. I found a relief that was beyond measure. My addiction to alcohol, the rapacious creditor, was the bridge that took me through a hell, far worse than what I had already lived, to a place just short of leaving me physically dead. Alcohol and drugs took me to a place worse than dead. My addictions brought me to a place of spiritual bankruptcy where there is no reason to live and every fiber that breathes wants to stop breathing. I would rather be dead. Before it took me there, it attached to me by taking my soul for saving my life. The paradox of my addiction story is alcohol saved my life before it very nearly took it away.

It gave me the ability to be indifferent; something that works before it obliterates whatever it frees. When I drank I didn't give a shit about my parents. I felt a bulging love in my chest. I felt giddy, loveable, and at peace. I felt comfortable around people. I had no fear, no anxiety, no self consciousness. I could make friends. When I drank I felt normal, whatever that was.

I was entering that time of life when so much becomes visible but yet inaccessible; that time when freedom is at hand and ten fence leaps away. I arrived convinced; hypnotized; brainwashed with certain definable attributes I held as my horrifying identity.

It was the ideology of a man named Hitler that created a nation of Nazis who were brainwashed to believe anyone not like themselves should be annihilated starting with the Jews, mentally ill, and gays. It was the ideology of a man named Joseph who, under the guise of the glorification of God, started a religion called Mormonism in which gross self glorification is manifest through his vision of what he sees as heaven and mans purpose therein. He calls, under the guise of his religion, to all men to join and take as many wives and bear as many children as they will bear. He calls women to bend to this Bull and cow like existence and be grateful for their child bearing privilege. It is their only way out of their inherent, sinful demise. It is the ideology of Osama Bin Laden that has the power to wash the brains of young men into believing there exists a God of love that would order terror and death to be inflicted upon the evil, who are people of any wealth, at the price of their own life for the rewards of that same beneficence they steal to be placed upon their loved ones and the promise that beyond this life, for their Godly service, they will receive ten thousand beautiful virgins in lust of their manhood. These young men blow themselves and everyone they can destroy into smithereens as a result of their rock-hard beliefs. It was the ideology of David Jones that led a couple hundred people to believe they would get to God if they all drank the purple arsenic. It was the ideology of Jesus that is a love ever so little understood, that Mrs. D followed that had the power to bring me back, ever so gently, from the sheer cliff of self destruction.

It was the ideology of my family, so deeply rooted in the bottom of my heart, that lay in a knotted heap like ropes tied in knot upon knot and soaked with a decade of unresolved tears until the ropes swelled so that the knots were so tight I could no longer breathe; until the sides and top around that knotted center shattered in a pile upon the base. The bottom line to all of my family ideology was; I was unlovable. Like every other human ever caught in the wash of anyone else's beliefs, I fit it together to make it work. Under the vision of any of those demonic leaders I may have done what anyone of those followers did. As a survivor thus far of my family I did what I had to do. Since I was unlovable, I decided never to look for love. Though it was all I ever wanted, I really had no idea what it was and the ways I came into contact with what I thought it was were always demolishing. I would guard myself from the hurt love implied. I never got too close to anyone. I never joined a group. I floated. I had the perfect remedy to quell my longings, my emotions, my fears, my needs. I got drunk. With alcohol in my belly the whole world and everything, everyone in it could go screw itself. Indifference was divine. Alcohol and drugs freed me from all ideology, all accusation, all assumption, all brainwashing. Alcohol gave me fists of iron and a heart of steel. It was my great survival weapon. With it I survived my passage from childhood to adulthood. The things that happened in those years cannot all be recalled. I did a lot of black-out drinking. By the age of fourteen I got drunk very nearly on a daily basis. It was wild, fast, and as furious as I could make it. I was living to die.

I was entering high school. My mother was right about boys. They did want something different. I liked it. Scot, the little boy from third grade was my age. He stopped wanting to hang out with C and started calling me. C was the only other person who knew of our secret rendezvous.

Scot would call me after school and I would sneak to his house when his mother went to New York City with his little sister who was still modeling. The first thing we did was go to his parents' liquor cabinet. He'd make us both a sixteen ounce tumbler of vodka and orange juice. We had both picked up the very common habit of pot smoking. With our drinks we'd go to his room and he'd roll a joint. We'd sit and talk and drink and smoke. There was a lot to talk about. We grew up together. Our families were well acquainted. His parents hammered booze as hard as mine. We often were vacationing in the same resorts at the same time in the summer. His parents loved money as much as mine. Our parents had a show-off relationship with each other. They got together on Saturday nights and played gambling games. It was before smoking was out of fashion. Scot's parents would fill our house with their cigarette smoke. My mother was a jealous type. So the best she could have with Scot's mom was a love-hate relationship because she was often jealous.

We shared a lot of family secrets. Scot had gone on vacations and to the Farm with us. He slept over and had dinner with us often throughout the years. We knew each other. He wasn't a brother but he was as close as he could get without making him off-limits.

I loved to look at Scot's hands. They were big and I loved the shape of his fingers and the way his thumb knuckle stuck out. I would just look at his hands. He had an artist's hands. I wanted them to touch me. They did. We spent many hours investigating each other. It usually ended with me running out the backdoor to the sound of his mother's arrival home. Scot was the guy I was with between boyfriends. I never had to be alone. He never seemed to mind when I was taken. He'd always be available again. Scot grew up to become a plastic surgeon.

At the start of high school I had some lingering grammar school friends. I did some double dating with a friend named Cindy and her boyfriend Bobby. I went out with a guy named Joe. It was an odd set-up. Joe had this concubine that he said, and everyone knew, he intended to marry. That was fine with me. I had Joe every Saturday night and for every prom. What we didn't do because of his concubine was have intercourse. That was fine with me. I was a virgin and had no desire to take the chance of getting pregnant. For me getting pregnant meant I had to commit suicide and I didn't want to die. We went to wild, raucous parties. We went to dinner, the movies, and basketball games. It seemed I got all the good parts of Joe while that concubine got no more than private meetings. It was weird. Joe had permission from this other girl to go out with me. I could care less that she existed. Joe was great and I got every benefit without having to put out at all. My drinking at this time was seen as cool and wild. It was accepted and condoned by my peers. We were all having a great time, Cindy and Bobby, me and Joe, acting hysterical together.

Over New Years of my freshman year in high school I took Cindy to The Farm. My whole family and extended family were there. My brother P had his lifetime friend Riker there too. There was about twenty relatives and friends staying at the Farm that New Years. It was like the top blew off Kilimanjaro. The champagne poured like Niagara Falls. Everyone got hammered. The next morning Cindy and I were each in our own hell, barfing our brains out. We didn't get better until sometime in the afternoon of New Years day when we managed to eat some bland chocolate cookies. We went out in the icy, crisp, clear mountain air and zipped up and down a huge open field until the fuel ran low. We drove my grandfather's snowmobiles for hours, revving those engines flat out in figure eights and giant ovals up and down the great field slope. When we finally came down from the field and got off the snowmobiles we were completely excited and invigorated. We were both deaf from the ringing of engines in our ears. We both forgot "the morning after" and jumped to connect the night before and the tremendous afternoon we had riding the skidoos. We couldn't wait to get drunk again.

A short time after that trip I was cutting through the woods to Cindy's house. I was just stepping onto the corner of her backyard when she stormed out onto her back porch and yelled; *get off my property!* I thought she was talking to someone else. I glanced behind myself and saw no one. I kept approaching. Then she yelled with greater vigor; *get off my property!! You're a queer! Get off my property and never come back!* I was dumbfounded and crushed. I wasn't only being rejected by who I thought was my best friend, I was being accused of being a queer as the reason. I stopped in my tracks for a few minutes to swallow what was happening but there was no swallowing this. I felt a seething rage come over me then a black blanket of shame strap around that. I turned and walked home in dead silence. By the time I reached my house I determined I'd find out where this came from. I had lost my friend. This was no small matter. At first I figured it must be those wretches who called me a queer when I was five years old. They scorned and ran from me because I wore a patch on one eye. They denied it and sent me to the girl they were sure made the accusation. I cornered Clark at school in the library. She denied everything. I had no re-course. Another nail of self loathing banged into my frame. I did not understand why I was continually thwarted. I was nice enough. I was dismally confused. I thanked God I had booze to quell my inner fury.

I went off by myself with a six of beer and sometimes a pint of brandy or vodka and sat against a tree or big rock and talked to God and got drunk trying to figure myself out. I'd try to figure out how to fit; how not to get thwarted; how not to be queer. I never knew what exactly I did to get people to come to the conclusions and reactions they'd come too. I drank and drank.

I decided my mother was right. If a woman likes a woman she is queer. Men could like men but women could not like women. Women could only like men. So, I could have woman friends as long as I didn't like them. It was a bugger. It was easy to not like my mother. She was downright nasty. My grandmothers fell outside the rules. I could like them because they were old. But, I had an aunt that I adored. This was a problem. Was I queer because I loved my aunt? This was a question that nagged me for many years. It was the question that, if answered, had the potential to unravel the whole confusion. The problem was there was no one to ask. It was a terrifying subject to even consider breaching.

My secret rendezvous with Scot continued, perfect in their way. He was completely outside of my life but played a part in the center of it. My time with him was a void where there was no pain. There was only pleasure and release. As much as I didn't want to get caught with him, he didn't want to get caught with me. To his mother I was a grossly inferior female. They were rich people. His mother was determined to make Scot a doctor. My mother would have galvanized me the slut she suspected. She wanted me to hurry up and get pregnant and get out but not at the expense of her dignity. Like I said; it was a lose-lose deal with her. I was either a queer or a slut. I only needed to make my choice. Scot and I talked about our mothers, and relieved our desires for pleasure and touch. I remained a virgin.

Sometime in the late spring of 1973 I met Tucker. He was adorable. I loved his muscles and his curly hair. He didn't play sports so my father had no use for him. We were allowed to sit on the couch with the family and watch T.V. or go for a walk. When we sat there I always wanted him to put his strong hand on my thigh. He didn't dare. So, we went for walks. We'd cut down to the woods and neck for awhile. We'd get our chance at all the parties where we could blissfully make out on a couch and roll all over each other. There was booze and pot always and pills had also slipped onto the scene. We dated throughout the summer and into the fall. Tucker had totally different friends who I never got friendly with. One night after I had been away at The Farm for the weekend, one girl informed me Tucker was with another girl while I was away. That was the end of Tucker. As it turned out his new girlfriend got pregnant. Better she than me. I had yet to lose my virginity.

In high school I got involved with softball and basketball. If not for those two teams I'd have remained as socially inept and alone as I had been when I arrived. I made friends with my team mates and we had great times going to and from games and practicing together. There was an undertow in my solar plexus when it came to these friends. If any of the girls seemed too friendly I kept her at arm's length. This was a fierce, and competitive group. These girls were suspect. They were not a feminine lot. I didn't want to make the mistake of getting too close to a queer or worse yet, being accused of being one. I had become quite homophobic. That being my attitude, still, softball and especially basketball were the best times of my high school experience.

My older brother S went to high school two years my senior. I was allowed to go out to parties with him. S barely drank and never did anything illegal. He wasn't particularly interested in girls but girls were quite attracted to him. S got his varsity letters in football at the end of his freshman year. At the end of sophomore year he quit football because when he realized the guys on the opposing team were actually trying to hurt him he thought it was barbaric. It ended my father's attendance at his sporting events. S became all county in track and his records still stand unbroken on the wall outside the gymnasium of his high school.

While my parents ungrounded, crushing opinion of me sent me spiraling downward into addiction, those opinions only made S more cemented in his resolve to make a clean and successful escape. He graduated Salutatorian of his class with high honors in Spanish and Math. His excellence in sports coupled with his 4.0 GPA made him acceptable to the Air Force Academy in Colorado Springs. When he left I will never forget my mother crying. I cried too. S was stoic. In his gentlemanly way he was very excited. He walked to his plane not once looking back. I thought, watching him leave, I wish my mother loved me that way. She openly cried.

After one year at The Academy S left. He told me; *because it is asinine to have to drop your books, for no reason, in the snow, and do seventy-five push-ups just because an upper classman can tell you to.* Abuse of any kind was always completely unacceptable to my brother. I never got that. How did he? S got self esteem from grandpa J. all those weekends, for years, spent at The Farm while the rest of us were home surviving a constant barrage of insults that became our inner frames. S went onto Notre Dame and Cornell School of Law. He paid his own way because when he left The Academy my father told him he wasn't paying. My brother was on his own for his stupid mistake. My parents were the first to brag when S held his law degree in his hand. As if they paid or backed him at all. Not one penny and not one writ of good will spilled from those two.

S took on a bit of a father role toward me in high school. When we went to parties he'd say; *Sue, if you get caught drinking that is one thing. But, pot is illegal. Don't do it. You don't want to get arrested.* Those suggestions he had didn't even put a ripple in my style.

I had a new friend, Ann. She had older brothers. We went to concerts and smoked bongs of pot and hash until everything was a hysterical rainbow. We smoked joints and pipes in a field behind her house. We drank beer or whatever was supplied. One day we were at her boyfriend's house. His parents let us party right in his room. There was about six or seven of us. I was seeing this strange little guy with no personality. I could beat him up but I didn't I just broke up with him. He remained harmless, good company. We were drinking and passing a bong around. Ann's boyfriend's brother was talking about doing heroin. He did it occasionally as did Ann's boyfriend. I asked what it was like. He looked at me with a grave expression and said one of those things that, with all the years of ensuing mayhem, I never forgot being said; *it is unexplainable but, having done it I can tell you that you are a person who should never do it. If I were you I'd never try it.* Everyone in the room heartily agreed on how dangerous heroin would be for any of them but, in particular, for me. From that conversation I never did heroin. I found hell without it.

There was a curly-blonde-haired, blue-eyed guy named Bobby I found to be irresistible. S warned me to stay away from him more than once. When he caught us upstairs, away from a New Years Eve party, making out he growled at both of us. I was told to get downstairs. My brother said something to Bobby after I left. I was too drunk that night so the next day my brother gave me a lecture about bad boys. Bobby didn't seem bad to me, exciting would be the better adjective. I never even saw that guy again. And I looked for him.

Spring track started and one night during the week my brother brought home three of the members of the team. I had gone to bed. My brother came to my room and in the dark he told me to get up and come down stairs and meet these guys. These were nice guys. I could choose any one of them I wanted. They were all single. I was resistant to say the least. I wasn't going to go down there, these guys knowing what's up, and pick one. How embarrassing! S assured me none of them knew anything. He insisted I just get up, brush my hair, throw some jeans on, and come down like I'm getting some juice from the refrigerator. Talk for a couple of minutes and go back upstairs. That's it. Then let him know in the morning. It will be a done deal. When I think of it now, it was a pretty incredible deal he set up.

I went downstairs and it took me ten seconds to make a choice. Willie was about two inches taller than me. He had shoulder-length brown-curly hair. He was the cutest guy I ever saw. The next day I told my brother my choice. I couldn't imagine that guy liking me but, sure enough, in a couple of days Willie called and we dated for the next two and one half years until he left for college. Those years with Willie were perfect. Everyone loved Willie. He was outgoing and loving. He hung out with a loving group of people all of whom were players in all the school plays. I was totally welcomed like a sheep into the fold. These were the people of coffee houses. They sat in circles and played guitars and sang together. They believed in the love of God and they loved each other and me. There was always hugging, kissing, and handshaking going on and Willie was one of the most pro-active stokers of all such interaction. Everyone loved him. I was very proud to be his girlfriend. Drinking was always a part of what went on in high school. When I drank too much and crashed out or puked out these people just took it in stride and wrapped a tighter hug around me. They were surreal. My relationship with Willie was the other half of the catamaran that kept me afloat along with sports from sinking into the abyss of imminent isolation. All the accusations of all my days that lay hidden, diminished during our time as a couple. We went to parties, dances, proms, shows, family festivities, ice-skating, and any other event that gave us an opportunity. My parents even loved Willie. When the end came it was a hard hit. I wrote him a poem and cried when I read it to him. We hugged for a long time and departed as friends whose lives just went in opposite directions. I made it to the end of high school still a virgin.

I had avoided a lot of trouble being in that relationship but, it did not stop the progression of my downward spiral. I drank on a regular basis, mostly every day. I smoked ounces of pot. I had gotten adept at stealing from my father's wallet. When I couldn't get any money the liquor stores I frequented gave me the booze on credit. I always paid them back. I hated my parents. I had no respect for them. To me they were total phony's. There never had been anything like a relationship and now what existed was akin to a dictatorship that had suppressed and tortured its slave for many years to the point the suppressed learned how to behave but, just give that slave a chance and they'll slit that dictators throat. I felt no remorse for stealing to support my relief measures. It was the least those fucks could do. Those people, as I began to refer to them, never had one good thing to say about me . . . ever. Their summary statements rang in my head, from my dirty choice of dungarees, to my choice of low-life friends, to my mental illness of volatile emotions, to my gay-tomboy-ism, to my inability and grave weakness of being able to let life flow off my back like a duck, to my insistence to speak out loud. I was appalling. There was something wrong in my brain that I couldn't just accept my position of inferiority, of inherent lacking and keep it to myself. Why couldn't I be a woman of honor. Why did I have to tell everyone how I felt. Everything about me was wrong and backwards. The repercussions to my not dying were steady and volatile. It became a family agreement that I was crazy. I fought that accusation in vain until I found booze. Then I proved them right. I lost my mind. At the cliff where suicide becomes a reasonable option the thread that pulled me from the edge was a good hard slug of Dewars White Label scotch. I chased it over and over with lots of beer. I blacked-out my existence and that was just fine.

I also kept dreaming. Between S's success as a runner, Willie being on the track team, and Frank Shorter winning the Olympic Marathon I was inspired to start jogging. Running immediately became both a relieving activity and a way to deny I had a drinking problem. It was, first of all, unquestioned alone time. I always pined for that. It was physically uplifting. It was emotionally uplifting. It used up a good measure of my bottomless rage-filled energy. I had a secret dream. I dreamed of running the New York Marathon. I never told a soul. They'd only think it one more crazy idea. S came to me after a short time of running and told me I shouldn't run. It's not lady-like. I should ride a bike if I wanted exercise. It wasn't the first thing I did that wasn't lady-like. No way was I going to stop running. I had a secret dream. I kept jogging and my alibi, running, increased as a force to measure against any question of my drinking.

In senior year of high school I was sixteen while most of my classmates were seventeen. The fact that I couldn't drive was a built in protection. Willie was gone. I didn't get attached to another guy. Though I dated I had no interest. My drinking and pot smoking had escalated to a daily relief. I had become very adept at acquiring, hiding, and consuming this life sustenance.

My home life was unbearable. My father's alcoholism had also progressed but I had acquired, from all my years as the inconvenient one, the scapegoat role. I was a much easier target. He was predictable, I wasn't. He was mean, abusive, and embarrassing to the whole family if we were in public. I might pee my pants in a most inappropriate place like the car seat or in the closet thinking it's the bathroom. I could be hidden. My father was a raging bull. A raging bull you can't hide. He made loud, nasty remarks to the waiter or waitress. He wouldn't leave tips or would refuse to pay for not getting a glass of water or some other inconsequential slip of the establishment. Often my mother covered the bill or tip while he mouthed off and stormed self righteously out like the drunken asshole he was. We never wanted to go to those dinners but we had to.

I was making scenes of my own by then. The fury my stress-filled family bore as a result of my father was beginning to double as a harbor of fury that swelled around me. My brothers backed off.

My mother was the broken bridge between it all. Outside the restaurant the twenty year brawl, my parents kept going, blew up the dirt in the parking lot. They had horrible arguments all the way home. We all sat rigid. If silence is stark enough perhaps it is actually emptiness. I wished I could puff into non-existence. I was sure I wouldn't be missed. If I hadn't managed to drink by that time I got drunk when I got home.

HIDING PLACES

WHEN MY PARENTS had a fight that escalated like the ones in restaurants the fight had the energy to boil up into such a steam we could all get scorched by the quaking overflow. If we weren't burned we'd be poisoned by that black molt. We all disappeared. I went to my room.

I had devised some never discovered hiding places for my stashes. Scot showed me how to hollow out a book to hide pot. That was a great place until I showed C. Then the whole book disappeared. Who was I going to tell he stole it? I should have known better. Scot also taught me to tape the bag under my desk behind the over-hang of the bottom edge woodwork. My rule for myself was to never tell a soul, not even P who was my most trusted person in the world, about my hiding place and to always put it away, no matter what. I was often in a black-out so it was very important to have the second rule or I'd lose everything. I kept to my rules through the darkest nights. My stash was always in its place when I went to check the next day. As for the booze, I laid the bottles on their sides all along my window sills where they would be hidden behind the window frame. In the winter it was great. I always had a cold drink. In the summer I drank what was there hopefully before it got too warm. It didn't seem to be a problem I can recall.

There was a huge bush at the base of the foundation outside my window. I was on the second floor. The window opened to the side of the house. After I picked up my libation for the night I sneaked around the side of the house and tied a rope around it that extended up to my window. I'd leave it there until, sometimes six hours later, when it was dark outside. I couldn't raise it in the light. The neighbors would surely see me and immediately turn me in because that is the way neighbors were, minding each other business all the time. I'd nonchalantly get up and go to my room and haul the package in. Then I'd go back downstairs for awhile to feel out the security situation. When I felt safe I'd go upstairs and get drunk and sometimes high as well. Then I'd pass out with no one finding out. That was as successful as my drinking ever got; to get away with it, not getting caught or hurt.

I was very good at getting my booze in without notice. I could get a flask past the family all sitting around talking with no more than a pair of shorts and a t-shirt on. Then I'd get drunk and they'd soon wonder how I did it. Alcohol allowed me to completely disassociate from my family. It put a fluffy barrier between where the exchange of insult had been a constant beating on my ability to even breathe.

MOVING DOWN THE BOTTLENECK

As for my brothers, I got high with P a lot. We laughed until our sides could bust but P wasn't me. He was greatly favored. My mother never stopped trying to keep us apart. She maintained that I was a threat to spoiling one of her prized princes. P was not void of self preservation. At some point everyone lets you get stoned to death as long as they are not the one. There is a point of self protection no one can be expected to go beyond. We both understood this unspoken truth. My mother had successfully created a monster and now she could rightfully call me what I was. I had become the monster. The recipe for that consummation started when I was a very little girl. C found girls and was never seen by me again for many years. PJ was a little football star. His innocence was delightful. He became the best athlete of them all. J, my baby brother, gazed at me with a wide-eyed wonder I wished could be multiplied one-hundred times. He was a beam of love, a love I treasured and never wanted to destroy.

I continued down the bottleneck. I recall a statement my mother made. It was the beginning of senior year. She came up behind me and said; *you're getting that cellulite on the back of your legs.* I was mortified. One more ugly thing about me I couldn't stand. I compared my inferior body constantly to my muscular brothers bodies. I was an 125lbs, athletic girl. That wasn't good enough. I went on a diet that very nearly excluded food all together. I could get down to 98lbs and not get any further. I had no energy. My calories came from booze mostly. I became so tired and my moods so morose between not eating and hormones and just being in my suicidal head, I made the most dire mistake of my life to that point. I quit playing on the basketball team. That hurt the whole team. Everyone mattered. It tore me up but I just couldn't go on. Another nail in the frame of my self-loathing banged into place. I drank.

I found a new group of girls to hang out with. They partied a lot. They'd find me a date and I'd go out with them. By then I was completely out of control. S was long gone. I had walked away from every friend I had ever made who questioned my drinking. Even these hard partiers didn't want to have to clean up the mess of me. Often times I'd pass out in the car before we even got to the party or bar and they'd just leave me out there and drop me off on the way home. I'd make scenes in bars and at parties that pissed everyone off. I made enemies of some, some would shroud me in a timed exile of silence, others would never have anything to do with me in the first place. They all wanted me to not drink. That I would not do. I drank alone a lot. Staying alone for awhile was a way to bank the fires I set. I'd be allowed to go out with the heavy hitters again. I was always funny. I always had pot to share and I always had beer money. There was something to miss not having me around.

One night I hit on the boyfriend of a girlfriend who was very good to me. She always stuck by me. She was a friend for sure. I never understood that. There were so few of those around. Everyone turned on me. Everyone loved this girl. She was a real sweetheart of a person. I was blacklisted and ostracized. The night it happened the girls even refused to drive me home and Steve, the boyfriend drove me home. That made for some heightened story line. I lost all those friends except for Kathie, the one I supposedly moved in on. As soon as I saw her in school I went to her and apologized telling her I never would hit on Steve. I only loved him because I loved her is what I told her. She said she knew. She understood. She wasn't mad at me but she couldn't help how others felt. They loved her too. We remained good friends. That was incredible to me. I never understood when someone was consistent, especially in a respect such as this.

My misery at home just kept widening and deepening. I learned years before how not to talk about anything. No one was interested in anything. If it was good I was bragging. If it was bad they were ten years past fed up. They wouldn't hear it. I was a molten ball of rage. My despair was profound. I had no purpose and no hope.

The suggestion to get married and pregnant hung in the air like a thunderhead in one-hundred degree heat. I would never be so selfish as to bring some poor soul into this horrific existence. That was the crux of disagreement me and my mother chiseled at our shattered relationship with. If I wouldn't even do that, how could I even be measured on a human scale. I was not only horrified at the notion of bearing a child, I was repulsed by the possibility of marrying a man like my father. As far as my mother was concerned, if that was my resolve, I might as well be dead. I agreed.

My whole existence was a mistake. My relief was alcohol and drugs which created a whole new realm of opposition to my life. The world fought against me. As I stepped further from my family and out into the world I was unable to step beyond the war. The levels I stepped down into sometimes were huge drops and other times paper thin. I was going down.

At one point, when I couldn't come up with any money I broke into a box of bonds my grandparents had been giving each of us, for many years, to put toward college. I found mine and took one worth about one-hundred dollars. I figured it didn't matter. I wasn't going to school anyway. That act was a fresh scathing of my scarred over character. I hated myself. But, what the heck. No one cared. I bought four ounces of pot with it.

At that time my friend Kathie and a couple of other girls had started going to coffee houses. She talked me into going. I was drinking every day at the time. We got saved. The experience was spiritual and emotional. It was a very uplifting time. P came with us a few times. What happened left an enduring mark for P and me. It was better than any drug or drink. I dumped the four ounces in the trash. I went back later but the garbage men had already come. I stopped smoking for awhile but I didn't quit drinking. Perhaps that is why that remedy was not lasting. We didn't keep up with the coffee houses. It was a fleeting time of love and joy I never knew existed. Because it didn't last I questioned its validity and I let it go as a whim. My drinking had escalated by enhancing it with valium, Librium, Quaaludes, or THC, whatever was around. The prayer meetings failed to be strong enough to pull me out of the despair I was in. When I ate I was afraid I'd get cellulite legs so I'd stick my finger down my throat and vomit.

Kathie really tried to help. She stuck with me way after everyone gave up. She never gave up. We partied a lot together. I couldn't walk away from it as much as she couldn't. We mixed the coffee houses with the parties. I made scenes and she'd cover for me. One night I raided a refrigerator for beer with the girl's parents sitting right there. They kicked me out. I started walking home. I lived about ten miles from where I was. It was the dead of winter. I didn't care. I knew how to get home. Kathie left and drove me home. We talked about my drinking. We talked about my not eating. If it wasn't for Kathie and the way people loved her I would have been completely cast out. She held onto me. God keeps the slightest thread about our wrist so we don't know we're being carried when we are.

I told her I had stopped menstruating for about three months. She told me I had to tell my mother. I had never been to a gynecologist. We had the conversation several more times before I promised to talk to my mother. I knew the outcome.

I approached my mother in great trepidation and just said it; *mom, I haven't had my period for three months.* She looked at me with dead black eyes and snarled; *well . . . what are you . . . pregnant?* Deflated I said; *I'm a virgin!* then walked away never to have the subject breeched again. Kathie never understood that. It seemed normal to me.

Later that same year a group from our high school class went on one of those spiritual retreats that were periodically offered. Kathie and I roomed together. The meetings and topics were very inspiring. They were always emotionally uplifting. It made me feel a giddy excitement nothing else did. Many of us, including Kathie and me had the time of our lives. We laughed and laughed.

The following week a rumor swept the class that Kathie and me were gay. I was whipped into a whirlpool of terror. What did I do wrong? Nothing happened between us. We were friends enjoying each other just like everyone else. I loved Kathie but not the way that was being implied. I began to wonder if love of any kind for a woman meant I was queer. I buried my emotions and steered clear of her for awhile. But. eventually, in a small school you run into each other. She said she didn't care what people thought. Let them think what they want. We are friends and I love you. I was not ever secure but I was so desperate for acceptance that I slowly relaxed back into the laughter and joy of our relationship. Damn we laughed hard together. From then on I always thought it was wrong that I loved her. There was always a knot of anxiety in my solar plexus. Kathie never changed her way toward me. For the next thirty years she had no problem loving me. I could never understand that. I had no idea what love was. I had to live beyond her lifetime before I began to find out.

I could be Chinese

Morning is yet a black dome, strewn
with stars, (freckles of character without a face).
There is no moon. The pressure of silence
sleeps hard against the shudder of a tree.
The sudden crack that breaks the air, skips
my heart three beats. The trunk explodes with
relief and drops against the forest floor like
a tidal wave hits the beach.

From the second story up, the mirror
does a belly flop, shattering its face
upon black-top, into bits bare feet can safely pad.

Not one single soul awakes to my
breath taking solitude.

I could be Chinese, in a suit of platinum
armor, riding bare back on an Appaloosa with
a painted lady as my scout and it would be as if
the moon is there, the tree stands firm and
the mirror shows true, my reflection to me. But
I am faceless, in a crowd and even
to myself. I garner the wear of everyone to
cover my empty plot and hover on
the edge of thought, in search of myself or
at least a knight, to rescue my nameless
fire that burns fierce
this arctic twilight.

SUMMER 1976

By THE END of senior year I was so far removed from who Susan was, a desolation panned out in front of me. The verbal tirade at home continued. I feared my father and hated my mother. I was a wild and ferocious, feral animal. What communication existed at all was completely annihilated. My life was a barren wasteland. I completely stopped talking. I entered the dark web of a self-constructed escape that accelerated the downward spiral I was already in. I was alone like a toad in the middle of the desert. I welcomed the predator hungry enough to imagine me palatable. To be eaten alive would be a welcome release from this place of such unquenchable thirst.

After being drunk at every graduation party I attended, with blotted out emotions, I turned, with easy absolution and walked away from everyone and everything and never looked back. My field of isolation locked around me as if I had the Amazon as a mote. I drank in the woods. I drank under overpasses and bridges. I drank at the duck pond. I drank in my room. I drank in parking lots, behind cars. I drank at bars. I drank alone. If I had to pee, I pee'd where ever I was. If that meant on the back of someone's house, in a closet, in the car, or in my bed passed out in a drunken stupor, I pee'd. I was beyond human aid.

My parents were beside themselves. I was a million miles from their grip. I was beyond reason. There was no reaching me. Any approach was met with volatile hostility.

My mother wanted to institutionalize me. She was sure I needed a lobotomy. My father insisted I needed AA.

In all this madness, I was preparing to attend college in Florida. Denial is a disease in itself. My father told me if I didn't stop drinking and go to AA he wasn't going to waste his money sending me to college. College was my only chance to prove I was worth anything at all. In my darkest despair I never stopped wanting to measure up to something . . . anything was better than nothing. College was my only hope.

I went to AA that summer. It was a dark, foreign place filled with strangers talking a language I couldn't understand. Everyone there was very nice but I didn't trust them. They were 'those people' my mother said I should be with; some kind of low-life society I better hope I was fit for. I wasn't fit for her world. That was for sure. I was filled with fear. I knew if the AA's got to know me they'd surely reject me. Only the women talked to me. No way was I going there! If I relaxed into that bullshit I knew exactly where that would lead. I just needed to get out of my life; figure out how to get to college; how to get out of here. There was a vague draw to those dark rooms and those shadowy people. They weren't pushy. They were welcoming. I couldn't imagine they'd let me in. They all seemed to like each other a lot. It appeared to be a very large click. I didn't have the energy to try and break into it. But, I did keep going back. I was seventeen years old.

In the beginning of August the family went to Hilton Head in South Carolina for two weeks. My parents owned a condo down there. I was doing well, keeping my drinking under wraps, not getting caught and going to AA. I had gotten all my paperwork for school in order. All I needed was my various shots that were required to attend school in that corner of the country. I even had corresponded with who would be my roommate. I was scared shitless and ready to go.

When we got to Hilton Head I fell off the wagon to say the least. In no time at all I was an out-of-control black-out drunk. One morning I was jolted out of my haze by my mother punching me and yelling; *wear is your sandal?* I was like; *what the fuck!* I got up to avoid the assault. I had no idea where my sandal was. My big toe was all bloody where a band aid had been sloppily applied. I had no clue. Mother blurted; *go find your sandal!* So, I went looking. Just to get away from her and into the silent morning air was a desperate reprieve. I had no idea where to begin to look. I could vaguely remember starting the night with my brother P. We went to the night club at The Hilton. There were two people we shared a table with. I remember the girl telling me her hair was a more realistic color than mine. Well shit, mine was real! I didn't like her. I walked around where I thought I might have gone. That night I had worn jeans I had sewn embroidery all over. I remembered she liked them so, we traded pants. I lost my sandal and my pants. There was a desperation in me that was that constant rock at the mouth of my stomach. I had to find that girl. I grew angry imagining I had been had. I found where she lived. Her father said she wouldn't come to the door. I begged to talk to her to no avail. The door was finally shut in my face. What was wrong with me I thought. It was as if all the curses of hell were on me. My parents were utterly disgusted. My brothers even stood apart. I still remember their looks at me. It was as if everything was spinning faster and faster and I couldn't stop it and everyone was just watching as I spun out of control right down the drain pipe, no one helping because they didn't want to be sucked down with me. I was in one of those nightmares when whatever is chasing you is about to get you and you are screaming as loud as you can but no sound is coming out and you are trying to run but your feet are in slow motion and you aren't getting anywhere.

I had gone on my final vacation before college and total strangers were slamming the door on me. The look on the man's face as he pushed the door shut was like someone who realized a wet rat was sniffing at his door and he needed to slam it shut so I wouldn't put his family in danger of infestation.

My drinking on that vacation was rampant and, in my shattered mind, totally justifiable. It was the only relief. It was *the only* relief.

Thankfully, that vacation ended. When we got back to NJ, even as I knew the repercussion of my insane behavior, I could not bear but deny it. I continued to prepare for school. My father came to me and said; *I'm not sending you to school. I'm not throwing my money away to a drunk.* My alcoholism had unleashed like the momentum of a fifty car train fully out of control on the downward side of a mountain. It was as if I had black rings around my view. My life was over.

The anger that swelled in me was a kiln that could heat New York. It was constantly kindled into a slow burn that was regularly given new wood and occasionally was thrown a big, dry, well seasoned all-nighter-log. Those are the logs that lay on the hot coals and appear to be so heavy they'll never burn. Those are the ones that end up creating so much heat, the sides of the kiln begin to crack.

This was the dark night of my life. Any hope of purpose vanished with the loss of a college opportunity. I was a piece of crap, not even measurable among humans.

If I could turn any further inward I did. If I could become any more silent I did. There was no more me. What was the use of utterance?

I was told to get a job. I got one I could ride my bicycle to. It was The Dairy Barn, a fast-food, ice—cream restaurant down on Rt. 17. It was when that highway had no cement divider but rather grass, was two lanes in each direction, and easily manageable by foot, two wheeler, or car. It wasn't unsafe to ride my bike on the shoulder going toward the traffic. Today on that same road you'd surely be killed.

The people I worked with were very nice. People always liked me at first. The sequence was always the same; like, then pity, then disgust. Since I was in such deep despair with no seeable way out besides total oblivion, the sequence was accelerated. These were all young people like myself. They liked to go out dancing and partying. At first I always felt like I found my niche. Well, it wasn't long before they dumped me on the curb in front of my house at 2am and left me there. It would have been earlier if we hadn't been in the city. I was lucky they left me there. It wasn't long before my boss took me to his office and talked to me about my drinking. He never fired me but, he did try to help. They gave me the intergroup number for AA and Laurie, the girl who worked there helped me to call. Someone named Marlene came to my house and took me to a meeting. Again, I was in AA. It was still dark and bleak. I still could make no sense of what was going on in those rooms. I couldn't imagine how it could be a solution. I was too deep in the well of despair to be able to bear the emotional pain inherent in keeping myself from picking up a drink. I couldn't talk to women. I thought all of them were queer.

I couldn't stay sober. Marlene was an enigma to me. Nothing about her made sense to me. She drove to my house and picked me up for nothing. She answered the phone when I called and was always willing to help. She listened to me and had reasonable answers for my concerns. She never asked me for anything. She never stood too close. She didn't repeat what we talked about. She understood me for sure. She didn't drink but she used to, a lot. One day I asked Marlene how long she was sober. She said seven months. I was floored. I couldn't imagine such a thing. I asked her to be my sponsor. She said yes. We started what would be a very short relationship. I could not stay sober. I knew there must be something to it but my life was too unbearable to manage sobriety and my circumstances at the same time. She continued to take me to meetings even as I drank. She was quite patient with me until one night I sneaked a bottle of Dewars in under the seat of her car. She disposed of the bottle and me. I endangered her sobriety is what she told me.

Just when I thought my self-loathing couldn't possibly get any worse, I lost my footing in AA and fell even deeper into the well I never imagined being so deep in the first place.

Back at work my boss found my bottle of Jack Daniels hidden in one of the ice-cream-topping-wells. It had been a perfect hiding place while it lasted but it hadn't lasted long. I got caught drunk because some nuns were ordering banana splits with special toppings and I couldn't remember what they were asking for long enough to make the mass. I had tried three times. All I can say is thank God they were nuns. It could have been worse. Another time I was on the grill. Under the grill top were burners to make grilled cheese. When the cheese started to burn I quickly squatted to spatula it out when I lost my balance and fell flat out backwards slamming my head on the shelf across the walkway. My boss just busted out laughing then told me to get out of the way. I never got fired. They just kept trying to help me. There were two bosses. I think one of them was in AA. Drinking put aside, I came to every job with the grandpa J work ethic. I was fast, thorough, efficient, untiring, uncomplaining, and always willing to work harder. I just couldn't not drink.

The worst day was the day I got so drunk my boss, Ken took me to his office. He was a big, strong, scary man. He was very kind. He talked to me about AA and my drinking. Then he put my bike in his trunk and drove me home. It was in the afternoon. My mother, of course, was furious. She came at me but, I had stopped paying attention to her existence some time before this incident. I went to my room and passed out on my bed. At about 8:30 I was jolted awake by my father punching me, ripping me off my bed, and slamming me onto the floor. My vision was cloudy at best. While my father was pummeling me I looked past him at the clock. It was 8:30! I still had my uniform on from the day before. I didn't hear one word he said. To me my father was no more than a self righteous drunken beast who only owned us because he had money. I vowed to never give any man that power . . . ever. He didn't own me.

All that was on my mind was; *shit! I've got to get to work! I mop the floors at 9am and thank God I'm already dressed.* I stormed out of the room, down the stairs, and out the door. I jumped on my bike and raced to work to punch in.

The north side of the restaurant, from where I approached, was a full sided picture window. As I got closer I noticed "Gerd" was there. She was a night person and I wondered why she was there in the morning. Then I saw Chris. I went in the back door. Everyone was happy to see me. I asked them why they were there. They told me it's 9pm not 9am. Everyone got a big laugh. I told them I can't go home. "Gerd" offered her couch. I waited out the shift, went home with Gerd, slept on her couch, and went back to work from her house in the morning. I didn't go home until the following night. My parents were volcanic. I was emotionless beyond the fear of being beaten to death. I wished they would kill me. I was dead anyway.

That job wasn't all that went on that year of 1976-77. It was a year of swift, downward spiraling wherever I raised my head to take breath. I turned eighteen that year. Alcohol had become my perfect delivery from hell and my doorway into its raging fire.

GLAMOUR SQUATTING IN THE CORNER

Through the thick cobwebs of waking up
my head is a vise under hammer attack.
My bloody eyes open to a
blinding beam of sunlight staging
glamour squatting in the corner
staring at me
waiting for me to wake.
Neptune slips out of alignment.
I fall to my hands and knees.
Close my bloody eyes.
Crawl to the edge of stage light.
Grab the quarter-fill.
Let the pour burn down my throat.
Crumble back against the wall.
Vomit where the long neck stood.
Wait for the rubber-bands around
my forehead to stretch loose.
Shake it off.
Start the day the way I always do,
ridding glamour's stare at me.

IN SEPTEMBER OF 1976, after having gotten my writ of consequence as a result of my insane alcoholic behavior, I had started my job and I met a few new friends. One was an alcoholic named Sue. Her mother was an alcoholic and we'd sit and get drunk and talk about her drunk mother and my drunk father. We met at some party and hit it off because we were two of a kind.

One night, at a party I met this guy named Jimmy. He really took a liking to me. It had been a dog's age since that happened. I was as hollow as a dead tree. I got so drunk the night we met, I passed out in the bathroom at a diner a bunch of people hit on their way home. He came in the ladies room and gathered me up off the floor, threw me in his 240z and drove me back to my parents house where he covered me with a blanket and let me sleep it off for awhile before he walked me to the front door and asked me for a date to the movies the following night. He called me the next day to check on me and make sure I was still available. By the next day I couldn't remember his name and I had no idea what he looked like. That was scary. Some downright wolfee guys had shown up in the past with a bit too much familiarity in their demeanor for me to be comfortable with. I was nervous to say the least. I informed my parents I was going on a date that night. I don't remember if there was any discussion at all. I just know they knew some guy was going to show up. My mother wanted to get rid of me so bad she didn't care who showed up as long as he did his magic and saved her from me.

While I was trying to figure out how I was going to introduce someone whose name I didn't know, as my date, to my parents, the doorbell rang and my father went straight to it. When he opened the door Jimmy immediately stuck out his hand and said; *Hi! I'm Jimmy Cook. Nice to meet you. If it's alright with you I'd like to take your daughter to dinner and the movies.* We all stood there agape. My father said; *Sure!!* This guy was handsome. He was 6'3", dark brown hair, crystal-light-blue eyes, a mouth full of perfect teeth, not a blemish anywhere. Holy shit, I thought, and walked out the door with him.

Well so much for virginity. My relationship with Jimmy was basically one of getting laid. We fucked every night we went out. He fucked me wherever he got a chance. That 240z he picked me up in was soon traded in for an SUV big enough for two people to use as a double bed. That's what we did. Every night we went out he'd bring me back to my parents driveway and screw me right there. I can't imagine they didn't know what was going on. My mother must have thought what her mother though when my father showed up at her door. This was my prince charming. Well I wasn't quite a princess to be had. I even asked him one night if he'd break up with me if I didn't want to have sex anymore. Without hesitation he said; *yes.* I at least got him to agree to not screw every single time we went out. Otherwise I wasn't going to go out so many nights a week. The only reason I think I didn't get pregnant was because I was drinking so much and I was completely anorexic and bulimic.

Taking me on dates meant we were banned from bars and restaurants. I made scenes everywhere. I'd get up and walk right out in the middle of a meal if he cut me off. When I finished my meal I'd go in the ladies room and barf it up. One time while a group of his friends and us were leaving a pool hall together I had to pee real bad. After I had started to get in his over-sized truck I said I have to pee. I promptly hopped back out, went around to the front fender, hiked my skirt, and peed right there. Everyone saw me. It caused quite a ruckus to say the least. Jimmy was pissed. I didn't give a shit. These types of incidents went on for about six months.

One night I was at a big party with all of his friends. By then everyone, with me completely unaware, was on high alert. I was drinking and drunk as usual. One of the girlfriends at the party had gotten sick and was in the bedroom lying down. I went in to check on her. The next thing I remember is her boyfriend was standing right in my face, as if he was going to rip my head off. He was saying he was going to beat the shit out of me if I came near his girlfriend. I was stammered. I had no idea what I had done to get this response. I was scared. As I was being backed out of the room Jimmy appeared. The look on his face was gruesome. He grabbed my arm and yanked me out of the house and into his truck.

When we started to drive away I asked Jimmy what happened. He was totally freaked out. Obviously, to me, I did something in a black-out. I needed to know what. I just blew Westwood up and I wanted to know how. All he said was, I have to take you home. He wouldn't say what happened just that his friends said I was crazy. The next day he called crying and broke up with me. I begged him to at least tell me why his friends thought I was crazy. It cost our relationship. At least he could give me that. He told me his friends said I was queer. I was baffled, but much more than baffled, I was mortified. What was this damned curse that kept whipping me out from under myself by my own tail. Who was this demon who lived and reigned beneath my skin. Is there someone here that I'm not aware of? How can I get rid of this 'me' that I don't know? Jimmy told me we could meet in secret for sex but his friends can't find out. We did but not for long. That relationship was over.

I settled in in my usual haunts. When I was alone I felt safe. When I went and got my booze and headed to one of my spots the act of getting and going actually gave me warm chills. When I nestled back into a corner under a bridge or a secret rock behind a tree deep in the woods, or behind a dumpster against a fence I felt so overcome with coziness, I wished I never had to come back out. I'd be very happy to die there. Those places were the wombs that gave me reprieve from my hostile existence.

My time between high school and college did not prove to be my darkest. As unfathomable as it could be, it got darker. That was a year riddled with drunken black-outs and sober despair. I raced through relationships. All trust in people was completely demolished. I could not take and I had absolutely nothing to give.

The Dairy Barn job had gotten me to go to AA. That was a catacomb of grey people speaking a jargon that could be Arabic as far as I was concerned. I was gravely isolated but for the threads I let remain. If hope could be measured on the head of a pin, what of it actually or seemingly existed came from AA. I had credit in a few liquor stores. I mixed up my frequenting; as if any of them cared about the amount of my consumption. My vehicle was a yellow ten-speed schwinn. My life was a circle of obtaining and consuming booze. My life was about getting obliterated. That's what I did.

By the end of that school year lost, it had been two years since I spoke to my mother. My father ordered me to talk to her. You can imagine how that order changed things. I was also ordered to go to AA. If I did those things I could go to college in September.

We all believed in the geographic cure. I began to attend AA regularly. I didn't stop drinking but, I stopped getting caught drinking. As far as everyone was concerned that meant I was staying sober, something that was impossible for me to do.

My mother and I went on a couple of college hikes. We went to see St. Lawrence, an all women's college nestled in the middle of nowhere in upstate New York and we went to see St. Bonaventure which was way out in Olean New York, a town close to Lake Eerie.

My mother thought St. Lawrence was the perfect fit as she pictured me becoming some kind of recluse nun. My oddity would surely be a perfect fit in this desolation.

Olean was a college town. St. Bonaventure was a basketball school. The campus was gorgeous. It was co-ed and heavy on men. It was my utopia, my salvation. I was going.

LAST CALL

I ATTENDED A midnight meeting, I had come to enjoy in Upper Saddle River, shortly before my departure. It was a young people's meeting. There was a young girl, my age, whom I hadn't seen there before, attending the meeting that night. I must say I never saw her again after that night. However, what she told echoed in my head for many years to come. There is a literary expression used when writing a story. It is called a foretelling. It was a word I'd not hear explained for perhaps twenty-five years hence.

This girl, whose name I don't recall, was back from college. She was very serious when she talked. That is perhaps why I listened a little better than usual. She had gone to AA before she went away. When she got to college she was swept up in the excitement of what goes on when bunches of young friends who haven't seen each other all summer see each other again. They party hard. She told how she got away from AA. She told how she got drunk. She told how she blacked-out. She told how she got raped. She told how she was grateful to be out of there and back here, safe, in AA at a midnight young people's meeting.

I listened and obviously I heard what she said because those words came back around. But, at that time I knew, it wouldn't happen to me. I had come to like the AA meetings. I had a boyfriend in AA. We went to concerts and AA parties together. He had good sobriety. I hadn't been to a meeting with a pint in my back pocket ever since someone mentioned to me he saw it. It never occurred to me everyone could see it when I had my back to the room getting a cup of coffee. Sometimes the meeting ended too late to make it to the liquor store. I had cut way back. In fact it had been two weeks since my last drink. I was well on my way to sobriety. It was perfect to go to college and get sober at the same time. I intended to jump right in up there. Jump in I did. I tread directly in that girls foot-tracks just as surely as alcohol has no rival.

THE GEOGRAPHIC CURE

IT IS COMPLETELY disorienting to go away to school. There are a lot of people there who already know each other. They are, at first, welcoming. That is to get a feel before the hazing begins. No one holds your hand. No one backs you. No one is your friend. You are an adult and expected to be able to stand as one. I could be likened to a rabbit set loose in a forest of coyotes.

I will never forget the comparison of my departure for college with my brother S's. We wept and everybody hugged when he left for Colorado Springs. When I was leaving my mother was folding laundry in the downstairs bathroom. I went to the door and said; *I'm leaving. good bye.* She just kept on folding. She didn't turn. She didn't say a word. I paused . . . then I left to catch the bus that left from Port Authority New York.

The campus was huge with one dorm set a couple of acres south of the main buildings and accompanying buildings that surrounded them. There was a chapel in the center of a great center field that I frequented often with a heart untapped and on fire. I recall one day a young man taking my hand in both of his, and looking straight into my pained eyes he said in a most soothing voice; *peace be with you.* With equal earnest I responded; *peace be with you.* Later I talked to him. He was planning on entering the seminary. I wanted what he had. I always looked to see him. I watched him. Peace shown off him like a low cast light. There were little prayer meetings he attended at the chapel. I attended them for a while but, I couldn't manage to make a commitment. I was too far down the well to take on grace as he had.

When all those students returned from summer break they were very excited to see each other. There were great dorm parties. The decision to stay in AA was washed away with the first garbage can full of bash; a mixture of vodka, some sort of powdered juice and ice. It was a thirty gallon garbage can full of that Godly concoction. Next to that sat whole keg of beer. Next to those two barrels stood me. I drank until I dropped my brand new beer stein and it shattered all over the linoleum. I had some new acquaintances with me. We were all raucous and wild. The music was loud and there were lots of guys. I definitely needed a boyfriend in this mayhem. The one I spotted had bushy blonde hair and a rugged beard. He was as cute as anything. We talked and laughed. I thought, this is easy. I'm glad there are so many guys it's not hard to meet one. Rudy suggested we leave the party. It was way too noisy and he knew of another party off campus. It was quieter and we could get to know each other more easily. I didn't know where my new friends went so I agreed. He was so cute and I was so excited. The next morning I woke up in my room to a disgusted roommate. I couldn't find my wallet. I couldn't remember the guy's name. And I was very sore. I knew we had sex. I was in a total black-out. I didn't know where we went or where or how to find that guy. One of the girls I recently met asked me how it went with Rudy. I told her; *not so good. I lost my wallet and I don't know how to find the guy.* With her help, in a couple of weeks we spotted Rudy on campus. Turned out he was a townie who hung out on campus picking girls up. I really had to push him to look for my wallet. The boyfriend dream was a rock at the bottom of a mud-puddle. With the added insistence of my girlfriend Gail he reluctantly took me to where we went that night. Rudy had taken me down a long two track dirt road to a pull-off near a river. I was far enough into my alcoholic haze to quell the reality of what I was seeing. This great guy took me to a party alright.

It was a one on top of one dead-end where the drunk girl, too far gone, is an easy lay. Rudy stole from me drunk what I never would have given him sober. Classes hadn't even begun. I never found my wallet. I didn't talk about Rudy again. I went through the hassle of replacing my I.D.'s in silence.

I majored in German because I got my best grades in German in high school and my parents seemed to agree on that choice. They were telling people I was going to become an interpreter for the U.N.. I couldn't interpret the face in the mirror. Somehow, in my parents ideology, that didn't matter. To me, it was all that mattered. I was screaming inside; *who am I and what is the meaning of this breathing hell?!* From AA I was left a habit of praying. I often begged. I had not known loneliness compared to the loneliness I swam in at college. It had only just begun.

Very quickly, I went through friends. I was totally unpredictable when I drank and I always drank. I could be the life of the party or I could be violent like a cornered wolverine. I could be peaceful company relaxing near a river or I could dump a waterfall of boiling coffee down an unsuspecting person's back. I'd be fine when something in my mind would snap because of something I suspected someone of doing and I'd fly off into a rage. I'd attack the person whether it was a male or female. I was fearless when I drank. My upbringing made me strong. My drinking made me feel unconquerable. I didn't trust women because past relationships had proven accusatory and I didn't trust men because they fucked me when I didn't want to be fucked. It became very important for me to *not* need anyone. I was willing to work the skin off my hands to make that need a reality.

I had certain rules for myself that were the measure that kept my denial of the cataclysmic sickness that had me handcuffed in its grip, steady, unmoved, and grounded in the self destruction that addiction is; If I made it to class I was ok. I always made it to class. If I always did my homework I was ok. I always did my homework before I went drinking. If I always worked out I was ok. I never missed my workout. I was running an average of forty miles a week and lifting weights. I worked out seven days a week. I had a lot to deny. I was the biggest I had ever been in my life. I had gone from ninety-eight pounds to one-hundred-forty-two. Most of it was beer-bloat.

I still had my new friends so, I had people to eat meals with. I was painfully uncomfortable with myself. I always felt that undertow pulling in my solar plexus. I always felt that rock at the mouth of my stomach. I always wanted to pop into non-existence. It felt like everyone could see right through me. I wished I was anyone but me all the time. The girls I hung out with were friendly and apart. I never felt like one of them. I always felt different, like I had a secret and no one else had such a burden to bear. One of them, a girl named Gail gained a small measure of trust from me. She had helped me in more than one debacle and seemed to be un-judgmental. I knew she could be gone with one mishap and it was only a matter of time before that happened.

Gail's best friend, another person in the group, came to college leaving the love of her life behind. All Sully talked about was Gibby. Everyone knew I was usually not in my room. What they didn't know or care to know was where I was. If I wasn't at 'The Skeller', I was at the end of the hall, downstairs, under the bottom of the stairwell, out of view of the outside door, with an eight pack of pony-bottle-beers. I'd come-too sometime in the early morning, like 3am, because I'd be freezing and I'd stumble up the back stairs and into my room. I'd collapse behind my bed because I was tired of having to change the sheets when I continually pissed in it. The back of my bed faced the dorm-room door. I slept right in the warm pee. When I got up I'd wash and change and leave the wet spot to dry. My roommate did not like stepping in that wet spot, especially with her socks. We shared a rather abandoned room. That roommate stayed down the hall somewhere except to use the closets. She couldn't move out until the semester break. She despised rooming with me and let me know about her disgust every chance she got. I had enough self-loathing to drown myself. Her hatred was like one more rock in a sinking boat.

With the situation as it was, all Sully saw was an abandon room. An abandoned room was an opportunity. We weren't permitted night guests because we all had roommates. It is a common courtesy. This seemed so perfect to her. She asked me if she invited Gibby up could they spend the night in my room. She offered me her bed in the room with her roommate who was fine with a strange guest for a night and most likely wouldn't even be there because she spent most weekends at *her* boyfriend's place. I figured I'd be alone in her room. It was my opportunity to secure a friend. I said; *sure!* So he came and that night, as usual, I went out drinking. As usual, I got smashed. When I stumbled back to Sully's room her roommate was in it. I expected her to be away for the weekend. That thing in my head that turned me into an animal clicked and every human quality that made me reasonable snapped into oblivion. No way was I staying with the hairspray queen. She had recently set her robe on fire lighting a cigarette because the robe was so coated in hairspray. I stormed to my room and barged in. The love-bird couple, all entwined with each other pulled themselves apart and asked what was wrong. I told them they had to leave. They were guffawed. They pleaded with me. They begged me to stay in the lounge if I didn't want to stay with the roommate. I could not be reasoned with and they very reluctantly got up and trudged together to the lounge. There they stayed at the edge of public exposure. Sully never looked at me again. A huge rock slammed the sinking boat of my self-loathing. Unto this day, I have not found the clear reason for forgiveness for my actions that night.

I maintained my dream of running the New York Marathon. One of my alibis to prove my wellbeing was running. There was a ten mile route that looped on and off campus that I had found. There were a few shorter loops that remained within the campus as well. I managed to deepen the tracks of all of them during my time at St. Bonaventure. When my running shoes fell apart I found duct tape and taped them. My fuel was mostly beer, some bar pizza, and some plastic smelling cafeteria food. I wasn't able to stomach much very well. I got myself down to microwave oatmeal and milk. I often suffered from liquid diarrhea.

While nearing the end of a six mile run one frozen, winter day I felt one of my uncontrollable urges come on. I jumped over the ice bank and ran in amongst the barren brush. I ripped at my sweatpants and shorts but I couldn't get them off in time. I shit all over myself. *How was I going to go back?* I cleaned myself as best I could with what wasn't dirty of my sweatpants then tossed them in the snow. I tossed my underwear and just wore the shorts back. They seemed to have gotten away miraculously clean. When I got back to the dorm a bunch of sophomores and freshmen were in a room right past the doorway. They were laughing and singing and when they saw me they called me to join them. I always got a positive response to my running so I felt proud to be seen. It was one of perhaps two things I did right. I didn't know what the other thing was. I told them I needed a shower but they said that could wait. So I went in. Within five minutes one of them screamed; *I smell dog shit!* Another one said; *Me too! Susan check your shoes!* Then they were all smelling the shit. I said; *Jeez, how disgusting! I didn't realize! I'm sorry I must have stepped in shit!* They all were saying, go take a shower and come back. I said; *I told you I need a shower!* And I scooted out. I threw out my socks and cleaned my shoes. I took a long hot shower. But, I didn't go back.

As for my classes, I had an 7:30am Latin class. I'd go still drunk from the night before and recite the Our Father in Latin drunk but, I never missed class. Sometimes I'd still be drunk for the next class which was German at 9:30am but, by the end of those two morning classes I would be sober enough to have a hard-to-swallow lunch and do some foggy homework. I never realized how horrible I always felt until I stopped feeling horrible and had something to compare it with.

I met a nice guy in my History class. We listened to albums together but he wouldn't be my boyfriend. He had a girlfriend at home. The good ones always had a girlfriend at home. Another guy I was attracted to reminded me of Willie. He had a blonde girlfriend. I went after him one night when we were both drunk and she wasn't around. He also refused my invitation.

There was another guy the sophomores warned everyone about. He was a townie. For some reason I took warnings as dares. One night when a group of us ventured out to an off-campus bar I spotted him. When I got drunk I'd take on anyone, any place, any size. I had come out of black-outs more than once having some huge guy tell me he was going to break my face if I didn't disappear. That is when I'd snap out of it, realize the insanity of my stance, and walk away. In that regard, I think being a female saved my life more than once.

So I approached this asshole. I didn't act very interested. But, I did intend to antagonize him. He was as arrogant as I was. We sparred verbally. Even as I was being physically pulled away from him I wouldn't give in. I wanted to humiliate him. I wanted to get him back for how he had disrespected and used women. By the time we both got good and drunk he had convinced me to leave with him and go to a party that was taking place at his and his roommates place. Against advise I left unafraid I'd be anything less than in total control. We went to a trailer where he and a roommate lived. It was freezing in there. I sat there watching T.V. with them, waiting for everyone to get there. Finally his roommate said; *I'm going to bed.* This guy, I'll call Ron said; *Well, I guess no one is coming. Let's go to bed.* I said; *I'm not going to bed with you. Take me back.* To which he said; *I'm not taking you anywhere! If you want a blanket, come to bed!* With that he got up and went to bed. It was freezing in that dump. There was already over a foot of newly fallen snow and it was coming down hard still. I was trapped.

I went into his room and his bed was a barren mattress. He was wrapped in a blanket. There was nothing for me. There weren't even pillows. I was drunk but not in a black-out and not without my wits. He was getting nothing. I was livid. I lied on his mattress and he groped me until he thankfully passed out. After a little while I fell asleep too. I didn't sleep long though. It was too cold to sleep. I was shivering. I was not expecting to get caught in such a cold dilemma so I hadn't worn enough warm clothes. I needed to get out of there before he woke up. I might not be able to get out of being assaulted twice. He was snoring. I listened to him for awhile, hating the thought of him, me, my situation, my stupidity. At around 4am I had had enough. I slipped from the bed so as not to wake the sleeping bear. I looked out the plastic covered window. The snow was up to the door which was five steps up from the ground. I had no idea where I was in relation to the campus. I had to walk back. I needed more clothes. I silently pulled open his drawers and came up with wool socks, wool gloves, a hat, a scarf, and some long johns. I put it all on then my stuff on top of it. I sneaked out as quickly and as quietly as a mouse when it scoots back to its hole, cheese in its mouth, right past the cat.

When I got outside I could just see the light at the top of the spire of St. Francis Hall. I hoped I was seeing from the north and not the south. If I was coming from the south the distance to campus was doubled. I started walking. The snow was up to my waist. The only saving grace to all that white is it made it light outside in the otherwise dark. I came onto the campus at the north edge where the cafeteria was open. I got on the line and went in. It was 6am. As soon as I hit the heat of the inner area I realized how drunk I was. My head was instantly swimming. I ate oatmeal because it was all I could stomach. I walked back to my room. Got my books and made it to Latin class by 7:30 to recite The Our Father like a drunken Irish dirge. I'll never know how I passed those courses. But, I did.

VALIDATION

I ride the white horse of omnipotence. My arms
shimmy from my silhouette against
the glare of sun.
I am a stick dancing in a heat wave neither
to arrive nor depart.
I joust between sky and earth.
There is no face for the clamber of
hooves to echo against. Breath without
mirror leaves no haze against the image.
I pass—
dimple the sand against a wind that
obscures my tracks. I catch the swords
of villains and the robes of lovers to
wear across my breast.

I am a glint shot from
a sudden angle of sun: gold, silver,
want—
the air in a dream—
the whisper muffled in a shout—
the immortal stealing mortality to force
skin against cloud for the sensation of bone, to taste
the sweet before remorse steals my tongue, to find
a backdrop to reflect existence, if only for a moment, to
validate my soul.

The whole semester was as if I had been dropped, delirious, and unarmed into a foreign land where every bend posed grave danger. There were no comrades, nowhere to get direction or aid. I was on my own. In this place there was no one to blame but myself for every single thing that happened to me. The depth of my self-disgust could only be matched by the confusion of my own identity.

My room had become a hiding place. I never wanted anyone to see me let alone me see anyone. One night, after consuming enough beer and pot to make my face feel a rosy warmth, I stood alone in front of my mirror. I didn't look like anyone I knew. A deep impending doom was gripping me. The lights were dim as usual. I looked like a demon. I talked to myself. Out loud, I said to the person in the mirror; *I've got to stop smoking pot. It is making me paranoid about my drinking.* It was sometime in the beginning of December, 1977. I stopped smoking pot.

I continued to sleep on the floor. My roommate was long gone, staying someplace down the hall, around the corner. To both of us I was a dirty, feral animal. Since I had never figured out who I was I was who anyone said I was. That description fit just fine.

As the semester ended I went home in a state of great trepidation. If I couldn't hold myself together over the month long break I wouldn't be sent back. The only place worse that college was home. That wasn't saying anything. I stayed sober over break and came back early so I could get to my room before I was seen.

I took the bus from Port Authority and had myself dropped in town so I could pick up some wine for when I got back to school. I had drunk a pint of blackberry brandy on the ride up but that didn't last very well over the course of a ten hour trip. I bought a gallon of white wine. I had two big bags I could hardly lift. I had to hitch because I had no money. The guy who picked me up was a little buzzed. He had a beer between his legs. It was common practice to hitch around in that college town but, that didn't make this guy appear safe. He was scary. I could look past that kind of fear. I got in. As soon as we came to the college entrance I had him drop me off. I soon discovered I had him drop me off at the southern entrance which was a couple of acres below where the entrance was to the dorm I stayed in. It was a long hard, cold walk back to my room. I always thought I deserved it. I welcomed the agony. It gave me more of a reason to hate my life, a feeling I had come to thrive on; an energy that made me feel like I had power without any outside threat or manipulation. It was my grizzly growl at breath. It gave me more of a reason to drink when I finally arrived. Nothing was open. No one was there. The halls were dark and quiet. The smell of the dorm shrouded me in its foreboding. There was no food but for a snack machine that had only a couple of stale bags of crap still hanging in its window. I was a ghost in a ghost town. I bought a couple of bags of stale pretzels and scurried to my hiding place. I wished anyone was there and wanted no one to return.

I couldn't imagine life getting any worse than the semester I had just survived. The geographic cure had yet to work its magic. Willingness is incredibly hard to come by. Denial has to be slashed. It does come. It comes in a way that is un-imaginable. My visuals of outcomes have always fallen grossly short of reality. Perhaps that short-coming has always been one facet of my fatal mal-twist. I never could have foresaw what avalanche of blows would come to pass. In no way could I have imagined where those injuries would re-direct me too.

My idea of self was a complete wasteland. But, it was worse than that. A wasteland is dead. I was alive. A desperate creature that skirted the edge of society, I was a despicable wretch. My ability to communicate was long gone. I wasn't even equal to a dog. My ability to have a relationship with any human being was long crushed. I couldn't remember ever having one. The memory of a girl I might have been was like some distant dream that must have taken place in a past life. I didn't know if I was ever anybody. I could summon up no memory of joy, no memory of the feeling that must come when I look forward to anything. I looked forward to nothing. I wanted to die. My heart was a shattered vacancy, hopeless of remains that might be salvageable. The fragments that lay around my soul-wilderness were like little charred bits of burned up stark scraps of a puzzle that lost too many pieces to ever be put together. All I felt was abject terror, ferocious rage, bottomless humiliation, and abysmal loneliness. There is no more unbearable state than a wasteland breathing through the prison of a human body. My only relief was oblivion of my consciousness; black-out drunkiness.

Lake of Alone

She walks the halls with empty eyes, spews
nothing nowhere; A shock of cold air
from the gray of her heart, a breath of ether,
a cloud of despair. A mouth drawn
slack, silent from years past, she,
never really there. Now here, she hides
in a shadow below the bottom stair.
Like an animal, a rat, she shapes her back against
the icy-stone corner of college life.
Bound to her fears she cements her
feet in the bottom of a bottle of liquid retreat.

Somewhere past the hour of two a convulsive racking
shakes her skinless spine. Her teeth chatter, like
an old engine, they grind.
A rats' ghost, she wobbles to rise to
crawl to a warmer lair. Unseen, unheard,
at the edge of humane
night passes to day.

She wakes in urine behind her bed drowning in
the lake of alone. Someone kicks
her shin in disgust and
the shore moves farther away.

She wishes the pump she hears in her head
would stop. The heat behind her face, fade away.
The cold from her heart, reach to her feet. Let
her hard lines disappear into shadow-less gray.

AFTER A COUPLE of interminable days my new roommate arrived. She was very different from the first one. She was happy. She played the guitar. She was part American Indian and very much into the spirituality. She didn't believe in alcoholism. She was determined to like me. She had a group of friends and they took me into their fold as if I had always been there, much like Willie's group had taken me in during high school. Their unconditional acceptance gave me a welcome calmness. I didn't understand it. I just went with it. It was water in the desert. I had many great laughs and times with them. They were strange, like a bunch of geeks and they were my saviors. One more unrecognized thread was cast about me as I hung from the edge. They were my campfire of safety in the deep forest of a black night typhoon. The hardened faces from my previous semester dimmed from my visual nightmare.

My drinking took off as hard and as steady as I had left it. This semester I hooked up with a couple of heavy hitters along with my new friends. It seemed as if my dismal existence had taken a step back from my throat and I could breathe a bit. My new roommate went home for the weekends and the dark pit would move up around me. One morning one of the Juniors came knocking on my door to make sure I was ok. Seems she had saved me from a bunch of black guys who were very close to having their way while I was in the floor lounge drunkenly flirting with them fully clothed in a sheer nightgown. I had no memory of the incident. That same person tried to intervene a few more times. But the downward spiraling was set in motion. Caring appeared fake to me. I didn't have the ability to be cared about. I was beyond human aid.

Half the nights of the week I couldn't find my way to my room. I could find the dorm but, once in the stairway, I couldn't remember where I was. I'd have to go back down, across the lobby, out the front door, and start again paying absolute attention this time. There were times I went through this routine more than once. I drank in corner-shadows in the college center. The bleachers were too wide open, and outside was *always* snowing and usually below zero temperatures. The campus was a maze of icy walkways walled in by seven to ten foot plowed up snow banks. Still, one of my favorite places was at the bottom of the back stairwell. No one ever went there. It was like a man-made cave. The stairs ended to go out the door but, there was a space behind the last set. The unfortunate draw-back was, it was not much warmer there than it was outside. After getting sloshed I usually passed out and was awakened by the intensity of my own shivering. In the grand canyon of my solitary existence, what people moved about me I paid little attention to. I never had eye contact. I didn't want to talk. I roved in a haze of despair.

But for those short, intermittent reprieves I got from my roommate and her friends I might have beat that semester to its end.

Unbelievably, all this time I maintained my dream of running the New York Marathon. My running held a major role in the fatality of my denial. It told me I was in control. I maintained the other requisites of my alibi system as well. I continued to make every class. I always did my homework before I drank. My roommate kept me from becoming totally isolated.

One weekend, alone in my room, I decided I'd try and stop drinking if only to prove I could. I knew, with all my alibis and denials that I was an alcoholic. I still didn't know what that meant though. That night, while I lied in bed, my room filled up with black Halloween cats. Claws fully extended they were hopping, stiff-legged all around me. All of their heads were cocked in my direction. They were all looking at me. They were getting closer with every rhythmic hop. Is was like they were all laughing at me. I jarred awake in a drenching sweat and stayed awake the rest of the night. I knew I needed a drink. I found some skunky beer and drank it, vomited, and drank some more until it stayed down.

SUNDANCE

is suave, the way a black man dances and
a white man can't move.
He struts the bottom of athlete's glory. They're
here for the game while his mind buys him a suit.
A salesman he is

At the Ratzkeller, she stuffs her face with a pepperoni
slice, after a pitcher of beer, bleary eyed for
the forth night.
He moves, like he does—
clear and ugly. Takes a seat beside her. Buys
her a beer, then a whole six to invite
her to his party.

Her first encounter with a black man her father
would call a nigger. She'll prove her father wrong.

She stumbles, but he is a gentleman and helps
her along the way. The party, at his dorm, is in the
community room; the one with the orange and gray, diamond
pattern, indoor-outdoor carpet and the infested love seat with
painted wood arms, inscribed with one hundred names.

He shuts the door behind and vises it
with a chair.
She's smashed, blind drunk.
He helps her to the spring-less cushion that permeates
the smell of rot and without eye contact, steals
a piece of life from her like slamming the head of
a fish on a wood rail until it is dead.
Only after he empties its bullets does she see
the black barrel of his gun as he stuffs it back in his holster.
He tells her to get up and go home.

She doesn't remember the walk to her room, but
vomits to the smell of gunpowder residue come dawn.
One time later he reappears to make a final cut; a warning
he gives, with the knife of his tongue, never to
tell of the scum he imparts.

She never questions what his real name is or
why Sundance for short or long.
She found out what she had no care to know; he shoots
his gun from the hip with rampant precision because
he fires on the run.
Sundance he is.

THERE WAS THIS black guy named Sundance who worked the snack stand in the Community Center. He was very friendly and outgoing. I liked the thought of us being friends. Everyone liked Sundance. He was getting educated on a scholastic scholarship. Obviously his upbringing was good. He was very polite.

I frequented 'The Skellar' often with my new drunk-mates. I saw Sundance there a few times. He didn't drink but, he would buy me a beer and talk to me. One night he told me there was a party back at his dormitory. He invited me. He bought me a twelve-pack of Pabst Blue Ribbon. He held my hand as we walked across campus. By the time we got to his room he was practically carrying me. We were both laughing and carrying on. I was quite drunk but, not in a black-out. His roommate was a big basketball star. He had recently been the talk of the campus for getting caught shoplifting in Rochester. When you are a big star you get away with things the rest of us pay for. He was still on the team and heading forward as if nothing at all had happened. He was 6'7" and black as the ace of spades. Sundance was a scrawny, brown rat in comparison to him.

When we got to the room Sundance went quickly in ahead. The roommate was studying. They had a little dispute and I heard the roommate say; *get the fuck out of here. Go to the community room.* I was wobbling in the doorway. He had the beer in his fist. He grabbed my wrist and yanked me to the community room. The room was empty except for a filthy, ripped-sponge cushioned, graffiti-covered wooden armed, love-seat-sized couch, and a hard wooden table and chairs set. He shouldered the door shut and jammed one of the chairs up under the knob to keep it closed. I just sat there like a drugged animal that couldn't combat its captor. *Was this really happening?* Then he was on me. He shoved me back on the couch, tore my pants down, opened his zipper, pulled out his big black penis and raped me. It only took a few minutes. When he was done he yanked me to my feet and said; *Get out.* His voice was barely audible. I was in a state of shock, not really sure what the hell just happened and knowing exactly what happened at the same time. It was one of the moments I wished with every fiber in my body I had the power to turn the clock back on so I could avoid it the next time but it was too late. I fumbled to get my pants on and left like the dirtiest little piece of living garbage ever conceived. I don't remember walking back to my room.

The next morning, early, I was jarred awake by a slamming on my door. It was my x-roommate. Trying to make amends, I had promised to cover her in a sporting competition and I was supposed to be there in fifteen minutes. I crashed to the door with the memory of the whole night between me and her glare.

I opened the door to her ugly mouth yelling at me, calling me irresponsible, useless, liar, etc. etc. I didn't need her to tell me. I knew it. At this point I was flat-line. I was beyond tears. I said; *I need a shower.* She said; *there is no time! You are late!* I ran into the bathroom at least to pee. Maybe I could still half save myself. I smelled like booze and sex. I stunk so bad I could smell myself. Sundance came pouring out. I wished I could die right there. My self-disgust was profound. My x was in there, outside the stall, pushing me to hurry. I changed into gym cloths and ran to the Community Center. With my help my team won. That's what my x wanted. But appeasing her gave me no relief. I was like a rotted body; a stinking living dead thing that had no purpose but continued to exist in spite of every dismal chance the world could erect to extinguish it once and for all. I hated myself. I hated that x-roommate. I had a wretched hangover but, who cared. The team wanted to go out and applaud themselves. I was included. It was good for a drunk but, I wasn't making friends with them and I wasn't going drinking with them. I was going back to my safe seclusion and try to rid myself of my sinful stench.

I had come to an existence of going to class in the morning. At 2pm I'd pick up my booze for the night. I'd go back to my room and place it in the window where it would stay nice and cold. Then, I would do my homework. After my homework I exercised. When I was finished, I'd get something to eat. Usually I got some sort of cheap delivery. Then I didn't have to leave my room. I could get take out from the bar. Sometimes I did that. I was totally paranoid and going to the cafeteria was out of the question. After I ate I snuggled into my cozy aloneness and got drunk. It was the only way for me to drink safely. I was open prey when I went out.

One night one of my drunk comrades and I were out drinking and she got us involved with a couple of guys. They were a little goofy to me but I went along. I liked my friend. We went back to their dorm and I thought; *oh no, here we **don't** go again*. As we were climbing into our respective bunks I feigned an intense need to urinate. The guy didn't believe me. I assured him I'd pee in his bed if I didn't run out and go. He let me go, promising I'd be right back. I ran out to go to the bathroom and didn't stop until I got inside my own room and locked the door behind myself. The next day my friend asked me where I went. I told her I had no intension of getting laid. There were no hard feelings.

The last time I went out I met this really nice, handsome, tall, athletic guy. When he told me there was a party in his dorm I said; *no way!* He was insistent and said; *come check it out. If there is no party, you can leave.* That seemed fair enough. We went to his dorm. Sure enough there was a room full of people. I relaxed a little bit. They were all sitting in a big circle. I'd say there were about twelve people all together. They were drinking from a keg and passing a bong around. John and I took our places next to each other in the circle. These were all his good friends. At one point, as I was in and out of a black-ou,t I was aroused to clarity by cheering; *Go! Go! Go! Go!* I realized they were cheering at me. I had the bong and was refusing my turn. I realized every person in the room was a guy. I realized, one hit off that bong and I was going to be out cold. I realized I was on the verge of being gang raped.

I told John; *I have to go.* He said; *you can't leave now! The party is just starting! If you leave now I'm not going to tell you how to get out! You're on your own!* The bunch of them were too drunk to stop me. They couldn't be sure how clear I was. If I could see and recall faces they all could be in grave trouble. I had to be passed out. I stumbled out the door, down the corridor, across the campus, and into the safety of my own room.

I didn't go out anymore that year. I drank in my room or a short distance down the hall in one of my drunken comrade's rooms. My roommate and her friends were a last reprieve. I got some semblance of fun out of being with them. They were an odd, backwoods group of girls. The qualities of being completely harmless, non-judgmental, and totally welcoming had everything to do with why I relaxed into their herd. They were a refreshing and much needed respite in the battlefield of humanity.

Once when I had no money I went into my roommates drawer and wrote out a five dollar check from her checkbook. I wrote it with my non-dominant right hand to disguise my handwriting. When she inevitably questioned me I went into a victimized speech about how some Sophomores had stolen a pair of my boots and a shirt once before and how we had to keep our door locked. The door was thence locked. She never moved her checkbook and the subject never came up again. I had become completely unscrupulous. I couldn't even be a friend to a friend. I was a liar and a thief.

The last two outstanding incidents to round off my year at college were; I had stopped attending English Literature class because the final grade was for an oral report. The thought of any kind of public speaking froze me in fear. One day, while walking back from my consistently empty mailbox I ran into my professor. He asked me if I was coming back to class. I asked if I could just turn in my paper and forgo the oral part of the assignment. He told me; *no. It is part of your final. But if you come to class I'll call on you next and you can get it over with.* The mere suggestion sent me into a spin of anxiety. I never went back. It was my one 'F' on a report-card of straight 'C''s.

Another time, walking down the same sidewalk back from the same empty mailbox, I walked, literally, smack into Sundance. Apparently our head-on collision wasn't by accident. I bolted erect and stared straight into his dead black eyes. He muttered so that only I could hear; *you keep your mouth shut or you'll be really sorry . . . mark my words.* Then he went right on walking like not a word was ever spoken between us.

I was in upstate New York attending school on a magnificent campus and I might as well have been in a jail cell siding the corridor of the green mile. The utter hopelessness, despair, desolation, and self loathing were like a case of unrelieved shingles, but there was no rash, no open wounds, and there was no name for the sickness that gripped me. There was no doctor I could go to for a cast or wet salve to give any kind of relief. Any soothing would have been a moment of affection before the last breath of a dying dog. The most unbearable manifestations regarding emotional sickness are; no one can see it so it's not neat and tidy like a broken arm. It makes people uncomfortable because they feel helpless and annoyed by the powerlessness it provokes. That creates an irrepressible need to deny the very existence of any illness at all and the denial is like gas on the fire of the force from within that is so destructive in the first place. No one knows how to deal with it, not the one who is sick and not any person who is affected. There are what—ifs, and way too many mirror images. And the result of these grave characteristics is the one who is sick gets slowly, or quickly if God is merciful, bludgeoned to death either physically by being raped, beaten or murdered; mentally by being slandered, mocked, coaxed, chided, blamed, accused, or looked down upon in any measure; or a combination of the physical and mental reactions of those who join the crowd like citizens in the great stadiums of Roman Gladiators blood-thirsty to see one go down. It's always easy when it's not oneself. It's easy to be one of the crowd and feel right in numbers. If the reaction of the human race is not enough to extinguish the flame of any mental malady then, in the end, to the agony and relief of every person of witness, the swollen misfit inevitably will find a way to commit suicide. Then society can move forward diminishing its claim to any blame by proclaiming; *what a shame . . . what a shame . . .*

FAST SLIDE

WITH MY ROOMMATE going home every weekend, I stayed in my room alone. One night, while I was trying to patch a couple of days in a row without drinking, I fell asleep on my couch-bed. I saw a great white light barreling toward me. It was a train. Its approach was rampaging swift. I was fighting desperately to wiggle out of its tracks but, it kept coming and it got roaring loud. As I was about to be demolished like a bird being smashed against a speeding car-grill, I bolted awake. I sat up panting, cold, and covered with sweat. I knew exactly what I needed. I gulped down the stomach wrenching remains of a skunky Molson Golden Ale. My favorite brew tasted like the worst rot gut I ever had cross my tongue. It was like drinking liquid sandpaper soaked in acid. I sat in the dark terrified. I calmed myself down drinking a few more, un-opened skunky Molson's. As the night wore on I knew I had to stop drinking. I knew I couldn't. I knew what alcoholism was. I knew I had to get out of this place. I knew if I lived to get out I'd never, never come back. I prayed harder than I'd ever prayed before. I sat there, unable to sleep, until it was time to go to class. Without any relief in sight I went through the motions. With all of my might, I went through the motions.

When the semester ended my roommate had gone early. I packed up my stuff and left through a side-back door so I wouldn't have to see anyone. I took the bus home. When I got there I stayed dry for a week. I met a girl my age who was living in, my childhood-friend, Mat's house. Her name was Mahla. I was a million miles from being capable of friendship. I guess she was very lonely because she was very insistent. It was ok. Her house gave me a place to run to. We were friends for about one month.

After a week I got ripping drunk on a pint of vodka and a six of beer. The next evening while I was sitting at the breakfast bar my father sat down next to me. He said; *I'm the best friend that you will ever have.* Hah! He said; *if you want help you have to ask for it.* That was the end of his talk. I hadn't said anything for years. I was well trained at keeping my mouth shut. Between the horrific beatings he laid on me and my brothers, the indifference toward any achievement I had experienced, and his constant barrage of demoralizing accusations I couldn't, for the life of me, understand why he would being saying what he said. I decided it was because it would be devastatingly humiliating to he and my mother if I committed suicide. It was a reasonable option in my shattered heart-mind. If I got drunk enough I would success; get out of this fucking-hell-hole of life for good.

Another couple of weeks went by. I had to get a summer job. My hollow relationship with Mahla was no more than an escape. She had no clue. My parents acted like they liked her. That was good enough. I just kept getting drunk. It was the only way I could bear to draw breath in what seemed to me to be one big fake existence. Everyone was lying.

On that Stoop

I remember the day I sat on that stoop
the way you did, then we all did. It was
a black, sunny day. The velvet green lawn
you extracted sanity from tending on weekends
was fresh cut and gave its breath to sweeten the
air all the way from the root.

I remember the day I sat on that stoop with
an ocean in my head. I didn't dare let
the pressure force a leak through my eyes.
I pretended to have interest in the occasional
passing car—the squirrel nibbling something
in the lawn.

I remember the swirl—everything moving in
a spin, outward, out of reach—me the
vortex forcing everything away, not knowing
how to stop the momentum that had gained
velocity, had become a tornado.

I remember you sitting down next to me, unafraid—
how the centrifugal force couldn't push
you away—how you reached your hand in, found
mine and held it long enough to offer help—
I remember how I accepted.

One Saturday afternoon in mid-May of 1978, at the age of nineteen, in a state of total handless, vacant despair, I came down the stairs and saw my father sitting on the front steps as he often did after mowing the lawn. I went out the door and sat down next to him. We sat there, next to each other, silent for awhile, just enjoying the fresh green smells, the warm breeze, the beautiful spring day. Then I broke the silence with just four words; *Dad, I need help.* We didn't look at each other. He just said; *Don't worry about it kid. I'll take care of it.* We sat there for awhile more like we never said one word to each other then I got up and went back in through the house.

My father set up a meeting with a counselor at a regional drunk tank/nut house named Bergen Pines. My meeting was a week away. I stayed sober until the morning before the meeting. I was all jammed up about it. Mahla wanted to go to the mall in the morning. It was perfect. This was one more excuse to get out one last time and have one more drunk before I started treatment. I'd have to control it but, I knew I could. While I was taking a shower I downed a pint of vodka. I usually could hold that amount just fine. I guess I drank it a little faster than usual. I went and met Mahla. The rest is a black-out. She told me on our way to the mall I started to act funny. Then I insisted she bring me home. I remember getting out of her car at the bottom of my parents road. She thought it was weird but really had no recourse but to let me go. When I got like that there was no stopping me. I was in one of those breaks from reason.

She dropped me at the curb at the bottom of the street. The road ran parallel to The Garden State Parkway. I hopped out of the car. I knew I couldn't go home drunk as I was so I ran down the embankment along the side of the road that met with the side of The Parkway. About halfway down the grassy slope I laid back in the overgrown lawn. I passed out. The next thing I recall a cop was picking me up. He threw me in the back of his car and drove me to the station. I vaguely remember being at the police station. They tore my wallet apart finding I.D.. The next thing I remember I was lying in a hospital bed and this woman was talking to me. She was asking me if I remembered her. I never saw her before. I couldn't imagine what we had to do with each other. She told me she was my counselor and that we had had a long conversation the previous day.

I didn't believe about the long conversation but she could call herself my counselor if she wanted to. I didn't trust her. She was way too nice and she acted like she cared; one of the first signs of trouble brewing.

There was a twenty-eight day program for alcoholism she offered. I accepted. I'd do anything. They did a lot of mental tests on me. This was a real nut house. I knew I wasn't one of them. All my life I could never be sure with all the convincing my mother had done of my insanity. But, hanging out in a day room with people zonked on thorazine shocked me straight into recognition of the difference between the sickness of chemical dependence and mental illness. I did not want to be zonked on Thorazine and led around aimlessly for the rest of my life. It was a scary and sad place. It was gray, dismal and dirty. Everyone was alone. There was a woman who roomed at the end of the hall. She kept screaming for her mother. She had wet brain, a condition I could get if I kept on drinking. I saw two different people have convulsions. That appears like an exorcism. The person jerks around and foams at the mouth like they are possessed.

A group of patients in the program at the time I was there went out drinking one night. I didn't dare go. I had no idea what was going to happen to me if I stayed with the program but I didn't want what going drinking gave to me. They all got caught. That was the night I saw one of the convulsions. I was having a horrible nightmare of my own. I was dreaming someone was breaking in through the window over my bed and they had a big knife they were going to stab me to death with. The girl who was convulsing was making guttural noises and it added to the reality of my nightmare. As the aids got her under control they heard me screaming. They came hurrying into my room which brought me out of my trance. One of them said; *oh, she's just hallucinatin', she'll be fine.* Me?! I was hallucinating?! What was happening to me?!

I was like a scared little girl left in the middle of a battlefield where bullets are flying everywhere and there is no one to scoop you up and carry you to safety.

I went to all the meetings. I did all the assignments. I was completely willing to let people save me from my imminent demise. At twenty-eight days I was ready to wet my feet in AA. I was filled with the relief of having found the answer. It was June 29th, my mother's birthday. When she picked me up I said happy birthday. She was surprised and happy I remembered. I think it was the first time I pleased her in any way in my whole life. The moment was glorious.

I went to AA and reveled in the confusion of my infant solution. I rode my ten speed bike to meetings all over the place including the ones at the rehab. That drunk-tank was the thread that snagged me as I dangled over the abyss of my last pass over the fiery canyon gorge of rock spiked addiction.

When I got home from rehab my parents were immediately on me. I was accused because I was me. They couldn't contain their rage toward me. It was like having my wounds washed out and then being thrown back into the cage with the same tigers that tore me up in the first place. I was a wretched, despicable, worthless burden they didn't deserve. I was an animal at the edge of humanity wanting to get in and run away at the same time. I was terrified. I had no identity. I was at the discretion of whatever anyone said I was. When I wasn't in an AA meeting I was on a quickly melting ice-flow in the middle of the Antarctic. When I was in an AA meeting I was a small child on a shadowed street of tall strangers. I was alone. It was unbearable.

It took about three days to drink. I met a kid in the neighborhood who had some pot. I had long since sworn off pot but after all I had been through it seemed safer than drinking. We smoked a joint and in just a few toques my throat was burning. The only thing the kid had was Schmidts Dark beer. It was like mud. I drank it. The combination did not put a dent in the relief I desperately sought and I fell into a black fear. I asked the kid to take me to Bergen Pines on his moped. I think he thought I was going to cop some more pot. He was wrong. When we got there I hopped off his bike and said thanks for the ride. He was a little dumbfounded by this turn of events. But he left giving me a strange look as he departed. I went into the emergency room and they made me wait two hours. When I finally gave up hope of help and started to leave someone chased after me. I went back and signed myself in. I wanted help. I signed myself back out the next day. But, I had no place to go. I couldn't be at my parents house. As soon as they saw me they'd start up. It was beyond unbearable. I hung out under bridges, behind buildings, in the woods, at AA meetings, and at Bergen Pines. I was beyond human aid. I wouldn't go near men for fear of being raped and I wouldn't go near women because anyone of them who was nice I assumed was queer. I signed myself in and out of Bergen Pines five times that July.

The last drink I had was on August 1, 1978. It was a pint of Peppermint Schnapps. I figured I could disguise it as crest toothpaste on my breath. I downed it with a buttered roll along the side of a baking hot field of tall grass swaying with bees and gnats. There was a small herd of cows grazing alongside me. I felt at home with them there. I dreamed of the farm as a white haze released me momentarily from my inner turmoil. When I was done I headed over to Bergen Pines. The rehab-center had become my hang-out. The sober alcoholics were always welcoming unless I made an uproar which I occasionally did at one of the meetings. Then, they would only tell me to pipe down which I always did, with great humiliation, having forgot myself,.

On this day, the woman who was my counselor called me into her office. I truly believed no one could tell I was drunk even as I crashed into her door on my way to falling into the seat. Since she didn't react I figured she didn't notice. I was scared of her because she acted like she cared. Caring was all bullshit to me. Even so, the caring felt good. It waked a much guarded longing in my ribcage.

She said; *you need long term care. We can't help you here.* I said; *I have no money but, I'll do whatever you suggest.* I was at a place of abandoned willingness. I knew I was going to die or worse, keep living as I was. I was in a state of terrified desperation. Whatever she offered I'd take. She told me there was a three month program in Jersey City at the Salvation Army. I agreed to go.

On August second, my first day of sobriety, my counselor asked me to tell my parents of my intention to go to Jersey City for the ninety-day program. They weren't permitted to tell because I was no longer a minor. I was nineteen. As far as I was concerned my parents could go fuck themselves. I hated them, had no respect for them, and had absolutely nothing to say to them. The counselor was insistent. Eventually I told her to do whatever she wanted but I would not have anything to do with them and I didn't want to ever see or speak to them again.

On August third, sometime in the afternoon, they showed up in their car in front of the center where I was staying, awaiting my departure for the Salvation Army Program. Someone told me they were there and prodded me to go to the steps. I went. My father told me to get in the car. I said flat out; *no.* I didn't have to do anything he said ever again. That car didn't move until I agreed to sit in the backseat with the door open just for a minute to hear them out. I was like a volcano without a hole to spout its lava. The rock at the mouth of my stomach was a hot boulder. The undertow in my solar plexus was a red rip-tide. This better be good. My face was stone. My eyes were black. My mind I was granite. I was absolutely ready to commit suicide if I had to remain one more day under their regime. They would not get a feathers weight in power.

My father said; *We're sending you to Alina Lodge.* It was a renown drunk-tank in western New Jersey run by a notorious woman named Mrs. D. I had heard the place spoken of many times at meetings. It had even been suggested as a place for me.

I told my father; *I'm going to the Salvation Army in Jersey City.* He said; *You're not going there. We won't allow it.* I said; *You can't stop me.* He said; *We are stopping you. You're going to Alina Lodge. It's a three month program. There is a pool on the premises.*

I asked; *what about school?* He said; *This is your school. It's coasting me 3,500/month.* Not feeling there was really an option, being absolutely defeated, and at least knowing I was getting out of my life and there'd be a pool there, I agreed to go and got out of the car.

That night, my grandmother's sister, my aunt Edna, came to see me at Bergen Pines. She had the name and phone number of a board member from the Lodge named Sonny. I needed to call if I was serious about The Lodge. The next day I called her and she came over that afternoon to talk to me. She knew all about Mrs. D and Alina Lodge. She talked to me for a couple of hours. She came back the next day with some papers of intent. Everyone wanted to be very sure I wanted what was being offered. They had no idea just how desperate I had become. Little did even I know, the tightening of my heart screw had started way back when I was barely five years old and now I was wound so tight the fact that I hadn't already snapped was a miracle only Mrs. D could see.

Every fiber in my body was starving like an emaciated animal willing to gnaw at a dried out bone from its own leg long bare of even a hardened strand of sinew just to free its mind of its obsession with hunger. I was deciding between life and death. This was the final turning point, my last chance to choose life. I chose life and I knew I needed help to succeed.

JUST TO GET AWAY FROM THE HATE

That night, the feeling of relief was the most
profound sensation I can ever remember having.
I lied in starched, white sheets, my head
on a too flat pillow, next to a roommate who
was a nun.
What we *didn't* have in common was a question tweaked
void in the talk we exchanged in the quiet after lights out.

Something was wrong when this nineteen year old kid and
this fifty year old nun needed to be shuffled away to
a secret place, become nameless, faceless to unravel
the knots of horror that made it a welcome foray to be
boarded up against life for a year.

I couldn't imagine how close to insanity I was until
years later, given the same eyes, the same mouths alluding to
my inferior confessions, my worthless endeavors that
I recalled how exquisite the idea of self-destruction
had become.—How I tried to blot my perception out in the
repetition of addiction—How I'd keep waking up, again,
with an ever tightening head—How life became
a game of chance I wished I could stop playing—
So,

the day I landed in that bed, put away from everything,
to say I was relieved doesn't come close to the shedding
of those years of pent up, hollow rage that eclipsed from my
shattered spirit, left bruised, abandoned for
a lack I never could quite figure out.
I knew that night it was over. I was getting
what I wanted though I had no idea what that was.
> Maybe just to get out, away from those
> people who bore me so and
> hated me for who I was.

Maybe it was just to get away from the hate.

On August ninth I arrived at Alina Lodge. I was strip searched right down to my shoes having the inserts pulled out. If it was possible to humiliate me any further, it was humiliating. But there was nothing left of a person at that point. So my entry requirements were just one more chain of events to withstand. I was incredibly tired. I just wanted to go to sleep. It was hot as Hades the day I got there. All of my secret snacks, even my hairdryer was sent home. I didn't wear make-up or have bleached hair so I didn't have to suffer those losses. I was given what was called 'a Buddy'. That was a sister woman student assigned to me to show me the ropes; the rules. She was way too friendly for my comfort but, she used a cane so how dangerous could she be? I'd role her skinny body in a ball and shove her behind a rock if she tried anything. In a few days I felt comfortable with her. It was quickly obvious she had no ulterior motive. We were in this together.

The first night I lied in bed in that place I can still remember the feeling. I had an overwhelming impression of being safe. It was a wonderful feeling. I knew, in the pile of my shattered heart fragments, that I was going to be alright. I could not ever in my life recall such a warmth. Even as the tornadic swirl of my mind whipped, vaulting the flying debris of my short life like a million daggers scratching to impale an opportune mortal wound at first chance, with great flotillas of disbelief keeping the whirl spinning in a down-spout, a pressure, like a herculean helium balloon, filled the space of my colossal storm, rose up with so a great a force it stopped the tornado and unraveled the twist in an opposite direction with an energy that had the impact to give me a glance at the possibility of rescue.

I was really here, in this bed, with this nun as my roommate. And she said; *I know exactly how you feel.* Oh my God . . . I wasn't alone. I slept in a fleeting peace it took nineteen years to find.

A BARE BEGINNING

THE PROGRAM WAS rigorous. There were three meetings and three meals a day that were required. We could watch T.V. from 8-10pm but, the night meeting was from 7:30-8:30pm and we were required to remain in the meeting hall until at least nine. Then there was no reception. The only reading material allowed was the AA big book and The Twelve and Twelve step book. We were given note books and pens. No one was allowed to carry any money. There was no phone and no contact with the outside world. All mail was checked. There was no fraternization. I saw people get kicked right out for even having eye contact with the opposite sex. Everyone got chores that rotated and we signed up for. Sheets were stripped and changed once a week. There was no sugar and no caffeine.

We ate separated men from women at round tables. We were served military style where each table got called one by one to get on line and walk up to the food counter. The staff sat at the head table and watched every person fill their plate. If there was suspicious eating behaviors they were promptly questioned.

I never talked. I had one expression; stone. I did what I had to do. I was deathly uncomfortable with the eating arrangement. Every self conscious thought I ever had ran rampant. All my defenses were up and running.

After just a couple of weeks of this I was called into my counselor's office and asked just how uncomfortable did I think my behavior was for those people sitting at my table. I didn't know. I was ordered to talk. Just say anything. I was told I was scaring everyone at the table when I sat in cold silence. This was my first big hurtle; talk to people I was having a meal with. Talk about a bare beginning.

MEETING THE LADY

JUST TO BACK up for a moment; the night I first saw Mrs. D is engraved in my mind. It was the second week I was a student at the Lodge. I was still on 'Buddy'. That lasted for two weeks. There had been a constant buzz about this God-like person since I had arrived. Mrs. D was away on a routine trip to Oklahoma. No one knew when she was coming back. There was a palpable anticipation that hung in the air. There wasn't a person who wasn't in awe of this enigma that could, at any moment, appear in our midst. Even the staff showed signs of fear. Wariness was never completely gone. This woman had ways of appearing when least expected. My fellow students spoke of how Mrs. D heard everything, saw everything, and was everywhere at once. They talked about how people were kicked out for breaking her stringent rules; how she could see right through a liar. This was a whole institution for the reformation of liars. Alcoholic and liar fell under the same paragraph of similes in the thesaurus.

At dinner men wore suits and ties. Women wore dresses. I thought we were lucky. Those jackets and ties looked boiling in the summer heat. This night was no more uncomfortable than any other except that this night the Lady was coming home. Everyone did a little more spiffing-up than usual.

It was at dinner that Mrs. D arrived. My heart was pounding out of my ears so that I thought those at my table must hear it. I suppose their hearts were pounding too loud to hear mine. There had been a short warning. We knew her arrival was imminent. When the lights of her Lincoln shined into the front of the dining hall, silence fell like a tree in the forest; whether it went still abruptly like the explosive snap of a branch breaking on its slamming stop short of hitting the forest floor or whether it was more like a wave; like the crescendo of a chorus when it rises up to the sound of every instrument; the moment every last leaf on every last branch has finally come to its resting place and all the creatures of the forest sit stone-still as specters of what they now are not sure really happened or was a figment of their thought because the silence that quaked to loom is utterly deafening, I am not sure. What I recall is everyone just stopped and waited. No one was breathing. Silence is amazingly loud.

It was an eternity before the outer door opened and my potatoes lumped in the mouth of my stomach. Then Simone, Mrs. D 's driver, opened the inner door. I leaned ever-so-slightly forward.

Mrs. D came into the room like a shining star; bigger than life and life-size at the same time. She had on a purple dress-suit, a ten-gallon, grey-suede cowboy hat, and snake-skin gray heels. In her hand was a twelve foot rustlers whip. Mrs. D stepped in that door, stopped, squinted her eyes, set her mouth in those ways I came to know well, and scanned the entire room and everyone in it. Then she snapped that whip against the floor. No one moved. I still wasn't breathing. So, this is Mrs. D. I thought. She didn't really look scary. But it wasn't her appearance that scared people. It was her knowing that blew everyone into submission. Mrs. D had a way of telling the truth in no uncertain terms. That truth made denial run like a rabbit from a wolf. My life was denial. Could this woman get me to walk out of my life?

A different kind of silence befell me. Where I never wanted to hear anything, I hung on her every word. I was comfortable with her presence as long as she didn't come too close or have eye contact with me.

After coming to the 'Buddy' table and meeting the three of us new comers she kept a comfortable distance. The crescendo of events wasn't quite over though. At that infant dinner, in the presence of this daunting woman, one of the three of us bucked out of her chair and fell to the floor flailing in a convulsion. In what developed into a short stretch of mayhem, I couldn't imagine where I had got myself. What I knew was, it was ten worlds better than where I had come from.

RECOVERY

USUALLY, A NEW student stayed in their original room for a month minimum, often times longer. After three weeks, having gotten relatively comfortable with my roommate, I was called to Mrs. D's office. I didn't know if I was getting kicked out or not. I had kept as low a profile as possible. I didn't know there was no such thing as a low profile at Mrs. D's place. Everyone was buzzing.

Mrs. D's office was big. There was a lot of plush dark furniture. Wood paneling and shelves filled with books and owls surrounded the room. Her desk was huge and sat in front of a bay window that looked out on an array of humming bird feeders that had a lot of customers. There were a lot of healthy plants hanging. There was a shag carpet on the floor. It was surprisingly very cozy. I had to look around as I entered to locate her. She was immediately friendly. I didn't trust that. Friendly usually meant trouble. I was offered any seat I wanted. I chose a stiff wooden chair with a basket weave seat. There was no relaxing here. I wasn't fooled one bit.

I was right across from her and she was looking straight at me. *Holy shit!* I thought; *she's looking right at me.* I swirled down to something like a beetle under a farm boot. *Am I going to be stomped or set free?*

Mrs. D started; *Do you like my owls?* I looked around; *yes. You see* she said; *you have to be careful of what you tell people you like. I mentioned once that I like owls and they've been multiplying ever since. I am running out of room. I suppose I'll have to start giving them away. Look around. I'm going to let you pick one for yourself one day.* It would be much harder to pick one of these than to pick out a pair of sneakers in one of those monstrous sneaker factories. Wow.

Then she asked; *how close are you to your grandmother's sister?* I said; *I don't know who you mean.* Mrs. D replied; *your aunt Edna.* I said; *I have nothing to do with her.* I didn't. She was a wild-red-headed alcoholic witch I, as a child, ran up into the house, the barn, or wherever else I could escape to that was away from her horrifying actions. She was terrifying to me as a child. But, I didn't have to tell Mrs. D all of that.

Mrs. D asked if I thought it would hinder my recovery if my aunt came into the Lodge. I said; *no. It definitely will not.* Mrs. D told me we were to stay away from each other. That was no problem.

My great-aunt-Edna came in at the end of the same month I arrived. She got my bed and I was moved into the white house in the room with sliding glass doors directly across the twenty yard lawn from Mrs. D's bay window. Unlike every other student who was regularly moved and always had a roommate, but for the occasional quick-pass-through, I remained a single and a steady resident of that room for the next nine and one half months. I never thought much of it. In retrospect it was the first room I had ever had to myself; no baby, no brothers, no roommates, no body. Only in retrospect can I see what Mrs. D saw up front. Right from the start and way before, way, way before I could conceive the possibility, Mrs. D treated me like I was worth something. I thought I was passing unnoticed.

SHADOW

There is no doubt I am here.
My shadow spreads out before me.
No darkness before a crescent moon can cast
if not for a mass before its shade.
Or *is* it an "I" who stands behind this difference,
this intangible that suds into the slightest angle,
that disappears in direct sun or a moon overhead,
that vanishes into me if
I bend to touch its soft, blanket cliff?

If it were not for the ache of bone,
the hunger of flesh clinging there,
the dryness of my mouth at dawn,
I'd have no cause
to pour water down the gullet of my reservoir,
to hear the siren of my song,—
the chaos of the name flinging before
the flame inside my cave.

I would have no need for touch
but that my shadow casts an
impression of a self.

No one stayed with the same roommate for long. No one stayed in the same room for long. Everyone was always moving while I just stayed put.

At first I was assigned to answer the phones. I suffered such abject terror of people I was overwrought by that job. All I could do was be defensive. It came off as a fierce nastiness toward the caller on the other end of the phone. After about a month of torture for everyone Mrs. D. called me in and told me; *if you weren't such a bitch I'd leave you there until Hell froze over.*

I knew Hell would never freeze over. I was on fire up to my neck and I was told my toes haven't felt much heat yet. I hoped for the fires of Hell. That firestorm would be so great, the pain of one more breath would never be felt.

I can't have you answering my phone. People are in too much need of help. You can mop the kitchen floors every day before the morning session including cleaning all the mats.

This was right up my alley. A dirt-bag job is perfect for a dirt-bag. I washed all the kitchen floors, inner and outer, with a bucket of soapy water and cloth handi-wipes on my hands and knees for the next eight months. Then I washed the rags in a washing machine hidden in the basement. The perk was I did my own laundry in the washer/dryer as well. I never asked permission. The student who turned the job over to me did it and told me I could do it. *Just be cool;* she said. I figured I'd do it until I was told to stop. I carried my dirty and then clean basket of laundry across that bay window view in that place where Mrs. D. never missed a trick for eight months. No one ever said a word and neither did I.

Every day, as I was cleaning out the bucket to attend the meeting, the milk man arrived and rolled his muddy wheeled hand-truck in and out over my newly cleaned floor. I couldn't change the time I mopped. It drove me crazy until one day while I was on my hands and knees scrubbing around the oven bases, the kitchen lady, Dinny, supposedly inadvertently, clocked me on the back of my head with a flying carrot-end that shot off the chop-chop-block. I waited for her to say *oouu I'm sorry* or to ask me politely to get it from under the big oven where it darted to rest. She didn't even acknowledge the flight of the carrot chunk. Right there I experienced my first "letting go". None of this activity I took so personally even mattered. I left that carrot to rot where it lay. I scrubbed that floor to perfection every morning and when the milk man came it didn't matter if he made mud tracks or skid marks. I'd be back tomorrow. It was real freedom and I told the group about it.

I got a visit from one or the other parent every three or more weeks so either of them didn't have to come more often than every six weeks or two months. Into my forth month my father came to tell me it was costing him ten thousand dollars and that this better work because it was my college education.

At the end of four months it was Thanksgiving time. My parents decided I had had enough treatment. After all it was a three month program. I was called into my counselor's office and told of their decision. I was asked how I felt about it. I had not spoken to my counselor prior to this meeting. Up to this point, I'd be called in. She would ask me if there was anything I wanted to talk about. I'd say no and I'd be excused. Every time I went in I wanted to talk. Every time I was too afraid. I was trained not to open my mouth. On this day the prospect of going home catapulted me into a dissertation on my life with them. I told her everything and in the end I told her if I ever went home I'd drink. Those people made me suicidal. The thought of ever going back filled me with immobilizing anxiety.

It was in that counseling session that my recovery took off.

Mrs. D. was always making the women with long hair tie it back or cut it off. There would be no hiding behind hair. I had long blonde hair down to the middle of my back. She never said anything to me about my hair.

The evening following that pivotal meeting with my counselor, while I was on the dinner line filling my plate, I felt a great presence behind me, at my shoulder. Mrs. D. stroked the back of my head and down the length of my hair with one hand. With the other on my shoulder, she said in a voice just audible to me; *don't you worry. I'll take care of that witch. You're not going anywhere.* Then she moved away. It was an experience akin to a dream. It felt quite ethereal. I didn't see Mrs. D. until I sat down. She was across the room. There was the slightest eye contact and unperceivable nod. I ate my dinner.

It was Thanksgiving. At The Lodge there was a special gratitude meeting on the Saturday night of that weekend. About one hundred people from the outside joined the eighty students and some twenty staff members. Excluding the students (we were only to listen) anyone who wanted too went up to the podium and expressed their gratitude. It wasn't halfway through that meeting that I began to cry. I'd never felt gratitude before. On this night I was overwhelmed with it. On this night, in 1978, I realized, without reservation, I wanted what these people obviously had. I didn't know what it was exactly or how to get it exactly. I knew, from this night, from these people coming together in this very out-of-the-way place, to not drink or do drugs was the fundamental keystone to have any chance at it at all. That was the night I knew I'd never drink or do drugs again, never. That was the night I turned up my listening; the listening I have never turned down. People were to teach me. This was a big one. It was one of the uncountable spiritual awakenings I've come to on my journey. I suddenly saw and understood things in a way I had never seen or understood them before.

Christmas was a beautiful and special time. Before I knew it, it was Easter. As far as I was concerned I could stay at The Lodge forever. I found a place I fit for the first time in my life. The meetings, the anniversaries, the Saturday singing and the great singing at every celebration. It seemed life had become a celebration. Time was grand. I felt happy. I felt safe. There was palpable love all around me. The Lodge had become a Heaven of sorts.

In April I received a letter from my father's sister, an aunt who lived about forty-five minutes from The Lodge. She was inviting me to come live with her. I felt cautiously excited. She always seemed to like me which was a far cry from my parents. It seemed a reasonable option for re-acquaintance with the real world. I put a write-it in to see my counselor. When she was away, a different, much harsher, counselor was available. I was asked if I wanted to see her. She had quite a reputation for head bashing. Without hesitation, I said yes. Cynthia read the letter then said; *do you think this is a God send? yes.* I said. *Ok then, I'll show the letter to Mrs. D.*

In may my aunt came to talk to Mrs. D.. She came again to attend some al-anon sessions. There we all met.

I got out of Alina Lodge on June 10, 1979 a little more than ten months after I arrived. My aunt lived on an eighty acre ranch in Bedminster, NJ. There was an eight stall stable with warm running water and a plush grounds-keeper apartment over one end. There were three living cottages for renters, and a smaller barn for farm vehicles. They had their own personal gas pump with regular grade gas. The house had eight bedrooms and nine bathrooms. There was a front and back staircase, the latter of which I wasn't to use. There was a two room kitchen. The cooking area contained a stainless-steel open-grille with a double stainless hood with a stove and two ovens. There was a second area/room off the kitchen with a table that could comfortably seat ten people. There were two dining rooms, a library, and two living rooms. There was a pool table/game room with a muck area adjacent to it that lead out to the backyard where just beyond that lay a couple acres of open, fenced land where the horses could be clearly seen from the great windows overlooking them from the kitchen. It had a built-in swimming pool and tennis courts with an adjacent wall for a single person to hit balls against.

My room was the last one on the end of the hall at the far end of the house that overlooked the driveway. The head and toe of my bed touched opposite walls. I had a chair, a dresser and a closet that was really just a door to cover an ugly space underneath a slanted roof plank. I was very, very grateful.

The uncontrollable tears was part of the grieving process I had no understanding of. My aunt would ask me in complete frustration; *what are you crying about?!* I didn't know or couldn't explain. On nearly a weekly basis she sent me back to The Lodge for an over-night. I was always welcome there. It calmed me just to head in that direction in my car.

While at my aunt's my mother would comment on how it was terrible that I was given such an inferior living space while my aunt was appalled that at the age of twenty I had never been introduced to a gynecologist. My dilemma was I wanted to be loved. I wanted to be number one some place. That would never come. For the most part, no one wanted to be bothered with anyone who required so much attention. That of course meant any attention at all. My mother and aunt were a couple of paper-doll cut-outs; exactly the same. I'd never be one of them. During my repose at my aunt's place while I was swimming one-hundred laps at the YMCA pool in the morning, lifting weights in my body-length bedroom and running between six and twenty miles in the afternoons training for The Marathon, I threw out my back so bad I couldn't straighten my leg, stand from a sitting position without excruciating pain I had to slowly stand out of before I could move, or get out of bed without rolling to the edge and very carefully dropping to my knees over the side before going through my standing routine. To say I was not obviously injured would be like insinuating that two cars hitting head-on at sixty miles per hour probably would make very little sound if any. I was never asked by anyone in my family if anything was wrong. All I received was that sideways look I had never become easy with but had become accustomed to from all the years of being me. I was NOT going to be allowed to draw any undue attention to myself. So, As far as my family was concerned, I never said a word and I kept to myself. I felt as though I was disgusting to them. Helping me was obviously a favor being done for my father and it was the lesser of two evils so to speak as the other option would be taking the chance to have not done something that could keep them from the responsibility of having any attachment at all to a story like suicide. Both my aunt and uncle were divorced from alcoholics. Two resentful, self righteous co-dependents got married and here I was, an alcoholic allowed to stay in their house. There was zero leeway.

I was completely confused about my identity. It was drilled in at The Lodge that I should stay away from men. I didn't have much trouble with that. I was totally engrossed in training for The New York Marathon, going to AA, attending a couple of college classes, working part time on my aunt's farm, and delivering The Star Ledger. As far as romance was concerned, I was an obliterated human being. But my dilemma over relationships ran deeper than just burying it under mounds of busyness. I carried, in my secret stash, all the accusations my mother bore on me, all the accusations those little girls bore on me, the accusation from Cindy and Jimmy, the horrors of college, all the incomplete pieces. Love was an issue for me. I was afraid of it, afraid of my desire for it, afraid of myself when it came to it. Love was a sand pile of shattered glass inside me that was devastating because I never could digest it. I felt like the ugly mongrel who was kicked when it came near the food bowl while the less fearsome looking scoundrels could all get a bite to eat.

I was afraid of my aunt because I adored her. She was cold as far as affection toward me but, I fantasized she loved me by witnessing her affection toward her daughter, my cousin Nancy and her step son, my cousin John. Since I didn't get the same affection from her I feared my feelings toward her might be queer. I imagined she knew it and that was why she was so distant. When I went back to The Lodge nearly weekly there was a nurse named Mary-Jane. She had about nine children. She weighed about ninety pounds wet. She was almost always there when I went back. She hugged me and let me cry. She listened and talked to me. Because she was so loving toward me I feared she was a lesbian. But, I was in such emotional agony and dire need of human touch that I hoped beyond hope that she would always be there. I was always afraid of her.

I was pretty much left alone to go to AA meetings beyond an occasional *are you ever going to have dinner with us?* To which I'd respond; *not unless you can eat earlier. I have to go to AA.* Mrs. D. gave us all a legacy of resolve to surrender to the necessary.

In AA I aligned myself with two women I met in treatment. They had brought meetings to The Lodge while I was there as a student. They were Mrs. D. approved. They were eight and ten years older than me but that beat twenty and twenty-five years older which most people were. My friends had one and two years more than me. Late at night when I'd be overwrought and crying I'd call them. They lived nearby sharing an apartment. They'd say *come over.* I went and the three of us would sit in their dimly lit kitchen huddled in front of the opened door of the electric oven keeping warm while we talked and drank red zinger tea. They were one of my safe havens.

I was running a lot, yet determined to run that marathon. The whole time in rehab I did vigorous walking and exercise in preparation. After I was at The Lodge for several months I received a clock radio. No radios were allowed but I took that devise down into the dry basement on the far end of the white house, where I resided, and ran in place to the music for an hour every day. A lot of people saw me with the contraband. No one ever told. That was weird because everyone told on everyone in that place. I figured I'd do it until I was told to stop and no one ever told me to stop.

So, now I was in AA. There was a man three months my senior in the program. He ran too. We began running 10ks, 15ks, 5 milers, and 5ks like two runner addicts. In a while I met Bill's wife. With my insistence she joined us. At first she was icy. But when she realized I was not after Bill we all became lifetime friends.

In March of 1980 my aunt starting speaking of getting their sailboat-yacht out of dry-dock. It was costing them ten thousand dollars a month to keep it where it was. She and my uncle planned to sail down the coast of California, through the Panama Canal, and up the east coast to Maine. It was estimated it would take them two months. They were leaving in April and wouldn't be back until June. She told me it was time to start looking for an apartment of my own.

A cold desolation took hold of me. It was a feel of defeated anger. I was scared. Life always felt too big for me. I always felt at odds and in battle with it. Not one thing had been resolved between myself and my family. Now I was leaving and it probably would never happen. That wasn't the part that hurt. What hurt was no one cared. No one cared except me. It was the ever scream into the black void of no hope. And now, having screamed at yet another angle to no avail, I was on my way, defeated once again. The only difference, with nearly two years clean time, guidance, and inside work I could name it even unresolved. It was a loveless place I had come from. Long, long before I knew it, it was a life's work requisite that I come to understand. I would never be understood.

Every fiber in me screamed; *you're gonna fail!* as I pushed through. I immediately talked to my sponsor. She said; *first, get a roommate since you can't afford to live alone.* I couldn't think of one person. She thought of two and both of them said no. My aunt and uncle left in April for

California. I went to meetings every day sometimes two and three whenever I could. I was attending college part-time. I worked for my uncle a short time but answering phones was not for me. My aunt got me a job with a silk-screen printer. It was a very cool job. It was my first real full time job. I loved it. I saved as much as I could for a security deposit. While my aunt and uncle were gone I had to supply my own food. I went and bought some ground beef for hamburgers. When I left it to thaw in the refrigerator for dinner the house keeper fed it to the dogs. That was a good frame for the idea in my head of how they pictured me; I even ate dog food and thought it was right. I bought for me what my aunt fed to her dogs.

In May, still frantically seeking a roommate, someone suggested a person who was at The Lodge when I was a student and was still living on the premises in a halfway house apartment at Mrs. D.'s house. I'd try anyone. I called and Beth said; *let me think about it.* She was the first one who didn't say no but, would Mrs. D. approve of it? Beth didn't ask her. She called me back and said *yes.* We met and looked at a map together. It had to be a place that fell between our two jobs. Beth worked in Blairstown and I worked in Califon. That placed Hackettstown in the relative center. We secured an apartment for June 1, 1980. When my aunt and uncle came home early it was shortly before I was moving out. My aunt was thrilled. I had spied two or three unused beds in the attic. I asked her if I could have one. she immediately said *no. It wouldn't be possible. All these beds belong to someone.* She can't just give one away. I resolved to use my sponsors sleeping bag until I could secure a mattress. A few days later I guess my aunt had a change of heart. She said she had one old one she could let me borrow but, I couldn't have it and I would have to return it as soon as I got one of my own. I was very grateful.

The day I moved into my apartment all I owned fit in a jeep SUV. I'll never forget my aunt's face as I climbed into my little Le Car and a friend drove the jeep. Her face was unmoving, flat. She stood on the porch hard and stiff with her arms crossed in front and her feet apart. I spurted a few tears holding back as hard as I could. I went to give her a hug but she didn't want one. She had done her brother a great favor. She was done and free. No way was she going to draw one hair of me back in her direction. Her hands were washed. She had earned her chit for Heaven. I think she would have spit on me if she could. What in God's name made them hate me so? It was shredding me apart. My eyes followed her as I drew away but she never drew contact with my look. Denial served me well as I quarter-turned the obvious into some soft, placid explanation for her actions that day. The only difference between this day and the day I left for college was my mother gave me the back of her head while my aunt gave me the front. I drove away.

Beth and I had our apartment. We were on our own. Beth's departure from Mrs. D. elicited a warning. Mrs. D. told her; *you have another drunk in you.* Beth was sure of herself and unmoved by Mrs. D.'s warning. Freedom was singing in her ear like falling in love. No one could stop Beth. We were like the chipmunk and the fox living together. Beth ruled the roost. I was ten years from even beginning to stand my ground. I poured my energy into seeking approval and overcompensating to just feel a tweak of fleeting lovability about myself. Beth sought love from men. The only rule we made was, no necking in the house. So boyfriends were outside business. The apartment was to be the ultimate safe-haven. It worked.

We each had a two dollar beach chair. Beth dragged her mattress in and out of the room to watch T.V. We had a ten inch black and white zenith that got reception with rabbit ears. It was just before the time of cable. I had a stereo from high school that my grandfather had given me. We used milk crates and 4x8's for shelves. We each got and old dresser from someplace. We both had breakdown cars. We both got sober. AA was great. There was a large group of women twenty years our chronological seniors. We were welcomed into the fold with open arms. We went to Friendly's on Friday nights and ate hot-fudge-sundays for $1.75 which we saved for all week. No one had more money to spend. From the start of my time in recovery the values I was taught, the ones that nearly made me perish were subtly, inconspicuously, insidiously, completely rearranged.

My car broke down so often I got quite good at riding my ten speed over schooley's mountain and into Califon to work. It was about fifteen miles one way. The people I worked for @ $3.25/hour said they never knew anyone like me. I worked like a husky farm hand. I weighed one hundred twenty-five pounds. My energy was bottomless. When I asked for a wage increase because it was impossible to continue living on what I was making they said *no* but then reneged and gave me a twenty-five cent raise which amounted to six more dollars a week.

I had gone to a print shop with my aunt one time and was completely intrigued with the presses. The synchronized movement of all the gears and cams and levers was incredible to me. I wanted to run a press. I needed to make more money. I went to that print shop and applied but they turned me down. I went back to that print shop but they turned me down again. I went back to that print shop and they hired me because they couldn't get rid of me. I started at four dollars an hour. I got another paper route to supplement my income. While Beth got all her meals at work, I lived on PB&J and spaghetti with tomato sauce. While Beth went through boyfriends I trained for The New York City Marathon. She made a few comments about my disinterest in men. She carefully insinuated I was perhaps gay then resolved I was frigid. I only thought about it when she brought the subject up. Usually she wasn't around, thank God. She was with one of her boyfriends.

In October of 1981 my friend Bill and I ran The New York City Marathon. I was three years sober and twenty-one years old. It was the first sporting event my parents ever attended. My feeling was, you're too late. My aunt gave me a framed map of the course for Christmas. The knife edge of my relation with my family sliced ever closer to my heart. There was a steel wall, paper thin, before the place where my blood pumped. I wanted to get right with them since all time remembered. *Fuck you all*, rounded my head. As much as possible, which wasn't much, I was learning to divorce my emotions from them. I was still decades from a forgiveness I would never know until I realized it. The Marathon was a great endeavor accomplished by me, for me. It gave a solidness to my person that was untouchable as none before. Succeeding was not ever something I could share with my family. Bill and I and his family and Beth celebrated the Marathon victory. It was long in coming. It was sublime.

For me, recovery has always been a desperate need to escape the bondage of self. I was filled with self—pity, the very feeling I was told would lead me back to drinking. The only people I trusted were those that were indifferent as to where I came from, what I did, who I was, or what I fancied; people who wanted to see me succeed for the experience of succeeding; people who wanted to see me happy for the experience of happiness; people who wanted good for me for the goodness of good; people who were selfless beyond the fulfillment they sought to experience through the opportunity to be of service in the saving of a life; the flourishing of a life that at one time was very nearly snuffed out.

If anyone acted as if they cared I was immediately and desperately wary. I had not learned caring from where I came. Men would steal my virtue, my self-respect, and finally my sobriety and with that, any chance at happiness if it even existed. Women would steal my soul. Either of these thieves would leave me abandoned which was worse than death. I would walk amongst the living dead. I had already walked that path and I had no intention of walking there again. My life was going to be a road of different measure from any I had seen so far. AA was my map out of this maze of despair from which I was emerging. The reason my sponsor worked was because there were two. The reason I could have a man-friend to run with was because he was married. I had to be "one", the-odd-man-out to be comfortable. This is how I learned to relate. AA allowed me both a separation and a connection to the human race. It allowed me to fully entwine my experiences with the reality of life while it also allowed me to the identity and opportunity to relate and compare my human experience in a way that enabled me to unravel my knots of confusion.

In March of 1982 I met Matt. At first I would have nothing to do with him. I didn't want anyone to be interested in me. He was relentless. We began to date. It didn't take long for me to discover what I was missing. He was to be the kindest, most fun, most carefree, best sex relationship of my life. We laughed and laughed. But, Matt ended up going back to cocaine the following winter. When I broke it off in choice of my sobriety I told him I thought we would marry. He said; *I never had that intention.* I thought, of course I got it wrong. What was I thinking? I'm too ugly to marry. I pictured myself from a lower class. I was dirt poor at the time. I had learned the fine art of duck-taping my running shoes, wearing each pair of sox twice, and rotating my t shirts; most inner layer in the wash next shirt out becomes the inner layer. I cried and moved on.

The one place I had, the one place I fit, the one place I was safely loved was AA but, more important than that, was Alina Lodge. I got involved with the young people commitments. I went to the meetings at The Lodge. The Saturday night anniversary meeting continued to be especially uplifting. There was always over two-hundred people. Mrs. D. was always there. Everyone sang and got filled with the heart balloon of gratitude. People cried and laughed. Everyone loved everyone. It was a room billowing with goodwill. It was a palpable spirit. Still, as I write, I can feel my chest fill with that place. This was an immeasurable greatness to be a part of. In the great and devastating learning curve of my life-length disillusionment, with all the sincerity I always ever had for the manifestation of goodness in me, I wanted what Mrs. D. had. With all the wit, stamina, perseverance, drive, and blindness on this journey, I would never stop seeking it. In my most stuttering calamity, even as all possibility shaved down to a sliver of dusty light, I kept my eye, completely dried, wide upon that impossible path, less tread than any other.

I did not run The Marathon in 1982. My father ran it at the age of fifty and beat my time by twenty minutes with a sub four hour finish. My friend Bill ran a sub 3:10 which qualified him for Boston. I wanted to qualify. That meant I had to shave forty-five minutes off my time. I needed to break 3hrs30min for my age group. My focus intensified.

My father co-signed a loan for a new car. I ditched my Junker. I needed more money to pay the loan. I learned and mastered all the equipment in the print shop. I was always good with machines. That was an inherited gift from my grandfather. The only machine I wasn't permitted to touch was the press. *That was a man's job* I was told. Well, where I came from there wasn't so delineated a job. Men didn't do women's work but the women were all over the men's work. I had two nags. I needed more money and I wanted to run a press.

A friend of mine from The Lodge new someone who needed a press operator. The man worked out of his basement. He had two presses. I got the job for five dollars an hour and produced the worst printing job ever delivered in NJ, an even trade to my friend for having convinced this guy to hire a completely unqualified press operator. In the end instead of firing me that man taught me to print. I picked up a job in the main street Hess station to supplement my salary and delivered The Star Ledger seven mornings a week. I attended five to seven AA meetings a week and ran forty to sixty miles a week with 10k's on Sundays. I had a shelf quickly accumulating with medals, plaques, cups, trophies, and ribbons.

Beth continued her obsession with men. Her occasional derogatory remark about my disinterest was never missed. I dated a few guys but they were always a drain to my energy. I didn't want to get pregnant or married. I loved the peace my freedom generated. Even with my great need for support I was a loner. When one guy almost got me to sky dive I prayed with great earnest the pilot would announce a stop to drops because of wind. There was no wind. I kept waiting for the next flight. When it was finally our turn and no more end of the line to run to the pilot announced there would be no more drops because the wind had kicked up. I never went on a date with Pat again. He wasn't getting me back to that airport.

I was most content giving my time to The Lodge, being near those people that were growing in the abundance of Mrs. D.

In June of 1983 after co-habitating for three years my greatest fear came to fruition. I didn't believe I could survive on my own. I came from a large family and never lived on my own. Beth proudly announced she was moving in with the love of her life, Tom. Against his ever-insistence to stay single, Beth was determined to marry him.

The instant ballooning of my fear was popped when Beth informed me she had gotten a replacement. A young woman named Michele would move in. I knew who she was. She was currently living with a guy she wanted to break up with. We saw each other at meetings. She was friendly with Beth. She was a woman I'd never have anything to do with. Visually breathtaking, she had to be mean. She was a man-eater. It was unbearable but I felt I had no choice. I must be grateful to Beth for covering me.

Michele moved in like a grenade. I never lived in such a blasted pig-sty. The rule of "no necking" was gone with Beth, and the quiet reprieve of the apartment I once enjoyed was blasted out of existence by the speaker-shaking-volume of Pat Benatar's rock voice.

THE SUM

It takes a long time to put two and
two together when no matter which formula
is applied it comes to standing on an empty
street corner wet with black snow—guttered
with a pond of rust colored slush that
splashes up a clean pant leg so when
I get to the office it is obvious I
came the wrong way.

It only occurs to me to vomit when
my best friend yells from her back porch
not to step foot on her property again.
A bubble of snot rises in my throat when
my mother tells me I don't add up.
By the time Jimmy, the boy who steals
my secret, tells me he is breaking up because
his friends tell him I'm crazy, I just
get drunk and I stay drunk until
drunk is a rapist and its
pitted against accusation that is only a shadow.
Then I get sober and pay as little attention
as possible to the sum.

When she climbs into my bed, naked, I can't
remember ever feeling so graceless. I stop breathing.
I don't move all night.
Weeks later when she kisses me, I can't remember ever
feeling so many butterflies without breath.

I stand on the street corner alone, in the storm.
I hop off—right into the ankle deep, dirt mash and
wade in the splashes of the cars. I hope
they throw brown blobs in my hair like I've been
sprayed with manure. I hope the wave ruins my make-up.

When I get to the office I dance my
disaster across the clean carpet simultaneously
throwing three's under florescent lights.
Love does that you know—
makes everything irrelevant.

At five years of sobriety I was a bit of an AA guru. I never understood why people in the program took to me so fully. As much as it scared me, I liked it. It wasn't long before I was treated as though I had long term recovery. Even while I was no more than on the brink of application to a life-long endeavor to self-improvement, people looked to me for guidance. While I was in desperate need of guidance myself, people waited for me to share my experience. Though I didn't have a clear understanding I could explain that confusion everyone was confused about. As I was too afraid to expose my most inner secrets, people could understand that fear I could clearly explain the reason for having.

I always had the ability, in the extrapolating of my own unwinding ruminations into words, to unwind the knotted divides that swirled like tornadoes in the vise-like grips of the vast majority that sat without any other way to free themselves of their consummate confusions but to hear someone uncoil what was mercilessly rusted in place and subsequently junked as unfixable long before.

When I explained a thing for myself, I explained it for everyone in the room. This was my gift. AA was my place to let my gift flourish. I actually had to sit near the door or chance being held up by a line of people actually waiting to talk to me. I really didn't think more of it than it was a blockade to the next event of the night.

A certain woman, who I at first thought was crazy, became a very dear friend. She was my mother's age. We enjoyed, tennis, New York, and simple companionship. We laughed and talked and talked and laughed. We went to meetings together and spoke to each other on a daily basis. Carol was always telling me, even more so than others, that I should be writing these things I say at meetings down. I would need twenty years of testing, failing, succeeding, finding, losing, loving, regretting, opening, and closing. Only by trial and error would I come to know who I am. And, only after finally coming to rest in the nakedness of full exposure, would I be able to come to love that naked-self some time beyond that knowing when acceptance of my findings surpassed the 50% mark and began to out run non-acceptance. Not until then would I begin to know what freedom really is. When that point by point grade was met and overturned I was able to begin to be true to me. Not before that turning point could I begin to write for the crowd. Up until then I kept filling numbered notebooks piled under my t-shirts in my bottom drawer.

Right in the flaming center where the essence of the exquisite self burns; that is the all-too-close hiding place where happiness blossoms that everyone misses for all the outer dressings we all embellish ourselves with looking for freedom, that yearning phantom. What keeps us all looking outside ourselves to be fulfilled is, we all keep looking outside ourselves to be fulfilled. We search outside ourselves because we see each searching outside. Happiness is not about getting more for the self. It is about accepting the self. The prerequisite is knowing the self. That requires a certain, often painful, stripping of uncountable, insidious, persistent, and all too commonly denied veils.

A gift from my family was to never be a fit in the fold. It was a perfect set-up. I did not settle because I was never welcomed to settle. I looked in the opposite place everyone else looked because it was the first time I was welcomed to be a part of the looking. I looked inside instead of outside for happiness because there were a very few people who came before me and guided me there and I believed them because they didn't just tell me; they lived it. They showed me. They loved me too look there. They themselves were the proof. Happiness was inside. AA was giving me the blueprint to progress toward that illusive human dream of happiness.

I never stopped seeking what Mrs. D. had. I never had any other plan but to have the best quality spirituality/purpose for living that was humanly attainable for me. That's what Mrs. D. called it, *spirituality*. I had no idea what it was to entail. I just kept going. I had already gotten more peace than I had imagined could exist.

I didn't take on sponsees in the beginning because I was just a fledgling myself. I couldn't handle anyone needing from me what I was unsure of myself. I trusted only in the process. I didn't trust the people. Alina Lodge was my utopia. AA was not so perfect but a utopia in its own right. As flimsy as it appeared, I had found goodness. Even as I stumbled in the on-and-off validity of what transpired in those rooms, I witnessed alcoholics get sober. I witnessed the miracle of spiritual awakenings again and again. I heard locked-mind-sets, bogged in remorse, fall open in tear-full gratitude. I heard the words of hope from the hopeless. I saw, first hand, the self-righteous go out and get drunk only to return like snarling wolverines full of rage, self pity and blame confabulating like cool-soured, sticky-thick molasses running out all over the room while their tails were tucked tight between their legs, welcomed and loved back into themselves human-sleeves from which the hand of understanding reached out and clasped the one who could not otherwise be drawn out of the black isolation alcoholics perish in. They became the best examples of a program that worked to save lives.

I was swimming in the wave of an ocean that belonged to God. I wanted to make sure I stayed in the middle of that wave. For I didn't want to be washed out, pummeled under, or slung up and left on the shore. I wanted to be in the constant movement of a great tide no matter how unpredictable it was. I knew its unpredictability was not a lacking in the tide itself. That was for sure. It was rather, a paramount lack of wisdom on my part. I knew, the only way for me to gain any measure of the wisdom I so keenly desired was to stay in the movement no matter what.

It was the ones who stopped going to meetings who always got themselves into trouble. I resolved early on that I would never *not* go to meetings no matter what. That was key because AA has a way of not allowing dishonesty to expand to a crippling level, as it continues to re-manifest in uncountable ways in even the sincerest of aspirations. It's not lack of meetings but rather, an expanding lack of honesty that creates the overwhelming remorse that can only be quelled with a drink.

At five years the only thing I did with more fervor than sharing my findings was working at chiseling out what kept me from happiness and peace of mind. I knew it was all an inside job. A perspective change would bring into focus a purpose/a new spirituality I could not understand without that different point of view. I had to adjust the very source. Nothing on the outside would ever give peace to the yearning of my phantom. I was embarked to tear apart every lie I ever took on as my identity; rip out the stakes of scarlet letters that pinned me cowering under life; unearth the someone I am because I believed Mrs. D. when she told me I was special. That opinion, re-stated again and again and again, from this pivotal person in my life was much more than the cup of water that nipped me back from the edge of perishing in a desert of human self-centeredness. It was the sustenance I sipped intermittently and relished in the smallest curve of the inner ventricle of my heart. I dared not even let it circulate. For I did not trust the flow of my own blood. At twenty four to actually realize my own specialness and the purpose that must sprout from that clarified perception was my impossible dream. Who was going to understand that? It didn't matter.

As I trekked forward into the forest of wolves, open vista's of angels, battles of heart and soul, ripping away of flesh-lies and enlightening of the spirit that I could not avoid if I intended to come to the fire where my dream burned; the dead center where the flame is so hot it is blue; where all that is, is disintegrated into nothing and every breath is no more than a spontaneous and easy release to inhale the reality of my smallness and exhale the opportunity of my unique expression in a flash called life I fell in black pits and stood upon light soaked mountains. It was Mrs. D. who first served me the food that sustained me unto the resting place where I am me and that alone is my great treasure. With that treasure once owned I can feed the world. Oh great providence, can what I have so far discovered take me there? Can a journey to such happiness as this be forded. I bear not one ounce of indifference. That is my pain. I bear all the caring of the world. That is my joy. That gladness, lit with the fuse of understanding is a light shining without resistance for no other reason but to give light. It is in the light beyond pretense that happiness waits. From that light happiness is spread. There must be a true freedom of spirit; not one judgment set dim, self upon self, but only light that shines out and out. Five years was not even a wetting of my toes at the edge of a receding wave.

As Michele took over the apartment I let her have her way. I was terrified she'd leave if I didn't. Finance was a major source of anxiety. I didn't think I could survive on my own.

I often had to stay in my room while she and her boyfriend sprawled out on my couch and watched HBO on my T.V.. I spent a lot of time with Carol. She introduced me to her son Alan. He was very handsome. We began to date. He came into AA to date me. We went to AA, the beach, dinner, the movies. AA and my peace of mind were always more important to me than Alan. But, we had good times together. For about eight months we double dated with Michele and her boyfriend. When I celebrated six years he gave me a cross-ring I have always worn. But, Alan didn't last. He became too demanding of my attention. He got too pushy. I'd never have that in my life. When he made it requisite that I marry him or break up, we broke up. I was relieved to be rid of him. I was running, going to AA, and volunteering at Alina Lodge. My aspirations were not his. The Saturday night meetings at The Lodge were like flying wide awake. The only other times I flew was two hours before dawn, an hour before my alarm went blaring, when I'd be in my deepest sleep. My spirit-eyes would come into focus as my body, complete without wings, would ease off the ground in an open meadow, float up and fly across the tops of lush, green trees, swoop over the cliff of a great crevasse, and silently soar in slow motion over the high walls of a stadium. If I never woke from that dream it would be just grand. That's what I wanted; free flying.

Michele changed that focus. She had all the wildness in her that I ever had. When she stayed out until 5am I was jealous. I felt like I was missing something. As we began to know each other a little more she asked if I wanted to go with her and the group. People were always a little put off by me. Perhaps it was because I was always a little put off by people. I started going out just for the hopeful fun of it.

The first few AA dances were tortuously uncomfortable. One New Year's Eve I sat all night and cried in the car. I was filled with that old sucking feeling in my solar plexus. No one came back to the car until it was time to go. That was no less than four hours of cold waiting. I needed that lesson. It took many years, many repeated lessons to realize it is *just* to demand for myself; that I be around people who care about me.

Michele always had a couple of boyfriends. Men were all over her. I dated a few different guys. It always seemed to be all about sex and I wasn't too interested in that. So they came and went. I always maintained an apartness from the world about myself that was an inner life order no one would ever crack and I couldn't share because no one seemed to understand. They'd begin to get that strange look on their face and

I'd shut up. But I let myself relax to the young crowd with AA as my backbone. That was because I saw Michele receive more bouquets of roses from more different guys than I'd ever seen anyone get, ever. She was having a lot of fun. There was always one or two arrangements around her room at different stages between fresh and wilt. I asked her what it was about. She shook her bootie. I wanted to know what she found.

Our friendship was deepening. I slowly began to like her as much as any best friend I had ever had. We began to seek out each other's company. It's nice to have a friend to go to meetings with, double date with, go to dinner with, go to NYC dancing with. We did concerts, movies, plays and just hung out together. What was great was we had the same AA aspiration so we could talk on that level we found nowhere else. It was a center of fun during a time in my life when I was nearly overwhelmed by the constant grip of anxiety that held me unable to pull from its captivity. With all the fear I felt there was a lot of love in the air. I had friends in AA and a friend as a roommate. It was a step up from Beth. She was not so much a friend as Michele had become. I had great spiritual leaders in my life from The Lodge. There was one woman in particular at this time who moved me to tears by the strength of her spirit. She was eight years ahead of me in recovery. My mother's age, she had Lou Gehrig's Disease. I didn't want what she had. I wanted to know how she had what she had with such odds against her. My attraction to her scared me because I thought in order to gain the Divine measure of peace she had I'd have to suffer from Lou Gehrig's Disease. I only wanted the peace. I asked her to be my sponsor. For awhile she was. We remained lifetime friends which spanned twenty more years. The one question I'll never forget asking her was; *How does Mrs. D. know what she knows?* Elaine answered; *The only way to know what Mrs. D. knows is to live through what Mrs. D. has lived through.*

I sunk that wisdom into my brain. I couldn't imagine how I could ever manage to come by such an unequaled path in order to gain such knowing. Mrs. D. had thirty-two years of sobriety when I arrived at The Lodge. That was pushing seven years past. I had a long way to go to, maybe, come to that depth of wisdom. It takes thirty-two years of seeking to find what thirty-two years of seeking might yield. It takes every single day lived awake. In my deepest root of sincerity I resolved in myself, by that conversation, to get what Mrs. D. had. Little did I imagine what inner journey I was agreeing to embark upon. Peeling open to raw self and allowing the brazen light of the world to shine on it with all its barbed-chain-judgments is sitting in the middle of the fire. Over the course of burning years you've got to scream once in a while.

At seven/eight years sober I was twenty-six/seven years old and stalwart about my quest.

It produced a sort of magnetism to me. I was dreaming the impossible dream. Like Don Quixote, I was intent to go out and right all wrongs. I still hadn't figured out what Mrs. D. had found; righting all wrongs was an inside job.

Michele and I had become like two little girls together. We laughed harder than I could ever remember laughing. When we weren't with our boyfriends we were with each other. Then I became single. As usual, I filled my time with work, running, and AA.

I had gotten a new job and there was a lesbian working there. She insisted I was also a lesbian. I felt like I wanted to kill her. This queer thing filled me with fear and hate. This assignment had a sure and black history. She was unrelenting. I questioned her accusations because I had no grip on my painfully developing identity. That is what made her so ravaging to my peace. I was not one to fall head-over-heels for boys but neither had I considered girls. My main taproot was one of a decision to keep myself as autonomous as possible. No one could have me. I'd not chance being abused as my mother had been. My inherent tuff-ness gave off an appeal to those of her persuasion I suppose. In my whole life I'd never been able to shake myself of that appeal. It was my devil in the alley. I moved like a man, worked like a man, exercised like a man, fixed things like a man, dressed like a man, and took on the Alfa role like a man. I didn't think about it but, when someone defined that behavior as queer, I questioned my motives. I got closer to trashing myself. If that be the truth, I was unacceptable to me. That was my dire edge where self annihilation and self purpose drew the cliff line between the decision to live or to die. The horror is with no identity it's nearly impossible not to take on the one pounded into you from the beginning of time remembered. While I dated Alan, she insisted it was a lie. When we broke up she was convinced she was right. I never said much to her. If there was any way to shut her up I would have. Since saying anything only served to spur her on, I said as little as possible in response to her constant harassment.

Michele started dating this hot-muscle guy named Joe. They were seeing each other for a couple of months when his birthday arrived. He was going on a business trip for his birthday weekend and she was going with him. I was looking forward to having the apartment to myself. The night before they were to leave she told me she didn't want to go. I said; *don't go.* She said; *I want to stay here and hang out with you.* I said; *stay here and hang out with me.* Michele stayed home.

On that Saturday night we did whatever we did on Saturday nights; go to a meeting, go to the diner, and hang out with people from AA. We came home and went to bed. Just as I was dozing off she climbed into my bed. I was immediately rigged. I wasn't sure what was going on. Then I realized she was naked and I thought; *shit!* My eyes burned dry staring at the ceiling. My mind was like endless acreage of smooth, grittle-hot, white cement. I squished myself up against the wall and didn't move all night. She snuggled up against me like J did when he was a baby.

The next day there was an awkwardness about us but not a rejection. Fear shook me as it had never quaked me before. A bottom fell out and what was inside was pouring out so fast all I could do was let it empty.

This short lived relationship could not be avoided if my life intentions were true. This relationship tore something out of me that had lied in waiting for every year of question and accusation I had survived. Feelings came over me that I never knew existed. I longed for affection. I longed to be loved all my life. Even as a small child, knowing I was different, (the patch and being a girl amongst brothers), I had that ever-present-pulling tied to my solar plexus. I never fit. I never felt loveable, I never felt even a part of. This relationship gave me the satiation of being fed my first meal after decades of existing in near starvation. I was overwhelmed; mind boggled. *So, this is what it felt like to be loved.* Michele was very affectionate. I could have no idea I liked that. I had never experienced affection before. No one had ever touched me unless it was a guy and that was because he was horny. This wasn't sexual. This put sex in its place.

I went head over heels. I thought; *they were right!* Everyone kept insisting I was gay all my life. Now I thought; *I guess if this is gay, they must be right.* Without an identity anyone can tell you who you are. My identity was much shaped by who people told me I was and not who I said I was. To have what Mrs. D. had I was going to have to tear down the whole brick and mortar wall pre-built of myself and piece meal the whole structure back together, brick by broken brick into who I really am. I am the master of who I am only after I master me. It is not for the world to tell me my name but rather it is I who am to tell the world. At this point having thought I found an answer I grabbed hold and proclaimed my joy however short lived it soon became.

It didn't take long at all before Michele became completely paranoid about our relationship. She went and spoke to her sponsor who told her in no uncertain terms that I was evil; a manifestation of the devil. She told Michele to get away from me and stay away. I was a sinner and a disgrace. The fiery exuberance we discovered in each other's company was at once stoked into a flaming fury of blame and accusatory retribution. Michele came home with a guy who moved in and acted as a guard dog to keep her safe from what she persuaded him to perceive me to be. It was obvious and deadly painful to be treated like I was some sort of sex derelict who couldn't be made to leave but could only be held at bay by a body guard. It was mortally unbelievable to me. I was in a living hell in my own apartment. Since I had no belief in my ability to move out, I was frozen in that hell-fire stove. The two of them took over the apartment. I started seeing a guy and we went away on weekends just to be out of there. He was very supportive of me. The return was always the same. There they'd be sprawled out on the couch in the living room watching T.V.. The only place to go was to my room. I felt like I had big chunks of hardened rock-salt filling my chest.

In my life I was always the one who should have known better; the one held accountable. So was my position in this quandary. I was sober longer. I should know. When I went to my usual meeting I found that I was completely ostracized by the women there. Apparently Michele's sponsor had discussed it all at the diner. I was basically abolished at that meeting. My credibility was smashed. I was shattered. My self-loathing was breathless. Thank God for Carol, my best friend and mother replacement. She was understanding, non-judgmental, and completely supportive. I cried and cried. She said she had almost crossed that line with a friend once. Just move on.

This was the nightmare of addiction replayed. Alcohol gave me a false sense of love. Here I had tasted that mortal quench-of-thirst re-invented in the brilliant confusion of beauty. If this was love I didn't want it. What price we are willing to pay for love? That we give our very souls to be shredded for that relish, die, and yet can be healed by the turning of our mirror *in* that it may reflect *out* the whole of what we are which *is* love that can bring light, clear, dazzling, and diminishing of *all* shadow, that the fear of loneliness buffets to billow gray, is a paradox that insists we enter the turmoil of spiritual blindness in order to see.

I switched my meetings. I did fourth and fifth steps, went to confession, and after a few months of torture, when the lease was up, I kicked Michele and Bob out. Now I couldn't afford the apartment alone so I went in desperate search of a roommate. I found a room in a house in a nearby town and my boyfriend helped me paint it. I felt like I had fallen in a deep well and no one could hear my screams so there was no way to rescue me. The desperation I felt was profound. The reprieves I had from my self imposed panic were The Lodge, Carol, and my new AA meetings. I had fallen a few steps back as far as trust in people was concerned. I was edging on running into isolation from the human race. What kept me from that was my abject terror of drinking again. I never ran into hiding . . . ever. I just kept going through the motions even as my emotions screamed for relief. A broken heart is not relieved. It eventually wears down as a boulder to a pebble in the constant wash of tides. I had no idea who I was but, I knew I wanted love which I now defined as affection. With this uneven piece of puzzle, missing all other pieces that fit to, I was washed in and out like seaweed on the beach.

Seaweed

I never thought I would become
akin to a knot of seaweed tumbling
in and out with the tide. Scuffing
along the sandy ocean edge, taking
oxygen from the sudsy waves without
reprieve from useless movement.

I never thought untangling would
be wasted energy bathed
in the lifeless saltwater of my eyes. Leave me
a fruitless strand of indigestible sea grass as
welcome under foot as a broken shell.

I never thought of the erosion stuck
at the shore line without
a wave to carry me in or an
undertow to carry me out. I flop
trapped under the mood of a faceless moon.

7/3/01

SED

THAT EXPERIENCE OF affection became like a drink. I was engulfed in the illusion of having found a utopian relief in the arctic chill of life. So, just as I chased the deliverance the initial comfort a drink induced, I could not resist the chance I may have found what was so sorely vacant in that first delusion. Perhaps affection was the real solution to the insatiable gnawing I never could shake free from even as it nearly destroyed me. I wasn't going to so easily give up on the possibility.

I was shut down by the combination of accusations and my lack of self-knowledge. I threw myself into more volunteer work at The Lodge. Nothing of this was known there. I maintained a wary presence in AA, and I talked to Carol. My mainstays, very slowly, pulled me back from the edge.

As I was preparing to move to a different apartment, enveloped in a palpable fear of what felt like my imminent demise, my father called and agreed to pay half my rent so I could remain where I was under the agreement that when I got a new roommate I not have them split the rent but offer it to them for cheaper because the second room, which I had had, was no more than a converted dining room and much inferior to the one bedroom in the apartment. With great relief, I agreed.

Now, the problem with Michele was not that I hated her it was that I loved her. She was my drink. She was no less financially strapped and stuck than I was. I made the offer to her first. She took it. For three more miserable months I co-habitated with her and Bob. I was the in-house monster. It was a re-enactment of my family life. I could live anywhere while being deemed the monster. It felt like home though, I must say, it was much easier doing it drunk.

In August, 1986 a sponsee needed a place to live and I asked Michele and Bob to leave. Trish moved in without a bed so I gave her a months' rent free to buy a bed for herself. The first thing I did was tell her what happened. I explained that this was a hugely unresolved issue for me and I wasn't about to abandon it at this point. I was accused of being queer for as long as I could remember from my mother to the little girls in the neighborhood, to my best friend, to some shadowy people in high school, to my boyfriend, and now this. Maybe I was gay after all and I could find some peace and even joy by accepting it. Trish was fine with it. She was actually very supportive. She showed herself to be a real friend in a short period of time.

Around that time I was out on the front sidewalk stretching after one of my daily runs. A car pulled up alongside me and the woman driving said hello and started talking to me. We had a friendly introduction. She had two kids. She invited me for pizza. She was quite engaging and obviously harmless. I had nothing to lose so I went. We talked for hours. Her husband had left her. But, as women make do she made do and lived simple, comfortable, and in an apartment with a lot of love. She was sure she was a lesbian. I didn't know what I was but at this first time in my life I was open to suggestion so, in the company of my new friend, I began my dark days of dancing in the gay bars. Neither of us would have the courage to go alone. With each other's support we frequented those rancid establishments. The dancing was great. I could go on for hours on end. I loved to dance. That was the beginning and end of the fun. Little did I know what a long gauntlet I would have to run before I would realize that.

Janet and I would stand along the side and point out to each other who we thought was attractive. We didn't like the same type. That was for sure. My level of anxiety was at a constant edge-of-boiling-over level. The raging vulture in my head was always screeching; *what are you doing here?* I was in AA. I had a whole other purpose I was putting aside. I had a life mission and it involved Mrs. D. This was clearly anti-Mrs. D. behavior. I always felt as though my back to that was the cutting line between any reason at all for my next breath and my imminent demise. Impending doom was my ever looming black cloud. I never relaxed. But, I needed to experience this affection solution again. So I stayed the course and guarded my sobriety. That doesn't mean I didn't sell my soul looking for happiness in the wrong place. It only means I didn't drink or do drugs on my hapless quest.

My wild self was alive and well even after eight years of sobriety. I picked out the wildest, active alcoholic/drug addict in a bar of well over two hundred people. I was warned by the women who knew her. My decision was made. I could have just about whoever I wanted. New meat was exciting to hungry wolves. I hated being new meat or meat at all for that matter. But, it gave me an open field.

I was sitting at the bar when Marcia came up behind me and poured her drink into mine. I immediately told her I was an alcoholic. She was quite apologetic. That was the start of our relationship.

The next weekend we were to go to a state fare together. I sat in my car on a street corner for two hours past the time we were to meet waiting for her. We went to the fare. An explanation of the relationship could end there. But, that was the beginning.

Trish had a guy staying with her. I let her know Marcia was moving in. It was fine with her. Marcia was so volatile that Trish was afraid of her. One night after just a few weeks, the police called at around 2am. Trish and I had to go and get Marcia's car. She was pulled over stoned drunk driving and was under arrest. In less than a month I was sitting in the parking lot having my head torn off for not doing something when Trish came out the back door and warded Marcia off. Inside Trish told me she cared too much about me to stand by and watch. It was Trish or Marcia. I had to make a choice. Trish moved out. In a few more weeks Marcia totaled a borrowed car and was caught without a license. Every Thursday we went to court together. It was like being in my favorite chair for my favorite show each week. As odd as it was, it felt quite normal to be sitting in the courtroom every Thursday night. One night she actually called the judge "Your Heiness" because she was too looped to get it straight who the judge was. I drove her all over NJ to gay bars. I met a lot of people and had a lot of social friends but, I never felt like I fit. I hated the lifestyle. Now I felt trapped in it. I didn't know how to undo what I had done so I just kept going. The wild night life gave me raging headaches. I had no desire for the bedroom life either. Marcia taught me other things. My intrigue in her spirit was ravenous. Her view of the world was a place way over-loaded with stifling, useless, de-humanizing laws and rules that she was probably incapable of and refused to follow. She never could hold a job for long. When she did she was drunk or stoned on her paycheck. Marcia was a grifter. She had me, the ultimate care-taker and Bill, her co-dependent man-friend. The two of us didn't have a penny between us of self-worth. We both got conditional worth out of Marcia. If she was happy we were happy. If she wasn't happy we were tortured. She took and felt we owed it to her. We gave and believed she was right.

Marcia hounded me until I moved closer to the bar. I left Hackettstown and a loving piece of myself with it. I would always think of Hackettstown as my first and only real home.

My parents came on a surprise visit to my new shack-residence and very nearly did a pirouette right back out the door. Later that same day they called and begged me to get out of that dump and away from that woman. They were appalled. They were sure I had forgotten where I came from. I forgot my good breeding. All of this interpersonal mayhem felt quite normal to me. My parents were always appalled with me. I was wedged in a new resolve. I wanted to be fucking happy and I would be damned if those two thieves were going to step in and re-instate me in their lie. But, as I'll *never* forget where I came from, I agreed to go to their house for dinner and discuss their dilemma. They offered to let me move in rent free, free phone, no curfew, no questions if I just got out of there. I said no thanks. If they wanted to help me they could give me some money. That they refused. I left.

By the end of 1987 I had had enough. I came home from work and found Marcia passed out. All of her paraphernalia for shooting heroin was strewn on the counter. I didn't touch it. A homeless friend of hers came to the door. While we were sitting out on the front stoop talking to each other the beast woke up. She bounded out the front screen smashing it into Buzzy and attempted to attack me. She was always very violent in withdrawal. Buzzy stopped her. He told her she would have to beat him up first before she could beat me up. Marcia jumped into Bill's second borrowed mustang, peeled out and was gone. I gave Buzzy a much needed haircut, a pair of my jeans which fit him better than me. I fed him a whole pound of spaghetti with marinara which he downed like it was his first meal in some time, and he was on his way. I never felt the same about homeless people after having known Buzzy. He was a good soul who lived between the cracks in society. I met a lot of homeless people during my companionship with Marcia. They were the most human individuals I ever encountered.

After that scene I kicked Marcia out. I didn't want to get busted with nine years of sobriety. She moved in with Bill. Soon after, a friend of theirs overdosed in Bill's bathroom. They dragged him down the stairs and threw him on the sidewalk then called the police. Drug addicts understand that as acceptable and expected friendship behavior. It was agreed, if you go down, you go down alone. A month later Paul was dead.

I moved into a garage apartment on the same property as my shack-residence. It was across the sidewalk. So began the end of my fear of being able to support myself on my own. I had met a group of friends in the gay community. They became my support system. I was grateful for them. They filled the vacancy in my time and eased the loneliness in my heart.

Even after every indication that screamed get away, after being dragged through mayhem only an alcoholic could muster up, in spite of a very nearly immediate sexual disengagement and a clear notion that there was no affection in this animal, I continued to hang out with Marcia. I think I was addicted to addiction. The breaking point was one night after many, many relentless episodes in a relationship made of episodes of accusations because she wasn't getting what she wanted from me which was I don't know what; at 1am while I was trying to go to sleep because I was getting up at 5am to go to work she wouldn't shut up so I got out of bed and began dressing to leave. At least in my own bed I'd get a couple of hours before the alarm compared to not one minute with all this raving going on. It was an amazing experience to be sober hearing the "so confusing it's convincing" thought pattern of an alcoholic.

As I was standing on one foot with the other half in my pant leg, while she continued her drug induced ranting about how this whole mess was my fault, she shoved me and I fell backwards. I was overwrought with the fury of red. I was up across the space between us and had her by the neck before she could react at all. I threw her backwards knocking down a lamp and slammed her into the corner and down onto the floor.

I was choking her to death when my eyes focused on her silent, gaping mouth and terror struck eyes. It was the first time in our relationship I had retaliated. I was fierce. There was a part of me neither of us had known before that impact. My rage was embedded in me long before Marcia had spiked it. It was not something to be knocking at the door for. I released her and as she choked to recover from the spasm I induced in her throat, I growled; *don't you ever touch me again.* I drove home to my studio garage for three hours of fitful sleep before going to work.

My relationship with Marcia was volatile to say the least. I have only known what a person was to teach me in retrospect. That violent relationship taught me a few seemingly small perspectives that were key holes to the wings I was always seeking and never knew it. We both were very angry, frustrated, misplaced women. Marcia opened my horizon to some people I never would have met on my own. I was far too fearful and without confidence to ever chance such ventures as the ones Marcia fearlessly took me on. Marcia was from Vermont. We went there several times and I met a few very eccentric characters. One carved granite for a living but, his hands were becoming, too soon, numb from the electric tools he chiseled with. I met a lot of artists, musicians, and poets. I met people who lived in their world created of flower gardens. I met people of complete peace who lived simply in shabby clothes, with little money, and less cares. I met a beautiful woman with white hair to her waist who lived in a huge cave in the side of a mountain in the woods near a stream. Her home was insulated with straw and heated with a big stone oven that sat in the middle. Her bed was all straw and natural wool blankets. She was a magnificent spectacle of spiritual manifestation. I could sit in her presence for time uncounted.

All these people who had known Marcia long before I met her welcomed both of us into their homes. They welcomed her interaction with their children. There was a deep, warm-seated love that emanated from Marcia during these visits. She had a love about her that glowed like an encompassing aura, magnetic as food to the starving. People really loved and sought Marcia. This was Marcia's heart.

It was no wonder the manufactured world drove her to alcohol, drugs, and ultimately self destruction. The whole of society was contrary to the wisdom of Marcia's aching soul. This is what kept me at her side long into the pain of such companionship. Our relationship was neither sexual or affectionate. I forgot about those desires once I identified with what she knew. She didn't make strange eyes at me when I went into one of my spiritual spiels. Her eyes widened with delighted understanding. She was with me. There was a burning ember in Marcia that stoked the same burning ember in me. Never-the-less I had to break ties in order to survive. To take to the hearth of Marcia's sanctum was suicide. For no one could survive in the den of so fierce a lioness. In a world that was not hers; a world where she would not be fitted a part; a world she envisioned as all lies, Marcia could not allow herself the connection of love. Neither could I. There was no place, therefore, to be shared. If nothing else, I was a survivor. I had to get out.

Marcia taught me I could get the universe to take care of me and not have to work at it at all. I only had to believe. It was a new concept that would take another twenty years to seed a harvest.

It was the early spring of 1988. At a meeting one night a man asked me about my marathon running. I said my last one was in 1983. He responded; *oh you're just a has been.* No. I wasn't I thought. Between the emotions of my confused relations, the loneliness of living alone, my inadequate meeting attendance during my parley with Marcia, and my unresolved discontent with life, the amount of rage that flamed from me at ten years of sobriety was unbelievable. It seemed I had gotten nowhere on my quest for love, for peace of mind. It felt like I hadn't figured one thing out in ten years! I decided to do two things. I called and asked Alina Lodge if I could hold and lead a young people's discussion up there on a regular basis and I started training for my third NYC marathon.

Anywhere along the time line of life is a point of possibility; I could fade into a turning point and shrink until eventually I plummeted into hopeless despair, ultimately drinking for a relief I all-to-well knew was *not* forthcoming by such determination; I could trudge forward through the foggy fields of my shattered heart and continue to unearth puzzle pieces, soggy in the mud of my self—mortified tears that fit into the fearful mosaic that was Susan.

Even as I felt no worth in myself I focused on the one thing that *had* worked. I did what I was taught to do. I went through the seemingly ridiculous motions of being present, being of service, interacting with the horrifying human race and, with ongoing desperation, I pleaded from the core of my soul to God to show me a purpose. There was plenty of volunteer work to do at The Lodge. I did anything from stuffing envelopes and wrapping Christmas gifts for the students, to leading discussions and speaking. I became more involved with The Lodge than AA. I felt safer and more accepted there. It was a place that focused on purpose-out from the individual rather than the individual as the soul-purpose. It was the manifestation of principles over personalities. It wasn't so much who I was, though there was no other core intent in anyone's stay than to come to terms with one's self, it was more a matter of how I put that self into service for all that I was. Alina Lodge gave me the means to discover the tools (the tools are my million puzzle pieces of character) to fulfill my purpose. That Divine place gave me the time to figure me out. There was no pressure, no accusation, no questions. There was good will. There was a large body of people all intent on the same outcome; spiritual enlightenment—clarity of a Divine purpose.

With the world and all its intrigues and illusions removed and with no pressure to find my gear point in that drive-train of life called society, it seemed quite clear and easy to get in harmony with the joy of saving lives, my own being right up there on the list with the rest.

To Come Upon One's Self in the Dark

To come upon one's self in the dark
and find no trace of light in the shadows cast
but only silent, enveloping darkness.
To find not a hand to grasp
nor a space to stand upon, left
pondering the setting of the situation.

To come upon one's self in the dark
in search of something to believe.
To find the heart, the soul and the mind (a crumbled puzzle),
where once existed, to some extent, a self
striving to be whole, slipped on a ridge too narrow.

To come upon one's self in the dark
and examine, with broken intuition, the surroundings,
the heart, the soul, the mind, (the crumbled puzzle).
To discover still remaining, a warmth, a flicker of light, a hope,
a wreckage worth saving, a piece whole and comprehendible.

To come upon one's self in the dark and
wait patiently until one's eyes adjust.
To see—just a glimmer is enough.
To listen—ears need no light to hear.
To touch—fingers need no light to feel.
To salivate—tongues need no light to taste.
To sniff—noses need no light to smell.
To think—the brain is engulfed in darkness and still can bring light in,
always.
To find one's gifts ~ in the dark.

To come upon one's self in the engulfing darkness
and like a child in question and wanting belief
to explore
until the darkness subsides from within
and the power of lifes' song plays forth from the soul through
the hand of the heart and the voice of the mind.

To come upon one's self in the dark
and find light
of one's self
only for seeking its inevitable existence.
And in the searching and finding, discovering greater gifts that be.

All the flowers are for one's eyes to gaze upon and if seen
only once, they will forever remain a gift of one's
incredible mind to bring forth in sculptured visuals.
All the honey and sugar are for one's tongue, to fill one's
memory with sweetness to, upon recollection, re-quench.
All the rivers are for one's ears to listen to when
silence reigns, to find peace in flow and rhythm.
All the fields of grass, tall and green or willowing yellow sway scents of
fresh, wholesome air for one to inhale and delight upon.
All the cotton groves, mossy stones, prickly burrs and marble slates are
to touch, rub smooth with one's fingertips.

To realize all the world is for us to explore once or
one thousand times, to plant perennial seeds to
cherish the oneness with what is within.
To ever blossom
awareness,
silence,
a light filled soul,
a quieted mind,
a soothed heart in the darkest dark.

To come upon one's self in the dark
and find one's God there too,
to know all is well
and to relax.
Darkness is not aloneness but a blanket to warm the light.

6/10/1980

SED

THAT YEAR I ran my last marathon. After that I knew my best time would be 3:41. I ran that in 1983. This time I had run a 3:56. I would never qualify for Boston. That dream was done. I was sated and if anyone ever called me a has been again I'd just say; *you're right.*

The unparalleled events that made up my life continued to weave a tapestry that, if it weren't for AA, I never would have been able to sew into a pattern that knitted into a portrait of me. With all the judgment I put on myself, and all the judgments I assumed were put upon me, it could only have been the will of God that I bore forward on what turned out to be no more than a journey of enlightenment for the sole purpose of serving others. I prayed to have what Mrs. D. had. It is often said, in the circles in which I roam; "Be careful what you pray for."

I had a new job and I loved it. I was running two-color printing presses. I was right at home working amidst a bunch of men. It was a far cry from my days at the farm but, it was a re-enactment just the same. I learned a lot of things from those men. My young boss was very much like my grandfather. He was an uneducated genius. Just like my grandfather he taught me and expected me to do what he taught. I did. It was a happy time inside those doors. It was the best I'd ever been paid. We thought each other great. It was a place of fulfillment where I could forget myself and flow into the commotion of the job at hand.

I lived in the studio alone for two and one half years. I had made friends in the gay society. They supported me. They welcomed me. They called me. I hated the lifestyle but I liked a bunch of the people I had met. AA had no young people in it that I knew of. There was wild fun in that group that wasn't existent with the old women from AA. Since I had no idea how to change my life any better than where it had come to, I just kept going. It was as if I had embarked on a river-run. As the raft ripped forward with the current, having entered a gorge with no embankment but only vertical walls, seeing there was obviously no way back out, the only option was quite clearly to go with the flow. That's what I did. I wasn't happy.

I hadn't demolished the idea that it was the lack of nurturing love of a woman that had left me so sorely dismayed in an uncaring world. After all, I drank alcohol until it left me all but flesh and bone dead before I could be barely persuaded to give it up as a hopelessly wrong choice for a solution. It wasn't in my dire make-up to give up on what gave me even the smallest shake of a quake of remission from my feeling of inborn separation from the human race. I wanted to fit anywhere. The problem was finding a fit on my terms. Feeling love was like a skin graft on a stage four ulcer. Just because the first two didn't take didn't mean it was time to amputate. I had to try again.

While I was living alone I tried dating two more women. Both of them were disastrous. It was evidently impossible for me to be attracted to anyone who might be nice. These relationships with women showed me a new, much more complicated, sinister form of abuse than any man in their nearly readable, simplistic mind ever unleashed. I remember feeling like I lived in constant darkness. It was quite evident that the solution to my unresolved discontent was not to get in a relationship with a woman. I wanted to be single but I didn't want to live alone. It was a predicament. I was twenty-nine years old. I was ten years sober. I couldn't go back to dating men. That never worked for me. Those relationships were suffocating to say the least. Relationships with women were like relationships with hungry hyena's. I was stuck between two worlds. I had no place. That meant I had no purpose, and that meant I was spiritually bankrupt.

I was attending a meeting that was new for me at the time. I had a burning issue that flared above the other juggernauts I continually chewed on. I couldn't get over the fight I had had with Marcia. That I could become so enraged that I could grab someone's throat and very nearly choke them to death after ten years of sobriety was beyond my conception of where I should be. If I could do that I could get drunk. I was told ten years prior; *long before you pick up the first drink you are drunk*. It bothered me enough that I told about it at this particular meeting. I was sweating and shaking after I told the story because I was afraid of being rejected for what I had done. I told because I didn't want to get drunk. After I finished a few people shared about nothing in relation to what I said. Then a woman I will never forget shared. She sat very straight and crocheted except when she shared. She had long gray hair tied tightly back in a bun. She was as tall as she was round. There was a very sophisticated air about her. She did not look left, right, or at me when she spoke. She glared straight ahead or down at her developing masterpiece.

She said she was twelve years sober. She said a person with ten years of sobriety acting in such a way was not sober at all. I was a dry drunk. I obviously did not work the steps. I was a frightening example of the miracle of AA.

I was embarrassed and enraged. I left the meeting resolved never to return. I went back to my dimly lit studio and thought hard about the resonating truth of what that woman had said.

I was at another turning point. I still had no idea what I liked. I had no idea who I was. I was living relationships that were all recreations of childhood abuse. My way of dealing with it wasn't much different. I was still isolating. I just wasn't drinking. I had to stop getting involved with abusive people. Abuse was a trigger for self-righteous rage which was a trigger for self righteous drinking. I was a dry drunk.

Though I had never left AA, my time with Marcia, the gay scene, and my subsequent search for self in that hot bed of repulsive interaction where I had fallen in so blindly with the earnest quest for self revelation, I lost the inner comfort, the purpose, the spirituality level I had worked so hard for previously to come to in the program and fellowship of meetings.

From the time I was ostracized by the old ladies from the AA mountain meeting, the ensuing shut down, the determination to identify myself, to find love whatever it was against the damning sin of Catholicism, through the incredibly similar relationships wrought with vile emotional abuse, to isolation, a deeper shut down, and finally to a confession brought on by the coupling of fear and dread, I sat in my studio in the same winged-back chair I drank in; the one my mother gave to me to keep, and I prayed.

I talked to my friend and sponsor Carol. No one could tell me what to do. There was no more than a certain suggestion. I thought hard about how to apply it. *Work with others.* What did I have. How could I give without any belief in me? I had no identity. I jogged many miles for hours often aroused to the road by some sound, realizing I had no idea where I was. I lifted heavier and heavier weights. I worked like a dog. My energy was bottomless. My anxiety was topless. My only balance was the pitting of one against the other. My inner turmoil was like a washing machine that went berserk with a full load shaking and bounding all over the room spewing suds and water everywhere and completely unstoppable while it cleaned nothing and made an ever widening mess. It was noisy too.

I had also pulled away from The Lodge. The Lodge is what came to mind. It was the only place I had not been shunned. Well tested, The Lodge had seen me at my worst. All it ever did was open its door to me. When I was questioned it was clearly from a heart of concern, never contempt. I was like the prodigal son. No matter what; even if I drank I could go there and find a welcome hearth; understanding even in the height of disapproval.

In that year, 1988, at ten years of sobriety I called The Lodge and asked if I could run meetings for the young women there. I needed to save my butt. It took a couple of interminable days to get an answer. Mrs. D. was out of town for a couple of weeks but, I didn't have to wait that long. A message was sent to her and she responded in a few days. My volunteer work picked up where it had left off a few years prior. At first it was just the discussion meetings one Saturday a month. My involvement grew as time allowed. I was up there greeting on weekends. I did fifth steps. I stuffed envelopes. I spoke. I partook in the anniversaries. I brought speakers in. I took students out to meetings. Alina Lodge became my home away from home. I stayed as close to Mrs. D. as I could. I never stopped wanting what she had. I didn't ever realize I was always in the process of attaining that. In my silent place among the crowd that surrounded that great lady, I was insidiously enlightened and enriched by her generous spirit.

In 1990 I blew out a disc in my lower back. I hadn't made a strong connection again with AA. My spiritual focus found its vitality at The Lodge. I was still lurking at the edge of the fire where gay society roared.

Outside of Alina Lodge, the friends I had made at the gay dance clubs were my support. They supported me.

I couldn't convalesce alone in my studio. My mother insisted I come stay with her and my father. Since there was no other place I acquiesced. When I got there my father would have nothing to do with me. He neither spoke to me nor looked at me. My mother dutifully drove me to appointments but she never was my ally. In all the misfit days of my childhood, all the lost days of my adolescence, and all the hopeful days of my sober life, I never felt as unwelcomed as I did those three weeks. I hibernated and talked on the phone a lot. There was a group of women who planned to get a house together. One of them was a good friend. She asked me to join them. It was just what I longed for. One thing I knew from living alone was I didn't like living alone. I accepted. I had to clean out my studio thoroughly, top to bottom, to get my security back. I needed the money badly. My mother drove me to the studio three weeks out from surgery and on that cold April morning she sat in the car with the heat on and read a book while I scrubbed and vacuumed. I gave her money for her vacuum bag. We went back to my mother's house. I gathered up my belongings. A friend picked me up. Before I left I gave my mother forty dollars toward the phone bill and asked her to tell my father I'd give him the rest when the phone bill came in and he let me know the balance. It was like leaving for college all over again. I felt like a bug they just figured out how to exterminate.

I moved into a house with three women, one of which was my friend. The other two were beyond the dirtiest people I'd ever had any prolonged contact with. People as lazy as they were were incomprehensible to me. In no less than a month their dog had filled the entire basement, which they refused to clean, with shit and chewed every piece of furnisher in the house. My friend cleaned it up several times. They trashed what they touched, emptied the refrigerator, and broke what wasn't broken. My cats were running across the roof and the street. I don't think they knew what a closet was. Nor could they have possibly known what a garbage can was. To say I was living with pigs would be too kind a compliment. We had a one year lease we broke after two months. My friend and I moved to a two bedroom apartment across town. A third woman who had mixed into the mess came with us. The new apartment was cheap and extremely inconvenient as we had to park on a back street and walk through an alley and up four flights of stairs to get to the door. Shop rite every Tuesday was painful. My back never got a chance to heal even as my friend helped a lot with all the carrying and lugging that went on with that residence.

In the midst of all the moving and rearranging I got a nasty letter from my father. It contained a copy of the phone bill all marked up with red ink and stating I needed to pay up immediately. His accusation was clear and appalling to me. My father was treating me like the thief I was eleven years prior. I immediately wrote and sent a check with a note stating you need not treat me with such assuming disrespect. I didn't need to see the bill. Just telling me the amount would be fine. I reminded him of the forty dollar down payment I made as good-intention and payment thinking perhaps he had never gotten the money I left and I resolved never to go there for such a length of time again.

There was jealousy between the two women I lived with. I was disinterested in either one of them for what they wanted. However, one of them came into AA with me. She also did commitments with me at Alina Lodge. She considered me her girlfriend. I wasn't going to change my situation so I did nothing about it. The drawback was, being a habitual liar and gossip, she came up with fantastic stories that involved me. Well, those who knew her as well as myself just let her dig her graves. She was, for me, someone to do anything with. She was game. I guess I have to admit I used her for company. But it wasn't like she didn't want to be there and I always told her. In her words; *it was good enough just to be around me.* It worked. I ultimately liked being single. To be able to be single and have a partner was perfect. What she called it just didn't matter. My focus was what was going on at Alina Lodge.

I was getting more comfortable in AA again. With that and The Lodge, most of the time, I felt a strong God connection. That had become, without competition, head and shoulders better than any other competitor for the fulfillment of that hole in my solar plexus. I was successfully getting God-full. There was an immeasurable peace in that.

In 1992 I blew out my back for the second time. It happened while I was moving into yet another apartment. This time after surgery I had no place to go. My plan was to just stay in my apartment and convalesce alone. I'd be fine. I still had one of the two roommates. She was more than happy to lend a hand. Apart from her incredible ability to fabricate lies, she had a good heart, a good sense of humor, and good intentions.

My mother asked me to stay there again. I flatly refused. Then a woman from AA who I had recently started to sponsor, who had a huge house with several empty bedrooms called and said she and her husband had discussed it and wanted to offer a place to me for the time I needed. It was both comfortable and uncomfortable. It felt like a big step out into the open to me. But, Carolyn had a way of making a person feel at ease. I was persuaded into the best bet. I took her and her husband up on their offer.

GIFT

In a world
that can't
take care of itself
run by creatures
who only
take care of themselves
a gift
is a gift
indeed.

At thirty-two years of age with fourteen years of sobriety under my belt, though many inner conflicts had been brought to a dimmer resolution and the flames of inner dissension had been somewhat lowered to a high simmer that was a livable temperature, I was still years from the true-self-clarity that has proven to be my only river of real peace of mind. I was still, in a deep, marked degree, stuck in the identity that was summarily slapped on me from as far back as I dared not look. I still rejected being gay even as that scarlet letter had had its way with me for the past few years. It was as if society and family gave me three choices. Get married and have children. Become a nun or, go to that unspeakable alternative called 'the gay life style.' I'd never live the life of marriage and children. I was way too wild to consider the convent. That left gay. There must be, I prayed, a forth alternative. This was my life's plight. I had drunk over it. I must never underestimate the need to be accepted. That need is a sheer cliff; the earth breaking open that offers death as a viable alternative. I didn't fit anywhere. God knew, as much as I, that I tried, whole heartedly, to fit into the options offered. In fact I went way beyond where others would dare. I had more remorse than insight for my interminable searching. The place where my life had landed felt like I was wearing a full length garment lined with wool and sewn with thistle while I trekked across the hot sands of a desert. I often felt as if I had taken too much Benadryl and was shot stiff shaking with jitters head to toe in that painful state of inability to relax the full force of whole body muscle contraction. The fact was, fear had so rooted in my identity that I actually lived a state of anxiety like breathing. It was a normal way to feel for me. It would be nearly seven more years before I would recognize my anxiety as the soul-screaming discontent it was. I had no idea what comfortable felt like. I was living in a state of being without knowing what being I was; it was like being in the wilderness and not knowing if I was a grizzly bear or a jack rabbit; when *ever* do I run and when *ever* do I fight? What *is* my food?

The gay society, my latest, ongoing solution on my path of discovery by elimination, was in complete opposition to my quest. It created a block to my flow. I couldn't decipher the clues that would make that apparent. My quest was to have a sole purpose of 'pay-it-forward'. My quest was to understand. My quest was to be of service. My quest was to be of unquestionable service. My quest was to have what Mrs. D. had. Someone once asked me, when I was talking about my story and saying Mrs. D. never did this shit; *how do you know what Mrs. D. did? You don't know how she got what she had.* That was true. I never was a bootlegger. I don't know exactly what she did but, I do know that that woman had to go through some incredible shit to get all that incredible stuff she had. Wisdom and understanding are a result of living not watching. Let's say that again; Wisdom and understanding; unconditional love, are a result of living not watching. Mrs. D. was no watcher. She knew too much stuff.

I prayed for power. I put more hours into volunteering at The Lodge. I talked to Carol. I went to meetings and, I blew my back out beating the energy out of my body.

Providence has not once come to me in a way that I could recognize upon its arrival. I have, so many times, simply gone through the motions in a hopeful, broken faith. Even as my course took a sudden turn, I could not see the change of course until I was way down the road, perhaps even three or four turns beyond that original hard right.

At fourteen years, I had, once again, against my will, become a bit of an icon in AA. It was only because I had a knack for putting everyone's thoughts into words. My recovery has always been like that. I was never comfortable with the enamored response I got from baring my heart. I couldn't see, I was releasing a room full of hearts. That and nothing more was what everyone wanted for themselves; a freed heart. If I was the holder of the key then, no wonder they all waited for me to spring them. I'd leave the key on the table if I could. It just didn't work that way is all. But when I raised my hand everyone shut-up and listened. And after the meeting I couldn't get out of the room before a line formed to talk to me. In the first years I supposed they loved my youth, as I stood alone. At the seven year mark the mighty lashing and ostracizing I got bucked me up and landed me in a gully of despair. I suppose I'm an expert at coming back from despair. My great gift was, I could explain it. In rooms full of despairing people, when one person can put it in reasonable, understandable, and identifiable terms, that person throws out hope to the hopeless like holy water that instantaneously heals the sick. That was never my intention. My purpose was always so ingrained in me it was like being the one white person in a black neighborhood and never knowing why I stood out because I never saw a mirror and no one ever thought much of my whiteness so they never mentioned it. But everyone knew I was different. In this most inconsequential way was rooted, the way in which I never fit. I was different. I was inside-out. My heart was on my sleeve. The way I was told never to feel, I felt. It was what I did about that feeling. I told. When I told there was no black and white. There was a rainbow and it was pure relief for everyone who identified and never could tell. It was a healing flow that crossed all lines. It was me as you.

My intention has always been to find a harbor within myself where peace of mind could dock and stay afloat. Every boulder hidden beneath the surface, every shipwreck concealed, every storm yet on the horizon was never rectified until long after every one of them collided and battled with my alerted captain, subsequently to be taken to my roundtable crew, and further studied before my course could be corrected.

I have been in a constant mental rearrangement; always letting go; always coming to a greater acceptance of life on life's terms that is reasonable to me; always reaching a deeper and broader forgiveness right down to forgiveness of the agony of breath itself. My interminable drive for a greater peace, as blind and disheartening as it so many times has been, kept me going like I always took another drink to enhance *that* illusive serenity. I had found what I wanted in booze and drugs but it left me dismantled. The great and incomprehensible reality of *this* stark and unforgiving process was, I could never go too far. In this "long haul" solution my life could be expanded without measure, without certification, beyond the hands of any confines, and completely free of all and every repercussion and consequence of the myriad paths of immediate gratification.

I never could picture the path. All the time I've been in it I've been so wrapped up in my humanness and the faithless embers of my mortality, that when providence made its perfectly timed, mighty move I was unknowingly exposed as one pawn on a chess board while I supposed

I was the queen. There never was a time I imagined I had no power while all the time I was powerless. All the time I prayed to do God's will while all the time I was doing God's will. Never underestimate the process within the process. That movement inside the movement is called preparation.

When I went to stay with Carolyn and her husband Peter, my roommate took it upon herself to inform the couple about the lifestyle I had been living in. Her pronouncements didn't have the effect she expected. I didn't get tossed back to my apartment. They didn't care (or so I thought). During my three week stay at their house, my roommate/ friend (as I thought) spread her vile rumors all around AA. She filled Peter's ear with her special ripeness. Even in the realm of good will that so envelopes AA, juicy rumors are irresistible. The rooms rumbled. The murmurs were like the sight of wheat waving in a windy field.

One morning at about 2am Carolyn came into my room. She was very upset and wide awake. With great haste she said; *come on we have to go. Right now!* We threw all my stuff in a bag and she hustled me out and into her old but well kept Honda Accord. It was a cold October morning in 1992. In the dark she drove to her Deli, ran inside and got two bagels with cream cheese and some re-heated coffee. Then she drove us to a parking lot behind the post office. She told me; *Peter is really mad. He said; you better get miss Sue out of here before someone gets hurt.* There was a lot more explaining to do but the dilemma was, where do we go from here. Taylor was at my apartment. We had to sit and wait until she went to work. We sat in the cold until 8:30am. Then we went to my place. Thankfully Taylor was neat. She slept on the couch but she always folded up all the blankets when she got up. I appreciated her cleanliness as I had lived with some cataclysmic slobs. We went in and about 9:30 the Chemlawn truck Taylor drove pulled up in front. We sat ready to pummel her but, after awhile the truck just pulled away. We knew Peter knew where we were.

Carolyn went to her house later and got some of her belongings when she knew Peter would be at the Deli. She had to go back to work. She stayed at the apartment that night and Taylor stayed someplace else. She had been seeing someone I had not met and I figured that was where she was. The next morning when Carolyn went to work she arrived back at the apartment about two hours later. Peter had taken a righteous liberty and expelled her from the property which belonged to Carolyn. I was both confounded and incredibly calm. My experience of life was filled with these types of events. I was a magnet to troubled people. Though always unnerving, they inevitably turned out alright. The problem with Carolyn being ousted was she owned everything, the house, the business, and all the debt. I was just finding this all out and my life felt suddenly and delightfully simple.

In a couple of days, with Taylor in and out and Carolyn not moving I asked; *so, when are you going back?* she looked straight at me and said; *I'm not going back.* I said; *never?* she said; *never.* I said; *what are you gonna do?* she said; *I'm staying here.* I asked; *how long?* she said; *forever. I don't know.* I was on that raft shooting through that gorge. There was no turning back. None that I could see anyway. I was a bit dumbfounded. This wasn't a bad thing mind you. But it was a turn of events I felt I had to be wary of.

The next rapid to navigate was Taylor. She was driving a new car I had signed for that she made the payments on. I wasn't sending her off with my name signed on that loan. She was not trustworthy and quite vindictive. What Carolyn and I did was, we went to shop rite and bought a couple hundred dollars worth of food for her and her cat. Carolyn gave her an additional five hundred dollars along with her Honda which had a year's worth of insurance on it. We sent her back to Washington State where she said she wanted to head. Someone, her new girlfriend, apparently was chasing her for some money she borrowed. We inadvertently created a getaway while we ourselves were buying freedom. There was little resistance, few tears, and relief for everyone involved.

As I've reiterated I've never known what I was looking for until long after I have found it and I've not known who I am until I've taken much alert time in observation. My life has been a continuous assembling and stripping away. Eventually, drawn through enough illusions that I forged through as unrecognized gauntlets, I would be so naked to need no code and so disillusioned as to need no plan to move forward. That starting point is where I would blow into a clear and radiant light. In this way my blessed life with Carolyn began.

We talked to each other about ourselves. I told Carolyn about both my deep and current past. In those beginning days she didn't have a lot to say. My explanations neither dissuaded, frightened nor tipped her to question her actions in moving in with me. I continued to not understand. What I did see was a ticket out of the gay world that I didn't have before she arrived. That was enough for me to be *all for* her moving in.

We mingled briefly in a "the rite of passage". We were like two people with all left hands trying to get it right.

When I have a question it does not abate until I get some kind of answer even if its temporary. I needed to know why Carolyn was moving in. I needed to clearly know what she wanted from me. I did not want anymore gay relationships. It was not the answer for me. The anxiety it unleashed was unequaled even by my days of active addiction. That horrifying third option-final assumption had been thoroughly investigated with the blood and shatter of my own heart.

As clear as I was about what I didn't want, Carolyn was clear about what she did want. She wanted my spiritual clarity. She cared nothing of the rest. She was attacked and ostracized by members of AA, her family, and her friends. She was unmoved by any of it. I said to her; ok. *If you want what I have then I'll take you to where I got it.* I didn't know what else to do.

So began our journey together through the halls and caverns, forests, mountains, and skies into the shaft of light that illuminates the core of our breaths, our souls. I took Carolyn to Alina Lodge. While Peter took great pains to bankrupt her financially we rebuilt her devastated spirit into a fortress that would prove indestructible in time.

Carolyn met, became familiar with, and cried huge tear-drops of spiritual gratitude with the greatest spiritual giants I had known. I got to relive my awestruck senses by her experiences over and over again. We flew. We sang. We celebrated. We grew in overwhelming awareness of God's love. We were welcomed at the great hearth of Alina Lodge. We became missionaries as ready and willing as life allowed.

In AA we switched meetings to find an acceptance wrought of ignorance of the facts. We found a women's meeting that was quite motherly in its welcome. We were quickly summed up by a couple of old lesbians when Carolyn shared; *I walked out of my life and it has never been the same.* In that funnel view that runs most of society, they reveled in that statement for years. It is an incredible blindness the human race suffers to be so small minded in a universe of endless possibilities. I ask; *who can imagine this kingdom that has no beginning and no end? We live and die in less than a spark of its light. Why even consider choices? Light shines out as far as it can in a circumference only diminished by the diminishing power of the light itself. Don't measure by what you see. That is only a supposition. It appears wholly different to another eye. Measure rather by what you don't know. Realize your blindness and you will see. Measure not by the cast of your shadow but by the illumination of your light. Pray; be not blind; be not limiting.* As much as it was a continuation of the same old yipping dog at my tail, it didn't matter. We had found some friends. They were harmless and it took no work to fit in. We went to the diner after meetings with the group. We went on retreats with them. Eventually we took turns having dinner parties with them. We had a lot of laughs and underneath it all our common bond was AA. Behind all the surface squalor that screamed to be safe we all wanted serenity, peace of mind, sobriety; we all wanted a higher purpose and our sharing carried us to that end. They were easy and we had fun together. When Carolyn and I started to miss the company of men these same women allowed us to meet their gay men friends. We tried but this was too much for us. These guys were arrogant, snobbish, offensively rich queens. The men we had in mind were the gentlemen we enjoyed when we were at one of the innumerable events at The Lodge where women wore dresses and men wore suits. It was fine that our new friends lived their lifestyle but it didn't work for us. We soon cut those get-togethers out. We talked about how we didn't like anyone. We talked about how they were so annoying and assuming yet we continued to be a part of their crowd. We didn't want to become isolated. We didn't want to start over again so we continued to go to the woman's meeting and engage in some of the extra-activities that went on around them. It was social.

After two years in the apartment, in 1994 we bought the perfect house for us. It had two rooms, lots of closets, and big basement for my seven thousand dollars worth of workout equipment. The Thanksgiving weekend we moved in it snowed. That same Christmas we had a holiday party to welcome our social group and make a place to spread into where we took our turn to complete the welcome circle.

My job as a multiple press operator was great. I had gotten a bit of a crush on one of the men that worked there. He called me Susie which was always a heart-fall for me as some of the most special people from my childhood always called me by that endearing name. His name was Bob O. We worked and laughed and laughed. If he wasn't married we surely would have done more than that. I loved going to work. The men were great. They taught me everything. I was good with machinery so they were letting me run the big presses. The machines were so big anyone had to step up four feet onto cat-walks to reach the rollers, ink trays, or water troughs. They were awesome, exciting, and very loud. They were sheet fed presses that took paper as large 32 x 25. This was big stock to load and off-load. I worked like any one of those men and we loved each other.

Carolyn had gone to a lawyer and re-claimed the store. Peter stayed in the house until it was sold at a dismal loss. When she told him she'd be out on a Wednesday before the final closing to take some of her belongings he said fine. Carolyn took her sister with her. When they arrived with a small truck and went through the door, she found the house was no more than a shell. Everything, right down to the carpets and wall fixtures was gone. What was left was a butter dish and a weight watchers mug. She fell on her knees and cried. Yet the store remained. Peter could not be legally barred as they were still married and he continued without let up to try and bankrupt Carolyn. She finally hired a new lawyer. The two previous ones had caused more harm than good. And she continued to trust Peter. This one had a new plan; a plan with Carolyn's best interest in mind. While Peter stole the mortgage money from the register and spent it on trips to the Bahamas and presents for his latest hit, Carolyn waited, as she was advised, and worked managing a kitchen for a company that hired her dirt cheap.

After two years, as promised by her lawyer, the mortgage holder/owner relented and let Carolyn off the hook. She had invested over four hundred thousand dollars and now she was just grateful not to be going bankrupt. She had closed the doors, locked up and walked away and it took two years to be set free by that action. Carolyn lost the store to her great relief. We moved on.

We were more and more involved with Alina Lodge. It was a place of great solace and fulfilling joy. We knitted ourselves right into the fabric of a great common mission that Mrs. D. headed. That was who we were, unrecognized and boiled over with ever expanding fulfillment. It was a utopia obviously born of Divine intention. God's presence was palpable all the time. Hearts were exploding in service and lives were being saved. Gratitude was the driving force. There were many conversations about how we were so full we felt as if we would burst from joy. There was nothing Mrs. D. could ask us for that would be too much. She never asked for anything. She just welcomed our presence and whatever we did. Our time in service there was beyond unbelievable. It was indescribable, unspeakable for this person who could always put it into words. The only way to realize the possibility of such a reality would be to be a part of it. Carolyn and I had each other for mirrors of validation. This was real! All you had to do was want to be there and you were welcome. The joy of living manifest was its gift.

There would be well over two hundred people holding hands in a great circle that doubled up around the perimeter of the meeting room; the same room in which I first decided it was sobriety I needed ; the first room I ever felt and cried for gratitude in, that filled with the sound of angels, like the walls were humming, with every voice at once singing "Amazing Grace how sweet the sound that saved a wretch like me. I once was lost but now am found. I once was blind but now I see."

The unconditional love; the good-will of every person for every other person in the room was the most powerful sensation I have ever felt. I have always loved big meetings because of those nights at The Lodge; those nights of good-will buzzing, electrifying a connection between human beings that could only flow that freely by Divine intervention.

A Spiritual Experience

That is what this is—
all of it.
Once the volcano sends the mountain out
there is no way all of that can *ever* go back in.
Validate it!
Write it down!
When a crossroads comes, only hesitate to
imagine which road will be exciting enough to
make you willing to die to break clear the path.
Death is the turning point at which life's value clarifies.
Take the shape of form to the very edge.
Where the cliff falls vertical, lean out.
The body is the wings the spirit needs to live.
Fly.
Without reprieve, keep open eyes.
The rainbow is relief.
No storm reduces what is changed to black and white.
Listen.
Just above the breeze the forest sings.
Move fast and slow at once with open hands.
Keep them arm's length and free.
Outstretched arms with splayed hands make balance easier.
Breathe.
The feel of breath alone is sublime to
eternal mist that cannot, of itself, catch such wind.
Love like light.
A shadow cannot lean into light but only
disappear for its entire length to
reveal a greater space for anyone who
wishes to rest in the warmth of love's luminescence.
Go inside.
Pull what is inside out.
When feathers fall the face is gone.
There is no need for any of this when you realize what you have is

not a hiding place but a temporary resting place from which spirit can glean.
Divinity is utterly obvious.
Cry.
You've found your wings.
Don't waste one more moment of your momentary spirituality.
Let your spirit fly.
Your body is the wings the spirit needs to be alive.

This was life at its highest ability of appeal.

Mrs. D. illuminated for me and every other person in that room, spirituality; she lit us up with a purpose to exist; a reason to look not only inward to find ourselves for the sake of a healing process, but to take those findings and own them as the processed gifts of so many artists stuck in the shadows of impatient confusion released, exposed, refined, and finally, freely set forth for the salvation of anyone who might seek, even without knowing, Divine restitution of their life. I could not imagine what the enlivening of so much spirituality must have felt like inside of Mrs. D.. For the small part that I could give away I was exploding with joy. Sobriety was, by far, the better part of my life. Those years were the best time of my sobriety. I was excited and naive enough to fully open my heart. I was completely present in those piles of moments. I moved my focus and passion into what was happening there.

THE DUST CLOUD

As my involvement at The Lodge grew, the opinion of my family, what began to take place in my changing work environment, and the gay pushers in AA all echoed together into a low billowing dust cloud under a thunderhead on a distant hill. I could occasionally see lightning strike and the dust fluff higher. But for the time, I was wide open in an exchange I thought much more important. I ignored what would not go away. My unresolved identity would not cease its haunting. I was not finished going through it. That was the only way to get done with it. I've never learned one thing but by looking back and seeing clear through the length of the gauntlet.

My passion was clearly rooted in the carrying out of the old-timers AA tradition of *do the work and pass it on*. I wanted what Mrs. D. had and that meant; I must be a missionary. This was my purpose and it was all that mattered. What my story told was only as useful as were the tools for helping others it produced. Self was bondage or self was emancipation. I refused to look at what trapped me in me. I looked rather at what in me could be used to set me and, as such, all those around me free.

All this time I had one friend. Carolyn was at my side. She was the God-given calming influence I continually needed to keep going. My emotions, those horrid animals I was, so long ago, taught to never wear on my sleeve, were my driving force; my landmarks; my signature; the heart in me that spoke to the heart of each person who heard in every meeting at which I shared.

More and more I was being told to write the stuff I said down. I did but, not for the general public. On a grand scale the paparazzi show us how the public twists the picture into a story. If someone glued a shattered glass together they'd have me. I could stand on the shelf with the rest of the glasses but the glue hadn't proven hardened enough to allow me to hold water. I wasn't ready to test my integrity. People actually waited on lines after meetings to talk to me. They'd come with a pen and paper and ask me to repeat what I said so they could write it down. I would have no idea what I said. Speaking from the heart was a clear pathway for God. The words were not mine. I actually sat near the door so I could get out before I got swamped. AA was making me an icon again. I knew better than that. I knew I was shattered imperfection. But, I was eighteen years sober which was a lot of time for a thirty-seven year old. And virtually no one around had Mrs. D. and Alina Lodge stoking their fire. Just as I wanted what Mrs. D. had, these people were intrigued by the seeming ease of what I had. I was very afraid. I had a lot of un-named anxiety. I was afraid I'd find out it wasn't real. I was afraid I'd find out I wasn't real. I desperately needed to be real or I needed to be dead. There was no middle ground for me. Life was not good enough, by any measure, to be worth the burden of living it if I had no clear-cut purpose. Purpose was everything to me. But, the world insisted on an identity so I could not ignore the dust cloud. I wasn't certain of my identity even at that point because a large portion of my life hanged un-rectified and quite untouchable to me. The only way to get the world to stop defining me was to define myself. That definition was yet years away.

It was the low billowing dust of the lesbian accusation that continued to haunt me. I never could get free from its choking torment. It had been thirty-two years. From the time I was five years old when my mother teased me but could never stop me from wearing rugged jeans and sprawling on the dirt hills with my brothers even if I must be a dyke if I do that, through a typical teenaged homophobia coupled to the latent one-eyed-monster insignia embellished during high school, into my adult life when I finally tried it, to find it appalling, and then to never have been able to shake the reverberations of such a bad decision, like having sex and getting herpes on the first encounter, once again, as if still seeking to annihilate me, it reared its ugly scathing at my place of employment. I always tell my sponsees; *many things happen at the same time. It is never fix one thing then fix the next thing. It's more like the swirling of a million stars into a visible circle that works like the one on the big screen.*

After working at a much loved job for seven years, my enjoyment abruptly ended when a man with the personality of a starving madman, a friend of the boss was hired. I fell from the employee who received secret bonuses for excellence to the only problem the company generously endured. The man despised me without provocation. He was certain I was a dyke and made no secret of his belief. He aimed at annihilating a creature so disgusting to his masculinity. It was a bone-crushing, interminable attack that went on for eight years. In all my years of being accused of being a lesbian I never, from any accuser, got an explanation of how they arrived at such a conclusion. I read once in a book; people don't decide their judgments by our intentions but rather by the actions they witness. I never took into account how my persona might appear. I always just plowed forward. I would never not be tuff for anyone under any circumstance. There has always been a price for everything. For me it has become a defining characteristic I won't shake.

In my family, no matter how any one of us fell short, athleticism and strength were highly regarded. Being the one little girl with five brothers, they are who I competed with. I remember an incident at the Jersey shore. My uncle had come to visit. He was very handsome and very muscular. He was all about athletics and my father often bragged about him. We all looked at him with awe. He decided we were going to have a competition. The clothes line consisted of a stretched cord of course. But, either end was a T shaped pole cemented into the rock-yard. My uncle hung each of my brothers from one arm of the T to see how many pull-ups they could do. They weren't really interested but he made a big deal out of each successful chin-up. I wanted a turn. He said; *No Susie. Chin-ups are not for girls.* When I made a fuss he relented. He hung me up there and I did a chin-up just like the rest of them. My uncle yelled; *Wow!* and clapped and I felt glowing as the sun. That is the way it was; the way I became. As the girl I worked harder and longer than any of them cared to. I made up for the inadequacy of being female. I wanted the same recognition as the boys and I was willing to over compensate to get it. So, as an adult it was not unusual for me to get up at 4am and put water bottles out for a twenty mile run at 6am and it was not unusual for me to be bench pressing 135lbs.

By the time Mike, the madman, came along I hadn't been running for a long time but, after work I'd go home and ride my bicycle 40 miles then go into the basement and lift weights for an hour. What felt like breathing to me, I suppose, was a little unnerving to the onlooker. A guy like Mike might be intimidated. The only thing for a guy like Mike to do with something that intimidates him is destroy it.

I grew up with my grandfather who taught me I could do anything. I worked on a lot of farm equipment with him. At thirteen I was driving his tractor. He believed in strength and hard work without complaint. I worked with those Green girls. They were scary. They were strong. They were straight. They were the strongest farmers; the strongest women I ever knew. They were stronger than any male contemporaries that worked by their sides.

I loaded and off-loaded those presses and skids of paper. I trouble-shot my press problems. I fixed broken parts. I made jobs run that refused to run. I was a hammer. I thought I was doing what was right. I didn't think any of what I did was unusual. I was never a coy woman. I was never a deferring woman. I was never a run-of-the-mill female. I was well paid and given regular secret bonuses and increases in salary for my good work.

Suddenly the attributes that brought me abundance in the workplace became the points of character used as evidence for assassination. I was stunned and crushed. *This demon cannot be here!* I pleaded with my boss only to make it worse. I was sexually harassed in every insinuating and straight forward, vocally degrading way that that madman could think up. He did all that he could short of physical contact. He went so far as to block off the microwave so I couldn't heat up my lunch. He blocked off the bathroom. Tools disappeared that I was responsible for. I would come to work and find my area completely blocked off by 6' x 6' skids of paper. I'd have to climb over the skids or get the lift and move them which caused a big scuffle. He jeered and gawked at me. He cheered when I left at 4pm; *now it was the men* he'd say as I walked out. Not one of my fellow workers would stand by my side. Only one didn't turn on me but he'd have no part in it either. I thanked God many times for his courage to stand against Mike. I became the one bad egg overnight. One day this monster was actually barking at me. I just could not fathom it. I had never been treated like this by any man in my life. I thought maybe he is mentally ill and can't help himself. He had no cause for such outrageous and infantile behavior. He was a big, healthy, strong man with a wife and baby at home. His onslaught, without provocation, against me just made no sense. I talked about him as I had talked about every circumstance and emotion I came in passing with. I was seventeen years in AA. I knew the process well. I wore my problems right on my sleeve and people helped me solve them. I took advise.

I deduced he must have Tourette syndrome. The notion seemed immediately feasible. A forgiveness came lightly across my forehead. I went into the office. Against the new face of imprinted disdain on my boss I *coyly* inquired if Mike had Tourette's. It appeared my boss swallowed a hand grenade.

I needed my job and, in spite of what was building, I liked what I did a lot. I always was intrigued, even enamored by machinery. I could not be pushed out because this beast felt intimidated by my toughness or my highly skilled work.

I went to a lawyer. I was told I needed at least one backer. During my battle two men separately left. Both of them came to me before leaving and admitted to the wrongness of what was going on but neither would speak out. They wouldn't even chance burning a bridge. I understood. A third fellow employee suggested I just screw the beast and get it over with. That's all he wanted. Without a backer, if I weren't me, I'd be inevitably doomed. As I worked it out in AA I came to recognize the playing field. I could play. This was an exact re-enactment of my childhood. I was the outcast; the crazy one. No one helps the one pointed out. They are all silently glad it is not them. They all follow the leader; the way of least resistance; *The Lord of The Flies*.

I wasn't ready to leave so I dug in. I decided this man would be to me as an Indian cast from the tribe. This man was dead. This man I would pay no mind as if he did not exist. Like I did as a child, I shut down. I made absolutely no reaction to him at all. Slowly, very, very, painfully, slowly he self destructed.

RE-INVENTION

The dampened perspective evaporates.
No path discerns a windswept desert from a white sky.
The belt-horizon between them is like a mouth with
lips blanched to the clamp of closure to keep the secret hidden.

There is no more secret.
There are no more clouds.
The view is clear.
The horizon has no reason in regard to destination.
All that is, is here now.

The value of speed is measured by
    the accuracy of the description of the rose.
What do you see?
What do you taste?
How revealing is your touch?

Re-invention is:
One day awakening to find
    I am exactly who I should be.
I am exactly where I should be.

I evaporate into seed before
    I can hydrate into bloom.

Bloom is a light spiking a circle of
    illumination where everyone is
        welcome to enter and dance to their delight.
Re-invent into whatever they perceive themselves
    to already be.

So it was shown; what you pray for you get. There was a completely dichotic way of life happening without me being aware of it. I was being shown who I was and I was being shown who I was not. As the spirituality; the purpose of my life was being hammered home and blown through a horn by Mrs. D., Alina Lodge, and AA, the ever slinking snake of erroneous distinction pinned to my chest like a scarlet flag flapping since childhood was being shredded, thread by thread, by the whipping storms those snakes built up across my steaming breast plate. I was determined to tear through the words of my definition until I had no definition at all but only illumination; light revealed that is wholly revealing; one who has the power to touch without touching; one who can love without preconception; one that is free from the bondage of defined self while completely equipped by that same undefined personage for the very sake of passing on the freedom from definition that is the ball and chain of every heart ache suffered. I prayed to be a self that is at once all and nothing at all. That required both a grave humility and a Divine love of self.

My gaining clarity of myself dove gravely deeper that most young girls would dare chance a look and subsequent disclosure of. Oh, I was strong alright. The fact I didn't commit suicide; the fact that I didn't only *not* surrender but survived ~ I dug out and, with great help, I unearthed in me a purpose and even a mission smoothly paved. That I needed to die one-hundred deaths was proof of the loneliness such prayer might require for fruition.

I put on the cloak of coverage that was the armor of my underlying despair and crossed a line very few have the overwrought need, born of interminable pressure, to pursue for the final insight they need in order to overcome an accusation if only to live for one day in peace. I was exhausted from my mental torture.

I went to the end-rail of each parameter to determine my definition through relationships. If anyone ever actually experienced a snake pit I'd need no more words. For the rest, whether you take my word or not, you might take heed of its echo. That remedy for happiness definitely doesn't work. At least not for me.

I wanted what Mrs. D. had. She had a clear mission. That mission was best manifest by the abandonment of what most of the human race ranked in the top two. I had to abandon the pursuit/God of money. I never had that addiction. I had to abandon the pursuit of a one on one relationship. I was never able to lock myself into one. No matter who it was relationships always were a cramp to me. That left me in a good position to pursue my dream.

Yes. I was different all the way from the start. All the way from the start I took hits for not being a right fit. I almost self destructed. But, here I was. Alina Lodge became my main focus.

Carolyn and I had been being invited and attending Board meeting gatherings. In 1996 I was invited to become a board member. I felt deeply honored and privileged. I was allowed into the inner sanctum of what I imagined, the spiritually elite at work. I perceived these people as Divinely directed and in pursuit of a selfless purpose. They were on a mission for the betterment of the hopeless, a mission that shot like an arrow straight into what is without end.

In the spring of that year Carolyn got to meet Elaine, that spiritual giant who flourished under the rigors of Lou Gehrig's disease. When Elaine entered the room Carolyn immediately knew it was her. Elaine's spirit shown like a radiant aura that shimmered into light the beauty of her soul. We both held back tears. There was an exuberance abounding in the room. I introduced them. It was as if we all knew each other forever. Everyone was a person of honor coupled to service. We were all recovering drunks or family members that of. Being present was being a part of a phenomenal miracle and knowing it.

The core board meeting I attended without company. You must be on the board to attend. I was welcomed that first time as one of the two new inductees. I was quite intimidated. This was a group of about twenty people. Every one of them either owned a company like an oil company or a hospital, or was a doctor, professor, or lawyer. Everyone had a lot of initials. The only initials I had were AA.

There was talk of great change at The Lodge. I didn't dare say a word. I knew Mrs. D. was dead against it. She questioned the board's faith. They weren't thinking of faith. They were thinking of money. Mrs. D. exclaimed *I've been here forty years. Money has always come. Get small when you need to get small. Get big when you can. Just keep saving drunks. That's all that matters.* The board meeting wasn't particularly friendly but, it was perfectly polite. I witnessed firsthand how the very civilized-educated call each other asshole. It was the bare beginning of the peeling away of my corneas.

As 1997 bore on my work situation smoldered as fire-hot embers pulsate orange and red. Simultaneously my energy keened at The Lodge. Carolyn and I had become regular fixtures there. We also attended A A. The reaction there kept with the tide of earlier years. I never tried to bring attention to myself but inevitably, after I shared, people would pick up on what I said identifying and using my name as reference to what they shared. One night a woman blurted out; *is this going to be another Susan meeting?* I felt embarrassed and was quiet for quite a few meetings after that. It was a reaction to my sharing I wished would stop. It had followed me all my days. Obviously, as with the perception the paparazzi ignite, it didn't cause me to be loved by everyone. This woman's reaction was what I always feared, rejection for being me. After eighteen years I was just able to see an equal response of people who wanted me to write what I said down. People came to me after meetings to tell me how they wrote stuff I said down and they showed me. I'd always think ~ *thank you God for allowing such a gift through me.* Both reactions were as old as my days. I wasn't going to stop wearing my human heart on my sleeve. That was the path. So my journey toward full opening continued as my prayer to have what Mrs. D. had ripened toward full blossom.

We had our A A women friends. They were a good light social life for some good hearty laughs. We didn't get in too close though. Their scorn of men was over the top for us and our politics differed as well. Mostly, life was cherished as it unfolded in the mission of The Lodge and we were both grateful to have a friend to share it with.

In the fall of 1997 Mrs. D was 91 yrs old. She was beginning to fail. Alzheimer's was getting a grip on her. Our most adored mother needed care. At the October board meeting the new president took control. Mrs. D was the president emeritus. I was appalled at how the new president treated Mrs. D.. She was no less that completely rude. When Mrs. D asked to have the speakers on the microphone turned up because she couldn't hear the bitch scowled at her and bellowed *they are already up all the way!* I felt like I would rip her fat white neck out. I didn't move. I was completely intimidated. But, the lawyer who came on the board with me was not. He spoke up. The president had a lot of members already in her camp. John was unrelenting and he not only got the speakers turned on, he got them turned up loud enough for Mrs. D to hear.

There was a new agenda at The Lodge. It wasn't about the sick and suffering anymore. It was now about the money. Mrs. D. was stomped down every time she tried to talk. I sat silent, enraged. At that meeting opposing camps were drawn. In an office with a head counselor later, Mrs. D. said; *They've been after this place for a long, long time.* I was told a story of what happened some fifteen years prior. I knew all the faces. I had no idea all of this was happening back then.

Universal law is universal

Each atom absorbs a different degree of light measured by spectrum of color. What each atom doesn't absorb it reflects back. This is the color I see. Since no two atoms have the same spectrum no two atoms reflect the same color back. This fact is how one atom is distinguished from another. Since atoms cannot be seen they are discovered by what they do not absorb (by what they reflect back). By this finding of individual reflections each atom has been discovered and named.

Universal law is universal. So, I am discovered and named by what I do not absorb. I am defined by what I am not. I am defined by what I reflect back.

MRS. D. ALWAYS said; *when the inside and the outside match you will be at peace.* Rid yourself of your demons. Hang your secrets out in the open air. Reveal yourself until there is no more to reveal. You will know who you are. There will be no unchecked question. Then all you have to do is go with it. All the restrictions on you are taken on by you.

It took a quarter of a century before I could piece all of what she said together. The gateway to freedom of spirit/freedom of the bondage of self, she claimed, was to wear every bit of yourself on your sleeve; live inside out. She told us; *you will never get out of your own thinking with your own thinking.* Open to the realm of all possibility by walking out of isolation. Do that by falling open to suggestion. *If your thinking gets chewed to bloody shreds that's what it needs kids.*

I never felt more grounded, more free flowing than when I was involved with volunteer work at The Lodge. The more anonymous was my effort, the purer was my intention, the greater my fulfillment.

No family inheritance, no education, no money, no job, no new car, no marathon well run or maxed out bench press, no girlfriend, no boyfriend, no book, no world travel, no nothing delivered the immeasurable, untouchable full heart experienced as a result of freely helping another alcoholic. This was an illumination of a rarely flashed light. It is not one at all easily even realized too shine. And, if noticed, it is even less rarely believed to be real. I was in a great field of light. My work under such Divinely touched spiritual giants delivered the awesome experience of being a clear prism of light. If I could manage to stay open I could and did illuminate the path out of darkness to those still blinded by the shadow of themselves. I had found my calling. The ruthless testing ground of the world and its humanity showed me *what I am not* by bullying me into testing those accusations I carried like lead balls. The world could have itself. My mission was here. Mrs. D. never made one accusation toward me. I had not experienced such pure acceptance anywhere or by anyone. In the movie "The Lord of The Flies" I was Piggy over and over again. If it weren't for Mrs. D. I would have perished from off the cliff in one of so many chances long before.

I never fit in. I never conformed to fit in. The longer I stayed sober the less likely it was going to happen. What all of society did was what all of society cried about. Then, alive in the dread of their own conformed life, they all claimed they did it to be happy. Everyone did the same thing so everyone did the same thing. No one was happy. It was the same manifest illusion for centuries of generations. Why would I want to follow them? I didn't and I got bullied for my decision. I still couldn't conform. It was too blatant a lie for me. It would be diving into a double thick lie. I'd have to lie to myself to jump into what I knew was their lie. I'd rather run 20 miles, bike 50 miles, or drive 100 miles to help a drunk who has resorted to living under a lean-to fence than date, marry, get laid and have children. The first choices all fit me with wings. The latter I imagined would lash me with one harness after another. What Mrs. D. gave me was a purpose. By maintaining the *boundaries of me* I could embrace a life-mission of helping others. It has been incredibly fulfilling from the start.

While my world judged me and bullied me for what I was not, and the very acts I played out to rectify and define myself confused me about my very identity, Mrs. D gave my spirit a place to outshine all of my self-bondage. My light was great, clear, and steady. In a clear cut way the attitude of my world did not matter. What mattered was I found a peace that was real. I had found the path and knew the means necessary for me to attain that peace. I had a clear gift of delivery. My spirituality expanded into a vitality for Divine providence to have its way through my slight prowess and hesitant voice. I am not who you say I am. I have come only to do good works and be gone.

Though I had no credentials compared to all the degrees, I had an intimate understanding of Mrs. D.'s ideology. The battle of the board was gaining momentum. It was a great struggle for ownership of The Lodge. The executive committee had control of the money. They were very shrewd. They couldn't change the by-laws that protected the integrity of Mrs. D.'s program but they could change the interpretation. That's what they did. They set up, and undermined the CEO's position and fired him. They created lies about board members and had them removed. It was a politically ruthless time. I was in the middle of it all.

When the board found two men to vie for the CEO position I was asked to be a temporary member on the executive committee to be one in the vote. The executive committee knew exactly what they wanted and they were just as shrewd in their efforts to succeed. For me there was a lot of pressure from both sides. Phone calls and secret meetings, letters and emails burned my mind with information. My respected position connected to historical tradition coupled with my naiveté and my pride were a perfect mix to use me as a puppet for their final aim. I felt both proud and afraid. The people who had stood by me for nearly two decades were turning on me. The executive committee was stroking me. I didn't notice the tear it ripped in my integrity. As time bore on I became alone in my efforts to save the ideology of Alina Lodge. The old school ran away and cried. The new regime lied. I was witness to the collapse of an incredible utopia. The yet un-molded question had begun to take shape way before my great fall into the black hole of my dark night of the soul; *what is real?*

The two men were opposing poles. The first man was familiar. He ran a rehab that followed the same silhouette as Mrs. D.'s. The second man was a stranger having headed several rehabs previously. The first man wanted to combine the two rehabs. Money was not an issue to his signing on. The second man promised a great increase in revenue and required a salary that at once nearly tripled what Mrs. D had been allotted and subsequently returned every penny of for revenue to help others in a self help fund. The first man ran his rehab on the premise of 'helping others brings help from God' coupled with a business wise gift for organization. The second man was a sly business man able to get an organization rocking in a ruthless, money driven world.

I was put in a position where my vote was to be used as the spear head of right decision. We listened to both men. The first was much more humble. He was under the belief that all he had done was God inspired. The second was sure of himself, Mrs. D.'s ideology, and his ability to save a sinking ship. He was a much more smooth talker. While the first man spoke of aligning the common institutions of thought, the second man spoke of saving the great inheritance we were about to receive. He spoke of it being our mission; his mission.

The executive committee leaned very strongly toward saving the institution. They weren't of a mind to align themselves with what they perceived to be a much inferior rehab but rather, to stand alone, strong, and as it was for forty years, head and shoulders above the rest. They believed they needed money and cunning not faith and alignment.

In the end we cast our votes. I was convinced what mattered most, the ideology, could be saved and, with the right vote, we could also be saved from ruin. I voted first and the executive committee followed voting unanimously for the second man. He was hired by a nearly bankrupt institution for nearly three times the salary of his predecessor with a promise of a ten thousand dollar a year raise after one year if he delivered and if he failed he would be fired. I was unaware of the salary differences and addendums until after the fact. Many things were kept in secret from the entire board outside the executive committee. That included me.

The first noticeable change was the drop in discipline amongst the students. They were climbing out windows to secret rendezvous in the dark of night, an activity unheard of in Mrs. D.'s time. One time, when I was a student, a priest and nun exchanged a couple of words waiting for the car after church service. They were both expelled. The no fraternization rule fell flat since then.

The relaxation of discipline was nothing compared to the final dividing line. That line was giving recovering alcoholics and drug addicts drugs. This was a firm, clear line Mrs. D. explained and proved for 35 years. Alcoholics need to be off all mood and mind altering substances. *It doesn't matter whether you drink, sniff, shoot, swallow, or stick it up the south end. A drug is a drug and you can't have it and get sober or be sober. Feel your feelings. Depression is unresolved discontent. Look at your discontent. Change. Resolve your depression. The need to drink and drug will fade away.* That's what she said and proved. How could her loss of charge be so shadowed over was inconceivable to me.

A psychiatrist was hired to prescribe medications. There expanded a great chasm between the past and the future of The Lodge. It was a zoo to one camp while it was heading toward becoming a profitable institution to the other.

This man was officially recognized in his new role at the spring board meeting. I learned the difference between talking the talk and walking the walk. No one could be Mrs. D. but anyone who claimed to follow her ideology of strict, tough love, hard line discipline, and stone cold drug free recovery better, at least, come close. And where they fall short, be open to suggestion from those surrounding who have been enmeshed in that exceptional process. Helping a drug addict/alcoholic could never work and be about money. Addicts are too slick for that. If they perceive any alternative motive, other than compassion for their suffering, you've lost them. One quality alcoholics seem to universally share is profound self-centeredness. That has to be addressed as a seed that will germinate into recovery or a mutation of its inheritance.

Mrs. D. was greatly failing. After many resignations and many terminations from the board, being of small consequence and no power, I was the last root of her dying crop still on the board. Virtually no one from the old camp was speaking to me. I was alone. There were a lot of secrets that were obviously firing back and across that I was not privy to. I asked for a meeting with the CEO. I waited two weeks and was given a slot on a Thursday night following the evening session. It was the one night during the week he was at The Lodge. A fifty minute drive from my home, I arrived at 8pm. It was a tuff appointment to make because I had to be up for work at 4am. I sat in the hall for one and one half hours. At 9:30pm he saw me. I told him I was sorry to bother him and that I had only one question. He said; *no problem. What is your question?* I asked; *Is there any part of Mrs. D.'s program that you intend to implement besides the use of her name?* He told me he disagreed with her program. He had a brother who was a schizophrenic who died for lack of medication. He intended to use The Lodge to end the suicides of MICA patients. I said; *Mrs. D was a specialist, not a general practitioner.* He disagreed with her belief in drug free sobriety. We talked for a short while longer but it was clearly futile to argue with him. He was in power and backed by the executive committee which for all intents and purposes ran The Lodge. The rest of the board was utterly uninformed; a mass of puppets who could write in "board member" on their resumes. We ended by him telling me; *it's going to change here. In the future no one will be on the board who doesn't put up/donate to the lodge.* At that point I gave him a donation I had received from my aunt. His eyes lit up as he took the check only to flattened when he saw it was for twenty-five dollars. To close the door I finished by saying; *You don't have to worry about ridding yourself of me. If this is the way you're going, it's against the what I have come to know is the way. I will resign quietly.*

It was a volatile time at The Lodge. It seemed everyone was at everyone else's neck. Accusations were rampant. Secret meetings were rampant. Resignations were rampant. Coups were rampant. Firings were rampant. And student mischievousness was rampant. I couldn't imagine being witness to it all. It was Armageddon. It was the crumbling of a great empire, my world was coming down all around me and every person in it was dying a death not one of us could have been prepared for. Yet we were all prepared because everyone of us survived.

The teeth of so many spiritual giants was bared. These people whom I immortalized were all animals. This place I had come to call my home, my heart, my paradise in a world in which I found no pleasure. The whole fortress was crumbling and all the swords were slashing at the falling walls. So was I. The by-laws that protected the integrity of the institution could not be changed but one shrewd alcoholic-lawyer who put aside the fact his measly life had been saved by those very by-laws changed the interpretation. The Lodge mission was successfully overturned and rerouted to serve itself with the funds of the alcoholic as opposed to serving the alcoholic with its funds.

CHANGE

Mother dies.
The sash blows open.
Putrid air envelops life.
Earth fertilizes a tornado.
Nature runs and hides.
Night steals day.
The heart shatters.
Weapons become baggage.
Dreams induce nightmares.
Finally—
without permission—
a baby is born in the new light of an unscathed dawn.

On July 9, 1998, twenty four days short of my twentieth anniversary, Mrs. D. died. Mrs. D was fifty-two years sober. The incredible journey of our intersecting spirits is the tweak of profound refraction my arrow shaft of light unwittingly sought to clarify its purpose. She had devoted her life to the purpose of helping others. As I was one of the innumerable, fortunate recipients of her treasure, the greatest gem I inherited was a purpose of my own. I was yet years from what needed to transpire in order for my shaft of light to transform from a smoky luminescence to a stark beam, from a stark beam to an expanding incandescence that forces shadow into a clear cut delineation of reality, a reality that precludes the freedom we all seek; freedom from the bondage of self. Mrs. D. left me with enough light that I might buff into a shine that illuminates the inexhaustible love of God. Known as Higher Power, the river of such an infinite source was proven to me to be at hand. I had the means to make that apparent to anyone who was in a great enough state of abandonment to want to know. I had the ability to put it all into words. So I have become the pen of my purpose.

There was a small memorial mass in August. In September, following that summer, I mailed my letter of resignation to be read at the October board meeting. It had been a nearly unspeakable two years.

DEMONS

And when they come, those demons,
they call your name so thick it tastes
sweet as cherries ripe from the vine.
Wind whistles soft, warm nothingness across
your shivering, downy skin and . . .
you forget who you are.

Nothing is ugly because fantasy casts
a spell. It breathes like morning dew covers
grass. It keeps true color draped behind its silver sheen.
When day wakes to full height and a trickle
of salty sweat stings your eye, you look with
greater intent because you discover . . .
you can feel.
It's not so bad living in this pain ridden body even though
you need to eat, drink, shelter yourself, and find relief in obscurity.

The demons slip their arms around you. In the passion
of embrace, they render you handless. Then they
feast on your heart. When you wrestle momentarily from
their grip, discover you no longer have hands but wings,
it is good because the demons show you . . .
you can fly.

When they go, they leave your gullet empty behind windows
to the world. They return when your fields remain barren and
you lie prone in hungered sleep. They smile while they
remind you of the wings you gained for
the hands that lost your heart.

It is a strange bunch of should-not's we put on ourselves when someone dies. I lost my mother-source. But more than that, I lost my world. I tried to convince myself; this was not my mother-source and this was not my whole world. I thought I had no right to grieve. I took away my right to it but, that didn't stop my grieving. Rather, it stuffed my immense loss, like an unspeakable secret, up under my sleeve. I so denied the existence of my emptiness that the actions born of its experience that began to manifest out of control in me were unrecognized by me for what they were.

It was nothing outrageous at first. The underlying attitude was nothing new; *no one is going to tell me who I am.* I am going to *be* myself into being. It took twenty years for me to be catapulted once again to stand up in the grave world of life. Whatever the cost to come to a peace in being me, my willingness to pay the price included a willingness to die. That was nothing new either. There was tremendous undertow pressure building in my solar plexus. Die I would a death I never could have foreseen the need for if I were to meet my quest.

The entire sphere of relationships I had to my universe had to be rectified. This time of profound loss put the need for all-embracing settlement at hand. My family relationships were always an issue. My work relationships had become a dismal unearthing. Coming to appear turncoat, all of my supports from The Lodge had turned on me. Both Elaine my spiritual giant and Alice a much trusted friend for all twenty years of my recovery; my closest confidents, stopped speaking to me as did virtually everyone else involved in the final few years of the utopia we shared. That was a shattering blow to my belief system.

I learned that to have something to believe in is just as important as to be believed in. And it was more important to believe in myself than to believe anyone or anything or to be believed in.

At the time I thought; *if no one believed in me then what did I believe in?* It was a huge question that heaved up out of the fragments of my well glued glass integrity as a result of what I was just barely able to sip at let alone even imagine a glass full of.

I had learned to sport a cloak of armor in AA as a result of the inconsistent feed-back I found. Not having a firm grip on my identity, I reacted to the un-sureness it provoked in me with equal inconsistently which left me at times paranoid and then feeling loved. It was way too important to me what people thought. That was a clear indication of my lack of self. This turning point in my life brought every one of my lingering inconsistencies to the stark light of my forebrain eyes. I was going to move forward into the naked reality of who I am or I was going to shadow back, regroup, and figure out like everyone else, how to hide and exist.

Grief is a slow burn. I had to run through the gauntlet of purposelessness one more time. It had been twenty years. This time I was to emerge from the far end with what I could not have imagined to be a pinnacle requisite for the answer to my lifelong quest. I came out with an integrity that wasn't only not glass, it didn't need to be, nor could it ever be a container. I came out with a clear identity. I came out with a clear purpose. I came out with a God of my own. In the end, I came out with peace of mind.

I always wanted a truck so, I bought a Dodge Ram pick-up. As expected the question came at me again and again; *why a truck?* And the comment that so often followed the question teetered in my untamed brain; *it's so un-lady-like.* I was incensed by that lifelong character trait so negatively hung on my chest. So, without conscious intent I aimed at slaughtering it once and for all if only to obliterate its interminable hurt. I built brick walls and backed them full of flowers on my property. I worked on the lawn until I felt like a slave to my patch of earth. I went to meetings and talked about what happened at The Lodge. My feelings felt wrong. I was ashamed of my grief. At the time, of no help to me, AA had me on a pedestal again. I felt it wasn't fair. I needed understanding not glorification. I resented my long term sobriety. It held me accountable and kept me from the solace I once received as a newcomer.

I was entering the darkest time of my life. I was shuttering over the black-hole of my lost illusion and could not name it. If there was a perfect way to commit suicide and not die what was to transpire was a perfect path. I was spiritually bankrupt and twenty years sober; a vulnerable epitome. My purpose had been ripped out from under me. I could see no place to go on this dismal globe for solace for that. I had built my life on

Mrs. D.'s passion; on Mrs. D.'s God and now that she was dead I was left empty handed. I needed to find my own passion; my own God. I didn't know where to go so I went crazy.

I was enraged by the whole Lodge coo. I was heartbroken over my loss. I was alone on my pedestal in AA. My family began asking questions because they noticed a change in me. There was a change. I drew the lines of a new boundary never again to be crossed. I excommunicated them all from my life. I had had it with their opinions of me. My place in that family became utterly unacceptable. I would either abolish that assignment or abolish that family. I no longer belonged to them. To all of their years of derogatory statements I boiled over. My disdain was the drawbridge over the mote pulled up-closed. From that time forward I would be taunted no more.

Mrs. D left me to find out who I am. After two decades of preparation it was time for me to find out. If I had known, like so many times before, what beatings I would bear in order to get through this gauntlet, I could not have imagined or believed it could be true. I can only say; *the pain of a broken leg is of no consequence compared to the pain of a broken heart.* As I stand today, I'd take the broken heart. For the blood that it delivered is my own. I got every drop of me.

Mrs. D had a deep love for life and humanity that was rooted in a profoundly clear understanding. I was catapulting down a shaft of light that would take me to that state of being. The ride was grossly indelicate as a ride on a light-beam might *not* be imagined. It was not *too love* that required so much skin. *Too understand* is what left me de-gloved. I don't know what Mrs. D. did but, I can tell you what I did. First of all, it's not to plan for. I was given the tools. I knew the process. The time was at hand. My opportunity was fatal. I had to die to every self I eluded to, been fooled to believe, ran from, was accused of, gave in to, and fought to be free of. I had to free myself from the bondage of self ~ all self. As my mother has said time and again; *old age is not for the weak of heart;* neither is the long term, unrelenting gauntlets of recovery and search for clear purpose for the weak of spirit. The closest I came to throwing in the towel and getting drunk was at twenty years worth.

In the late summer of 1999 I had found new meetings. Carolyn remained my roommate, my best friend, and my confident. We had become companions in a common effort. She accompanied me since she left her husband and walked out of her life. She was virtually always there. She wasn't in the same anguish about The Lodge as I was. When I asked her what she thought she would astound me with the answer; *nothing. I don't think about it.* I had been her sponsor for years. She was the only person in my life who was there; who witnessed the whole process of the upheaval; the tearing down of a spiritual empire and scattering of its wholesome fruit. She had no words for me. I talked to my long time friend Carol but, she was in another world with a new husband. At meetings people sought answers from me. When I came searching for answers they pulled back as from a flame. I was completely invalidated. I was brewing.

One night a newcomer was in the meeting. After the meeting she approached Carolyn and me. She assumed we were partners. Of a sort that was true. We began driving her to meetings. I began to sponsor her. She had another idea in mind. We did a lot to get her life in order. We cleared her property of debris. We painted and fixed doors. We even changed the plumbing in the sink, tub, and toilet for her. We went to AA. She had a straight forward way about her that was disarming to me. I liked it. I wanted to be told the unspeakable. I wanted to be shredded, annihilated, torn from my emptiness. A newcomer, the first person I was told to stay away from all the way back to June 10, 1979 when I left Alina Lodge, did it.

To cross that property-line-of-the-heart was the closest to suicide I could get without a dead body to show. I was so filled with anxiety and so unconnected from support I was a time-bomb bulging to explode into a million pieces. I went back to that same meeting where we met many times. I pushed people and they backed away. Carolyn even backed away. I was crazy.

One night I was so distraught that afterward I went into the bathroom, looked in the mirror with horror at my image and prayed with an unmeasured earnest to God to send help. I didn't want to throw my life away and it felt like that was what was happening. I emerged and stood in the shadow outside the door for a few minutes to calm myself.

I wasn't ready to get back in a dead car and drive home with Carolyn to a dead existence just yet. I sensed someone was there. I looked to my left and there stood Jean. Jean was a woman in AA I had seen, heard, and talked to for a few years. She was my mother's age and shared the experience of long term recovery. She was definitely wise. She was wise to the point of scary.

At first I said; *I'm sorry. Did you want to use the bathroom?* Jean said; *no. I'm just standing here.* Somehow that wasn't unusual; Jean and I standing in the shadow outside the bathroom door like two sentries, neither one speaking, both observing. I thought; *God! Is this who you are sending me?! Shit.* Then I said; *Jean, can I talk to you?* Jean said; *sure.* We sat down at the far end of that damp room and Jean listened and responded for hours after everyone had gone and until the room was too cold to sit in any longer. Then she drove me home.

I told her all about The Lodge and she said it would be like losing AA. I told her about T and she said it's time for you to find yourself. To do that you have to step outside the lines. You have to live out of control.

LOOKING FOR YOUR SOUL

To go there you have to throw away your soul, not
in safe keeping but in a blind act like
the act of falling in love when absolutely
nothing matters.—
Shades are drawn. Faces fall blank.
A siren scream is a silent sound like
the one in a dream when soft thought
turns hard and cool sleep becomes soaked
night sweats, helpless under the grip of
some nameless feral animal. All you
do is grab for more because you forget
your own name. You forget your face,
your lineage. Reason is incinerated in
the puffed blaze of smoke that rises
from salt scented sheets.

Your soul is gone and now you hold on.—
Become the white trash. Cling to your
last cigarette. *Drag* the dead out of life.
Stink like the matted bed while you gaze
directly into the eyes of heaven and hell.

Try to pull yourself back together but it's too late.
You've fallen in love with the drape of a ghost, a
heartless flying thing that casts a magnetic
shadow you resurrect uncivilized within—
Die one hundred deaths below and now
you want to live because something switched the light on.

There you are
in the garbage strewn by your hand
looking for your soul.

I HAD A huge dilemma. I was edging on getting involved with a newcomer (the cardinal sin of all sins in AA). It was AA social suicide. And it was like a drink I could not stop myself from taking. I was skydiving without a chute and there was a majority of me that didn't give a shit while the rest of me oozed with a self loathing that wanted me to kill myself for such uncontrolled lust. On top of that my big slide made me volcanically nauseous with an anxiety I could not name. This was a woman.

Jean's reply was; *you've already done it in your mind. There is no stopping you. Do what you need to do.* I said; *but what if T drinks over it. I don't want to hurt her.* Jean said; *T is not the one in danger of drinking. You are. T is not the one who is going to get hurt. You are.* I was confounded by these statements. But, upon those words thus spoken while we both listened I dove into an relationship that crossed every line, clear or blurry, ever set or painted to keep me in check. I went wild. The experience I lived with this woman was breath taking. I had definitely met the tiger.

I MEET THE TIGER

It is at the time, half way through my life
I come to a place of nothingness.
I meet the tiger.
Being of immense feline sensitivity,
I am taken just short of immediately.
Its suave motion and its unrelenting persuasion
Draw me like dew to a morning field.
I fall in its grasp; surround myself with its passion.
Into the forest of unexpected pleasure it
Caresses my needy secrets, kindling
A fire that always leaves me wanting more.
It quiets my apprehensions as they rise.
The tiger instills trust as sure as its kiss of death.
I meet the tiger.
I am overwhelmed.
I hand my life to the beast.
My life is accepted.
The tiger takes my heart and eats it without regret and
I, so enthralled, enjoy its contentment.
When the meal is through, so is the tiger.
As sleek as is the arrival so too does the beast depart.
Oh yes,
I meet the tiger.
And now ~
I am dead.

I BEGAN WRITING a lot more poetry than I had written in a long time. I was meeting with Jean on a regular basis. This was the most desperate time of my life. Writing and talking were always key in the AA process. She asked me if I was writing and I told her I was writing poetry. She said: *oh, you write poetry? Maybe you will let me read some of your poetry some day.* From that she prodded me until I relented. I picked out eight poems and brought them to the diner where we met. We ate dinner and I hung on her every word like each was the most important ingredient for my mortal survival. I was in a chasm of self defilement, and completely hobbled by my relationship with T. It is interesting, my drive to choose something completely and utterly destructive and my inability to stop myself or let it go.

With Jean I was inside out. At the end of our meal and after the table was cleared, with the reluctance only a great fear of rejection can cause, I took out and handed her my heart-stash of words. It felt like ten hours went by in one. Then she just sat there. I was furious with myself that I let her read my stuff of secrets. Finally I asked; *Well, what do you think?* As usual her response was slow. She said; *Your family really fucked you up.* I was immediately, flat-out seized with the size of my mistake for having let Jean read my writing. After a few more moments she said; *I think that you are a genius. This poetry is brilliant.* I didn't believe her but I kept writing and she kept reading. In the end I wrote over twenty books of poetry. We traveled all around the state and I read my work out loud at poetry meetings. It was a new and glorious venue of release. I was well taken wherever I went. The response was much like that of AA. This was an important piece of what was happening to me. Unbeknownst to me, I was healing from my core out. I was finding out who I am. I had to pull the whole mosaic of me apart and fit all the puzzle pieces together with my hands alone. In the end the picture of me was a whole lot different from what was originally glued by every association I ever had.

At home Carolyn fought her own battle. The world she knew was gone forever again. My disappearance was her loss of The Lodge and Mrs. D. The agony she withstood is her story to tell. I can only say we moved around the house like two ghosts, obviously present, obviously absent.

My involvement with this newcomer was no less than horrifying to the women we had become acquainted with in AA. The gossip grapevine spread the hot topic like wildfire. I was ostracized yet again as *these* women waited like hungry hyenas for me to drink. Then they could sit on their thrones of safe resolve and spout about how good and right they lived their lives; use my transgression, as they perceived it, as a lesson for what *not* to do. Not one of them tried to help me or Carolyn. Jean saved my life. Carolyn found a sponsor who saved hers. I learned more during this time than all the years before. As I taught a lesson to those women they also taught me. It was one lesson out of many, many insights I came to even as my heels dug in deeper. They could wait and drool for my demise but you see, in all my confusion about my identity over all my years of hard-knock mistakes in recovery, there was one thing I was sure of; I could not drink or do drugs. On that issue the hammer was down. Way past that original realization, way past many spiritual awakenings, past many whole new ways of beholding life, I had been dropped on my knees to encounter an experience that was beyond right or wrong. It could not be judged because no matter how it was viewed by the great source of definition that is the human race, it was absolutely necessary for me. It was necessary because it was the undoing only a relationship can undo that cut me loose from the brig of definition once and for all. That was one key in the lock garden of prerequisites to the free flow of my purpose; to the free flow of Susan. Some quite profound and unexpected results of such an immoral relationship were, I have not, to this day, had the slightest need to be right. I am open wide to suggestion and nearly crystal clear of judgment. The freedom to be and the peace of mind born of these outcomes is immeasurable.

If lust is one of the seven deadly sins then perhaps sin is not sin at all but rather one manifestation of the uncounted human frailties that can only be known by bearing the tear it incurs. What price is paid for that rarely understood, Divine quest, humility. Who would imagine such a pay-off; sin for Divine quest fulfilled? Only by the experience itself can one see the guideposts, as horrifying as they need to be, to get one's attention that one might gain the insight needed to surrender self sufficiently enough to head back toward where one has come. I needed to be redirected back toward God and my true purpose. I have learned far more by the mistakes I have made than by any of the quietly acceptable, correct decisions I have made. Who is to say which of these is which? Is what is correct the acceptable and what is incorrect the unacceptable? Who decides the line of demarcation between right and wrong? I once took a course in maladaptive psychology where the class discussed an experiment that was made. An entire town of schizophrenics was assembled. There they co-habitated successfully, which is to say, in harmony. When a so-called normal-minded person was introduced into the community that person received the definition of mental illness. So I learned, it is society defines me according to how well I follow their rules. If I am so fearing or submissive as the majority then I live my assigned role. What if, no matter where I squeeze I cannot fit? Am I crazy?

My family, while I was yet a child, pigeon-holed me mentally ill. I didn't fit their mold. My mother threatened more than once to get me a lobotomy. The little wenches in my neighborhood cast me out for wearing a patch on my eye. They screamed *queer* at me. I didn't fit their mold. When I drank I found complete relief but I couldn't get long lasting relief. Unable to maintain that calm the alcohol gave me I became an alcoholic chasing halcyon. Life tumbled around me like an avalanche of rocks. It didn't work. AA was a bleak last resort. As a teenage child I couldn't fit in with the forty year old divorcees whimpering over their various demises. The Lodge was my first fit; the first haven where I wasn't crazy. It worked for twenty years then it crumbled. I wasn't crazy. I was berserk.

There was, among my one-handed-count, something I've always searched for. One of my un-named quests has always been self-love. I was under the same illusion as everyone else. I thought if someone, anyone could love me then I would, in fact, be loveable. On that premise I could love myself.

Woe to those who seek love from a mirror. There is no replica of what we are. Love is a light. Light does not reflect back. Light shines out only diminished by what power it lacks. All power comes from God only curtailed by the greatest endowment of being human, self will.

As short as it was, just a couple of months, my relationship with T catapulted me forward in clarity faster than any person or circumstance thus far in my spark of existence. That relationship was the most intense experience of my life. T was a passionate-breath-taking lover. A person so scarred by childhood and dredged by the human race, alone, had the power to dredge out the bottom rot of me for our equal lot. The point at which I dove in was a point at which I had never been so bared of heart armor. I was wide open. I jumped in with open arms. I was dying. I could go no further in the reality of a world without love; a world that had revealed itself to be no more than a self service maize of gauntlets that left everyone eyeless to survive in the end. We both loved so hard my teeth ached like a cocaine addict jonesing in withdrawal for a fix. I was magnetized and obliterated. I could not pull away. It was physically painful to me to have to leave T's presence for any period of time. We talked for hours. We entered the unspeakable abyss of each other's scarred heart chambers. I abandoned everything and everyone. There was no calmness across my land. I didn't care what storm erupted. I was ready to sell my house, quit my job and lay down and die in the teeth of this monster. T empowered my womanhood. I felt, for the first time, incredibly beautiful, even radiant. I felt brilliant, perfect, and adored. The intensity of our love making blew my mind, obsessed me, and tore my heart to shreds. In our shadowed lair she managed to implant deep notions of my powerful, brilliant, and abundantly superior womanhood. She gardened my ability to write and connect to our like source. She laid deep roots of my courage and strength to dare beyond the average man-fearing woman to entrust myself with one of my own.

One day in mid-spring 2001 T informed me it was over. Just like that, I was asked; *what did you expect? You got what you wanted. Now go. I'm going back with my lover of thirteen years.* I was flabbergasted. Just as magnetic was the coming together, was the splitting atomic. Just as every preceding gauntlet, coming out the far end left me in great need of great caretaking to survive. It had taken twenty years for me to prepare. In three months I had gained and lost the earth. I was de-gloved. I stood wholly exposed with a blank slate to contrive my human idea of God.

The Sea Lion

I lift my dress and the Sea Lion
slips from a glacier into my bed.
Within the curl of its wave
I am hidden from all alleyways and main-streets,
forests and fields, dogs and foxes.
The immensity of the world is within the embrace of my open arms.

The caress I smooth along a satin arch breaks
through the wave's white-wall like a ghost passes
through a closed door.
Bridges erect and disintegrate at once.
Parliamentary guards stand staunch.
I am struck blind. The volcano ignites night into day, spews
the entrails of a mountain into heaven's release.
White ash, hot as cold snow, covers ancient
scars cut across my abused earth.

I wake surrounded in ocean.
Salt stings my skin.
A shiver shakes down to a soft breeze across wheat crowns.
She breathes into me.
Her air through my hollow ribs is breath through a lute.
The delicate resonance of woman is sweeter than
the universe of lilacs played in one orchestra.
My senses are drunk.
I throw myself with abandon onto one million living daisy petals.
Unchecked, I drink more than my ladle can hold.
Bankrupt, I run from my nakedness.

The mirror stands; an expression identical to the storm.
I tear the breach-of-contract against my heart to shreds.
Rototill it into the garden.
Fertilize its decomposition with my tears.
Tie a knot in the severed umbilical cord.

A kitten kneads the armor across my breast.
Music is a solid, resounding purr.
A broken dream is no more than a missing step to navigate.
Love is a rainbow over a fog cloaked sea where
The Sea Lion slips in to take me out.

When searching do not follow the rules. Those rules are exactly what keeps you from the finding. There is no black and white. There is no grid. There is no right and wrong. There is life and there is death and there is being alive and dead at the same time. There is fear and submission and there is chance and freedom. Just live.

I was as open as could be and a direct hit is what I got. I cried on my hands and knees in the center of my living room. The snot stretched from my nose to a blob on the carpet. I couldn't breathe. The great gasps that broke the silence of the long taught sobs felt good. It was excruciating and liberating. At the time I had no idea what was happening. I cried at meetings and those women waited and waited for me to drink. I cried at work and they waited and waited for me to quit. I cried in Carolyn's arms and she waited and waited for me to come back. Jean spent hours, days, months listening, talking, and reading my poetry.

A friend I loved dearly from high school called me one day. She was one of the few people who loved me. I thought my gratitude for that was a love I must never admit.

I told her the entire story; all about my heartbreak and how I had lost a soul mate. She said; *Sue, every guy I ever gave a blow-job to thought we were soul mates.* We laughed and then she told me she was dying of breast cancer. Shit!

I took off work the next day and went out to The Black River. I walked down the trail to where the river was isolated. There was a huge boulder out in the wash where the river swept violently around. I hopped and waded out and climbed up and sat on the rock. It was raining. I sat there and wrote about dear friend K. It rained for all the hours I sat there. It felt good to get soaked. I cried with the sky for her six years before she died.

There were a few things I always wanted. While I was turning inside out I got them. I bought a twenty-two pistol, a three-fifty-seven pistol, and a 9 millimeter pistol. I also bought a twenty-two two-fifty rifle. I got myself a Honda Rebel and a full leather outfit to ride it. I wasn't suicidal but I certainly appeared to be. I was a grizzly with newly sharpened claws and teeth and I was hungry. I had picked up smoking again and I was killing off a pack a day, by far more than I ever smoked. I lost twenty-five pounds and I cut my hair off. I had no intention of ever fitting again. I had no idea what all of my actions would turn out. For the first time I didn't care. I was just going to do what I wanted to and see what happened come what may.

I switched my meetings. I went home to Hackettstown. There I got support without knowledge so there was no judgment. I told two of my sisters-in-law what happened. To my amazement they were relieved. That they could relax in my truth rather than be in constant threat from my obvious unresolved rage changed those relationships forever.

Because I was so emotionally out of control I worked harder and with more focused attention than ever before. The pressure created at my job by M mounted. I stopped talking altogether there. It was a re-enactment of my childhood response to my family. But this time I wasn't moving toward self annihilation. This time I was moving toward spiritual emancipation. That was because my tool wasn't alcohol it was AA. I didn't know any of this at the time. I growled from the depth of my soul bottom. I went to the firing range and hammered out thousands of rounds. Wow, how empowering that was! I dared anyone to face-off with me. With help I could glimpse what was happening. I demanded; what chance had anyone taken in their life to gain the access to both separation and actualization I was in the midst of journeying. I took guidance with the intensity needed to survive the wilderness of my heart. When one night, in a fit of remorse, I scoured the closet for a pint of Jack Daniels I had kept for when my grandmother visited, Carolyn had poured it down the drain, and I had gotten through my darkest hour with the help of God who works through people. I had met my greatest demon and I lived. Now what?

I never aligned myself with men or women again. They had both served their purpose. They had both served their capacity to show me who I am by showing me who I am not. The carpet of time began to unravel. My family showed me I am not who they say I am. My job pushed me to show them I am not who they say I am. AA took its shot at defining me. It can be said; *I am an alcoholic.* Is the ocean defined by its fish? In the end there were two people open and waiting for me. They were Jean and Carolyn. I went to two different counselors. Both of them thought I should be taking medication. *I shouldn't feel like I feel* was their mantra. My tool was AA. With that applied, I felt my feelings and that is how I came to intimately know myself. It was Jean and me and long rides into PA just cruising and talking for hours or going to meetings. I wrote and talked and listened and listened and wrote and talked. I put it all out on my sleeve and slowly Jean helped me to heal from the very first secret out.

I wrote a poem that was posted in an area newspaper and my brother's father-in-law read it. He made a big deal of it. He sent a copy all around the family. Everyone read it. That is how my family found out I wrote poetry. At a family gathering soon after, with much prodding, I read quite a few of my poems to an astounded dinner table group. It was the first time I was ever heard by these people who grew up with me and who watched me dying to grow up and never able.

I'll never forget my mother's comment; *here you are a genius while we all thought you obtuse. You must have such patience to put up with such ignorance from us all your life. I feel like a fool.* From then forward their perception of me transformed. I put together a booklet and gave it to my mother for Christmas.

In all my poetry I wore my fears and fantasies, I wore my rage and glory, I wore my guilt and resentment, I wore my sorrow and joy, I wore myself right out on my sleeve. I read at poetry meetings, at AA meetings, at family gatherings, and I began to assemble and sell my secret self to an identifying world. Fear of who I am subtly, very, very subtly began to give way to an insight that so connected me to life that it gave me a freedom like flying.

Neptune Blue

When the garden snake with yellow diamonds
becomes your bird in a cage and all the feathers
shed unexpected like leaves from trees in spring

When the Black Panther in the alley is
really a gray wolf and you hear the last
good-bye though you have no words for proof

When your fist of strings breaks loose from your grip and
your rainbow of balloons explodes to plastic shreds,
you contemplate the skeleton that just crawled from your bed.

Is it you or is it me?

Your world turns too cold not to submerge from its icy wind.
Hold your breath while you fall and the planets rearrange.
Detangle from the grip of bony knuckles you mistake for a hug,
this

Anchored illusion that drowns you in thief's love, this
wingless angel that makes you want to forget a fool's bliss, this
shadow that makes you hope you forget how to dream because

Now, at the edge of reckless release you see
the bird, not a bird, never was yours and
a snake cannot break the nature of snake.

You've been there. Everyone who goes there and
lives, comes up empty handed at some point.
You broke the galaxy with the red ricochet of

Your heart, ripped off star tails cutting light
into dark. When you hit the crust of hot air on your thrust
back to earth, all that got through was your soul.

Romance that tears away flesh and crushes bone
leaves you an aura with a much softer hue, one
the powdery, cool atmosphere of Neptune Blue.

I WAS SLOWLY beginning to see that reality is no more than a dream. That it is completely contingent on perception. We are all puppets living in a group illusion of what the group perceives to be real. The fact that every perception is changeable and the fact that every different perception creates a reality that follows it proves to me there is no reality. All of life is a dream. With that in mind, I began to dream of flying, just flying. I began to realize glimmers of ecstasy as I began to cut the cords of all the illusions I had inherited. From the excruciatingly blatant chains to the incredibly obscure threads, all ties began to snap clean. I was literally changing color. My aura was coming true. I realized I could be whoever I always dreamed of being. That person is actually who I am. I had to be willing to go through the agony of letting go of any form or need of approval. I had to lose the false safety I bent myself into hiding in. Every single thing I did is every single thing I needed to do in order to actualize. I got what I prayed for. Make sure when you pray you are willing to pay the price. By the way, the price is worth it.

Happiness, self actualization, freedom from the bondage of self imposed by a suffering society held captive by the insatiable need to be accepted has to be met head on and overthrown. Every piece of armory devised was thrown in my life path. I was at odds with every aspect of my world. I had no intention of surrendering. To have *me* free and clear was worth all the dying for.

I walked out of every definition ever put on me. Not one ever fit right. I am not who anyone perceives me to be. I am who I dream of being.

I was exercising, as usual, like a person with a cause. Exercise has always been a great outlet for all my emotions for me. No one was ever near me when I worked out. It has always been my great time of solace.

There was a bike ride for AIDS from High Point to Cape May, NJ. It was a two and one half day 260 mile fund raiser. I signed up. It helped redirect my focus to service. My friend Carolyn joined my effort as a volunteer in a sagg vehicle. There has not been a thing more exuberating than the total utilization of my physical prowess. Pushing my body to exceed its limits has always been a great gift of living for my spirit. I've never felt more alive than just before the summit of a steep 2 mile uphill when my lungs are inflated to near bursting or the deep curl of a 45mph dash down the backside of the same mountain with the controlled tension of every muscle in my body excited. Every person I was ever in a relationship with tried in vain to steal that time from me. Carolyn was the only person who never tried to curtail my work-out time. A gift from God is often missed. I am glad I can see what a God-given gift this great friend is while she is still in my life. For many years, even through the darkest nights, this person has persisted, without my deserving, by my side. I have come to thank God for my silent angel again and again.

In the meantime it was the late spring of 2003. I was standing at the scrub sink at a job I had worked at for fifteen years. It was effortless and devastating. I was an expert at my trade but, the last eight years had been an increasingly sexually abusive situation. I was filled with anxiety every day all day. I was gravely distraught. M had successfully turned everyone on me but one guy who simply wouldn't take sides. Though he did not lend to my demise, neither did he lend to its fruition. He was the frayed thread I had to hold. I was clammed down and I worked my ass off so there could be made no reason to fire me. I needed my job. Anything else offered me less than half my wage of 21.00/hr. When all my overtime was cut and even my fulltime wage wasn't meeting my expenses I began using my savings and selling things to make ends meet. They were trying to starve me out. I was in a time of financial and emotional desperation. I vowed never to live on overtime again.

As I stood there washing my hands as I had done for so many years I fell into total surrender. I prayed with an abandon I understood for help. I prayed; *God help me. This job is not who I am. This does not serve my purpose. I am here to do what Mrs. D did ~ help others. This is a re-enactment of the rejection I learned to grow up in. It made me suicidal then and now that I see it, it is every bit as much unacceptable now as it was then. The difference between now and then is now I'm not suicidal. I am not who they are saying I am. It is not ok to abuse my spirit anymore. I prayed; God, please get me out of here in any way that you see fit but please God, don't make it hurt too bad.*

I shut off the water and resolved to wait. That summer I worked like a dog. I went to AA. I wrote poetry that came like a flood. I talked to

Jean. I began a long amends to Carolyn who never held me accountable for the understanding she had which I never understood. I peddled my booklets at poetry meetings and AA meetings. I gave copies to my mother and she read them all. She was rearranged in her perspective of me and a lifetime of misunderstanding began to unravel into a friendship neither of us ever imagined let alone considered. She would say; *You're brilliant and I think you are a genius and why didn't you ever tell us?* I never nailed down my exact reaction to this change in mindset. I only know it felt good. My brothers and their wives fell in agreement with my mother and it seemed I was risen out of the family ditch. It was a flame I would enjoy but not dare touch for fear of snuffing it out. There was yet a lot of shadow leaning in on the still-flickering luminescence.

By long battles of resolving overwhelming discontent with an assigned lot I found completely unacceptable, I was finding myself. Every person, every institution that ever took passage in my life was part of that assignation. All of it was malevolent to me. This was the time of my great vomiting of the world. For the first times I was experiencing moments of a quiet stomach; moments without ballooning anxiety. I was divorcing everything to put my puzzle together.

In August of 2003 I celebrated 25years in AA. There was a big celebration. Even my parents, who have never sought to understand one thing about the whole AA answer, attended. There was a woman recently back from across the country I had coaxed into sobriety. I was sponsoring her. She had an uncanny resemblance to T. So much so, we assumed she was T's mother. The women from the meetings I left were at my anniversary. After what I had gone through and what they had witnessed it was a miracle to witness me celebrate 25 years. As this new comer sat next to me many people asked me; *What is T doing here?* I said; *It's not T but I think it's T's mother. She denies any association.* The day I first heard this woman share I recognized the story. I immediately asked God; *What is this? Is this what T was about?* I was completely intrigued to find out about this consummate human-devil. I had spent hours in dim light, selling my soul, listening to stories told about her by T while she growled and cried, and I desperately tried to understand her. I forced up the nerve to ask if she was the mother because I felt overcome with an intention that was other than helping her. She flatly denied being the suspect. That is how it ever remained. T never got sober. Because of T I have a special love for this woman who denies obvious family ties. I went beyond the call of duty to bring her into the glory of gratitude that AA delivers for giving up the drink. This woman has remained sober and become a very dear friend ever since. God is so generous. I have received the gift of two friends now. They each have come in a most unexpected way.

I clearly recall in a meeting one night a young man asking if he should get in a relationship or not. He was newly sober and didn't want to endanger his recovery. A man in his late forties responded. He said; *Whatever you don't rectify now you'll rectify later. Have your relationships. Make your mistakes. I didn't. I protected myself. I found myself doing things at forty-two that I could have learned not to do at twenty. If you don't do it now you'll do it later. Just live your life.* That was profound to me. It was my life. I had run from my fear of self until I ran smack into myself. At forty-four I was passing through the far side of a personal drama I might have rectified half a lifetime sooner if I wasn't so manipulated by popular opinion. I also might not have lived. So who knows what is the right cut through time and what is the wrong timing of the cut through?

QUESTIONS FOR AN ANGEL'S CARD

In the wanton lust of emancipation
I sell my soul to desire.
Walk directly into darkness,
without concept of any grid.
Is desire a trek in forest green,
an aimless walk in wildflowers?
Must the sky be crystal blue and
accompanied by a cool breeze?
Or do I seek a truth: A secret
hidden beneath a breast that
rests secure behind the flesh
of blackened sin? Does it
spew from luscious lips where
words shoot scalding fire, burn
the skin around my eyes, steel
the relief of God given lids?
Do I continue blind,
down the path of mud and
rutted rock on feet with ankles
faulted from unsure gate?

When the plain falls open beyond the wood,
do I scream across its emptiness, in hope
a mountain will catch my
sound to give echo to my humanity?
Is freedom found in the sting
of poison from the scorpion?
Must I lay myself naked
cast cold of any bones and let
the brutal march upon my
soft back to earn my wings?
Or do I just fall from the edge of the cliff
offered in my name and take to the earth as
a door to heaven's gate?

My search for meaning lead me through a search for self that, half way through my life, stripped me of every sequin-flashing scarlet letter of which I ever was pinned and laid them out across the table-top to be spat upon and polished, crushed under heel and hung on the wall so that when I stood up in front of 100 people to tell my story there was no glamour, nothing profound, no great feat, nothing but the raw-cut meat of a groveling idiot spelling out, from an unfit path, the dirty-rotten exile route; the confused unraveling of a trashed mind; the projected fears broken by the bareback riding of twenty appaloosas; the dirty experiments that were thieves of merit; the humiliated voice of profoundly proven imperfection; the disjointed conclusions that were the captains of each sprinting lead into the walls of stone that shouted again and again; No! Your self is not this! Your self is not here! Whenever I spoke my heart pounded. The story of my life resonated in the lives of those who could hear. I had the power, from my wasteland, to reach a heart and pull it free from its wasteland. I trudged forward in my ever-dream.

With this Devil-come-alive-new-comer, I crossed property lines for the last time. I learned what I needed to learn. In my unresolved quest for self-understanding I needed to know why this person even appeared. I received a clear-cut clarity of my scathing self centeredness. My disregard for others was a razor-sharp cut in my ability to love me. I was twisted into a harder right angle. Today I often tell; you cannot picture recovery(spiritual growth). I didn't imagine the answer to my question "why" to be in the form of a cold hard, freeing insight. I continued to talk to Jean and I wrote like a fiend. There was no end to this. All of life, I resolved, is a revelation of self-will turned inside out. That's if you work at it.

In September I did my bike ride. I was fit as a derby horse. I came back to work on Tuesday after the ride and was assigned to off-load and label 280 boxes to ship UPS. There was 70 to a skid. Each box weighed about 30lbs. I worked like a man off-loading, labeling and re-stacking the skids. The next day my back was blown. I rested but it didn't get better. In a couple of weeks I went to the Doctor and he subscribed vicoden and flexoral. I was in excruciating pain. I couldn't straighten my leg, get out of bed or, in and out of my truck without a full load of pain killers on board. The pain was unremitting and worsening. I told my boss. I knew I was going to have to be out of work. He didn't respond. Two days later, in mid-October of 2003 my foreman came to me with the first smile I'd seen coming toward me in years and said; *I have an early Christmas gift for you.* I waited a moment. *M just got fired. He lost a forty-thousand dollar job twice. I told Jr. it is either M or me. He told me to fire M and I did.*

My heart sank into soft music. The scar of what had taken place over the previous eight years wasn't going to just disappear. I had a deep hurt and resentment toward these guys.

The next week or so was like heaven there. Everyone was very nice to me. The guys treated me like the cute young girl I once was. But it had been fifteen years and I wasn't cute or young anymore. I had deep wounds embedded with resentment. Furthermore, I needed surgery for the third time on my back. That meant I was getting out of that place. A distant dream I had often pondered had come under my feet and I was walking. As I left that place I thanked God for taking me out and giving me complete vindication as I took my leave. I knew I wouldn't be back. God had answered my prayer. I didn't know where I was going but I knew what I needed to learn I was finished learning there. I had new, well defined boundaries.

DOLPHIN

When I break from the lies of
the misinformed book, I am
a dolphin breaching full-body
from the sea. When air comes
between my fin and
the mirror broken, I blow
my whole breath and
I am seen to fly. But
gravity insists I curve my dive
back to the welcoming mouth that
quiets like lips to ice cream, slips
closed behind my tail.

Under the umbrella of predator and prey,
I swim just beneath the ocean's distortion and
wait for lightning or storm to rage.
I race until
I know I am safe, then
jet my fins and
breach again, never
gentle to the sea.

IN THE END all I ever wanted, from as far back as I can remember, was to be believed; to be believable. I needed to believe myself. I needed to be authentic to me. Mrs. D had said; *When the insides match the outsides you will know you are on the right path.* I never understood one spiritual concept until after I had lived it. As the experience of life transformed more and more into spurts of metaphors strewn about from one awakened breath to the next, ever so slowly, painfully, my grip on definition loosened and my arms opened to the exquisite movement of me from the inside out.

I recalled a man at a meeting quoting The Big Book. He was talking about himself, identifying with the sentence written, "I wanted to be judged by my intentions while my actions were what everyone could see." I was smacked keenly, like running head-on into a brick wall, stunned. While I was filled with self-pity over my assumption of what I thought people thought of my actions, most people didn't even know, some didn't care, and the ones who made a fuss were just busy with the latest place to point their finger. It was my own self-opinion I needed to change. I disagreed with myself. My actions were unacceptable to me. I was my own bad actor. I had gone way outside my own lines to discover the definition of myself. I had listened to the voices of those I thought knowing and had taken their obscenities to heart. I had acted them out and it was me who suffered the consequences of my actions. I needed to make clear what was right by me for me and then live by those principles that make up my heart. I wrote . . .

New World

When you were here, we owned all the mountains of
the world. We plotted their divide, traversed their cliffs not
once acknowledging where our shadows might cast.
We were one. We moved as cats move, along ridges,
through crevasses so small whiskers need a soaking-
wet paw to smooth them back to white.

We were not once careful. We stole when the moon
rose high. Light is not so clear then. Sound is muffled by
darkness and platinum, your favorite metal, illuminates a
spectacular luster on naked skin no matter how bubbled with
sweat or pocked with acne.

We chewed each other's flesh and damned those
who were repulsed. The blooding felt good.
The momentary flood of pent up rage spurted upon
each arrival of breath to the air we panted.
We discovered a new world beyond the mountains in
the cleavage where babies are born.

When we finally lost our strength for all the bleeding,
we let the voices close in like storm clouds. Flood our
new fields. Split our seed with acid rain.
We believed the voices the truth and not
what we discovered.

While those voices that turned us into ghosts fade like
the edges of shadows under snow-blasted moonlight,
I stand,
separate,
etched by you like chiseled granite
in a new world.

I was finding out who I am by discovering who I am not. As the world screamed reconciliation for its forty-five years of accusation, I was slipping out of that coat of thorns by my every failed experimentation of every soul-crushing expectation. I was more alive than ever before. As the clamor of self-righteous accusation relaxed all those name callers into the fog they felt comfortable picking up speed in

I was coming into the light of my own reflection. I was a bad actor. I didn't have all the subtleties clarified but of the larger acts I could stop immediately. In those movements the hardest swallow to take was forgiveness of myself. As I backed away from the bonfires of so many chunks of my soul, what each fire illuminated was both devastating and glorious. It wasn't so easy to walk away. After twenty-five years of sober searching and forty-four years of definition that suspended me in impending doom, I had arrived at the door where the freedom from the bondage of self, peace, astoundingly floated within reach. All I had to do was let go.

LETTING GO

Maybe it's because in my wildest trappings
I never get to where you take me. I never
find someone who conceives of going past
the far edge of shadow. I never hold
someone who, before touching, removes my
surface, deforms my name, shaves
the corneas from my eyes so I can't
see the crows perch around the dead
bodies strewn along the silent path you blaze.
The siren I hear is my own scream.

I never entangle with emancipation so
exquisite as to welcome the cauterizing
rod brand tattoos: ugly scars of proof across
the writing on my face.
No one ever flies me to the precipice where
to vanish in a firestorm is sexual—
Where satisfaction is above the law of any price.
No one ever bathes me in their river where wet silk
rinses away every bit of grit, cools the steam
that hangs about my skin, strips the armor
from my childhood.

Maybe it's because in my wildest trappings
I never get to where you take me—I never find
someone who disarms me of every weapon, turns
my book upside down, walks
me clear out of my life.

I never find someone I actually die for whom
leaves me, still breathing, to
reconcile my entire lie.
Maybe that's why there *is* no letting go.

EVERY SINGLE RELATIONSHIP was necessary. Every single place I went was necessary. The decision for independence was born not of desire but of desperation. Every moment of my life had meaning. All of life is poetry. Its meaning is determined by how it is interpreted. It has always been up to me to make sense of it. It was up to me to give reckoning to the spirit that enlivened me; that unremittingly sought itself in every ignorant human breath dissolved. I was never without means. I was given a process long before I had any idea what it was or how to apply it. I would, in the end, free myself from the coil of human entanglements that partitioned me from a harmony with the flow of the universe I could only know as separate and whole. I never would have conceived this to be what comprised the joy of living I so fervently and blindly sought.

In spite of me or perhaps because of me ~ I don't know, people kept coming . . . inquiring like I knew something I didn't know I knew. In AA the rooms still fell silent when I spoke. People still took my lead when they shared. I was still surrounded before I could escape out the door. Didn't they know I was broken? Big chunks of me were falling off right in the open. I was in the doorway not knowing how to be.

I got a call one night while I was recuperating from my back surgery. It was my mother. She suggested I go to nursing school. The Doctor had warned me, in no uncertain terms, that if I didn't leave that job I was bound to end up in a wheelchair. I had no other career; no other trade. I responded to my mother by telling her I had no money to go to school or support myself while I went to school and that, furthermore, I was too stupid to be able to pass nursing school. She was ready for my response and said; *I'll give you 1000 dollars a month. Go to school.* It was an offer I was in no position to refuse. A few days later I mentioned my intention at an AA meeting. After the meeting a man came up to me and told me there was a program in the state that would pay for my schooling under the disability act. I followed up and consequently discovered everything would be paid for as long as I got C's. Even my books and the NCLEX would be paid for.

I had all my credits from attending school throughout the years. There was a battle-ax in charge of the nursing program I had to go see.

She was one of the roughest people I've ever come across. She hissed; *You haven't even completed your sciences!* I asked; *What do I need to do? I'm out of work and time is a factor.* She growled; *Get your sciences done! And get A's!* I answered; *Thank you,* and was on my way.

The sciences were filled for the spring semester so I took maladaptive and child psychology courses. Both courses required research papers and proved to be perfect for how I was moving internally.

I describe the depiction of the evolution of spirituality to be quite like the swirling of stars on the big screen in a movie theatre coming into a circle for an Orion film. Everything is in movement at once. It takes more years than anyone would care to imagine, dare to count, and for the vast majority, go through the pain of unraveling, for the stars to swirl into what could be considered a spiritual harmony.

While I was unable to drive after my surgery I had started a meeting at my house. It was at the request of a sponsee who wanted to go through the steps. It became a place where I was a teacher, like it or not. I got the great opportunity to change a few lives forever at that meeting. Usually it takes no more than the turning around of one poorly rooted attitude and that person walks forevermore with an adjusted gait. I had acquired an uncanny ability to listen and hear between the lines. The answers are hidden like golden eggs in the sun right there. All I ever had to do is read them back. They each told me what they wondered how I knew.

I remember a conversation with a very long term friend. I was telling her how the admiration from people couldn't be real. They didn't know me. She told me my feelings were a lack of humility. *People made a big deal of time.* I said; *Time does not mean wellness.* Yes, she said; *People got hung up on time but you have to let them. No matter what you've done that you think is wrong, they see less than you think. They see what you've done right. You haven't taken half measures in your program. That is obvious. For that you have something they want. Give it to them. If they want to put you on a pedestal let them. Running from it is a lack of humility. You know you are just as they are . . . human. Humans need heroes. You know you're not a hero but to them you are. Just be who you are. Don't get caught up in self-destructive thinking. You have a purpose. Your message is clear. You are a guide post. Don't think more of yourself than that.* So, in the melee of my clarifying self-image I imagined myself as something of a landmark that if unseen could leave the seeker wandering off into the storm of anxious confusion I so recently pulled myself back from the edge and away from.

Carolyn stood firm by my side. The grace of her friendship gathered clarity. I needed and wanted a friend. We began to refer to ourselves as Don Quixote and Sancho. I had an impossible dream and she just liked me. So, the meeting at our house went on. I took Chemistry and Anatomy and Physiology 1 over the summer and got A's. I took Microbiology and Anatomy and Physiology 2 in the fall and got two more A's. I had a 4.0 average. I got my Professors to write my letters of recommendation. I was set to enter nursing 1 for the spring semester. It had been a year. When the letters of acceptance began to arrive I ran to the mailbox every day. I didn't get one. I sent applications to three other nursing schools in the area. By the first week in December I was getting pretty nervous. I couldn't not get into school. I had been out of work already for 14 months. I went to see the Battle Ax and make my plea. She was like rubbing coarse sandpaper on my cheek. I asked what happened. I told her I did what she asked. My sciences were completed . . . with A's. She hissed; *You don't even live in the county!* I lied; *Yes I do! I live on the border. I've attended school here for many years!* Then she snarled; *Everyone wants in! Why are you different?!* I said; *I'm not different. I want to get in just like anyone else. I've been out of work for over a year prepping myself. Time is money and I can't afford to wait another year.* She hissed; *Everyone has money problems!* I answered; *I'm here because if I don't come and tell my story I don't have a chance at all. I'm hoping if I come and ask maybe there is a way I can be considered at least.* She softened ever so slightly then barked; *The program is full!* After a few moments of just looking at each other she offered; *I'll put your name at the top of the waiting list. That's all I can do.* Not knowing if she just wanted the meeting over or if she meant what she said I thanked her. She wasn't used to a person who didn't fight. I reasoned and that's as much as I could get. It was better than nothing. As I left her office she said; *Someone usually drops out.* I hoped with no greater hope than I ever hoped before that she told the truth.

I heard nothing. I called the other colleges. I'd have to wait until September. I went to the campus and signed up for spring courses to hold me over. I'd keep cleaning houses with a friend who was giving me some hours. The state would continue to pay for whatever courses I took as long as I continued to get at least a C.

That was the darkest December I could remember for many years. On a weeknight, the 23rd of December, I came home from my favorite meeting and there was a message on my answering machine. The call came in at 7:30pm.The person said; *You've been accepted into the nursing program. If you want the seat you need to get in touch at this number immediately. Call back first thing in the morning.* I busted out in tears. I called my mother and she yelled to my father. I called first thing in the morning and confirmed my acceptance then got in my truck and flew down to the campus to drop/add the courses and get my instructions of requirements. I had a lot to do in a very shortened period of time. I was scared and excited. Could I succeed? This was the first thing in my life everyone, everyone was in agreement with. I was 46 years old and everyone, if only this one time, agreed with what I was doing. I could see how people could be such sheep. For how little it mattered to be approved of, it felt glorious. I could get addicted to that.

I had to end the meeting at my house. The studying was overwhelming. I attended night school because that was when nursing 1 was offered in January. It was perfect because it gave me all day alone to study.

One woman from my meeting insisted we continue to work together. She wanted me to be her sponsor. She wasn't going to just stop coming to my house and walk away. She wasn't finished. She wanted what I had. She was willing to meet any time, any place to get it. After discussing it with Carolyn I agreed to meet with her once a week on Sunday evening. With all the crying, stomping, fighting, and letting go, the work we did together dragged us both to higher plateaus of increasing ownership and acceptance of ourselves, our places in the universe, and life for what it is or isn't worth. For nearly three years we met. In the meantime her mother died and I became a nurse. By these absolutely unreflecting experiences we both got some freedom from the bondage of self; she by coming to the understanding that we own nothing and me by realizing the very body I live in is the universe. All answers emerge from the inside turned out.

Nursing school opened my eyes to the miraculous human form. It gave me a whole new perspective on "normal". I learned that not only are my fingerprints unique but that every cell in my body has an exclusive and unique code. This is true for every person ever to breathe or never to take one breath. By the laws of nature normal is to be unique. That meant that every time I wasted my energy on the sorrow that gripped me for not fitting in I was denying access to the gloriously life giving chamber of the spirit that set up house in this body shop and has waited ever since for an opportunity, one beam of light across my self consumed brain, so it could spread its wings into reason; so it could illuminate the simplicity of a purpose that has so far been too obvious for me to see. The dim wits I have gathered of my spiritual abundance have been, for every flicker, hard, nearly impossible to come by.

During an externship as a nursing student there was a young man, 26years old, from Central America, I had the great opportunity to care for. He had come to the U.S.A six years prior and at this time, with all his great and glorious dreams dashed in the new world, he was dying of AIDS. One day I went into his room and he was standing, delirious, beside his bed. The entirety of his frail body was shivering. He was covered with his own feces from head to toe. He was trying to get it off himself but was just spreading it more. My preceptor RN and I walked him like a bag of cracked sticks to his bathroom and gently cleaned him. Then we cleaned his bed, the floor, the walls, the chair, and the night table. We helped him back to bed. Later when I came to check on him after his dialysis he had done it all over again. When his sister came to see him. I asked her to ask him if he was in pain. All he did was wince and mumble. He spoke no English. When his sister asked, the man broke out in tears. The RN immediately got him something for pain. On my way home and in bed that night I cried. This was life's brutal disregard. As much as we are responsible we are also ignorant. As much as we are all victims we are all judges. No one learns from anyone else and we all learn from each other. Every student is a teacher and every teacher must be a student. There is not a way to avoid ever being an example. I knew then; I was the one who could learn from my experience. I was swirling; awakening. I was looking intently, that is with the intention to learn.

Into wings

When I get to the ridge
The unscathed view reveals
Nothing is real,
Only wild imaginings, dreams, and ideals.
Fields are green
Rich with trees and
Silver-blue streams—
Eternal as time, just as certain.

I am aloud to see and feel.
Wonder at my own imaginings.
When I grab
I discover
None of it is real.

When I get to the ridge
The unscathed view reveals
Scarred mountain peaks
Dragged out river-beds
Black-burned fields.

I want no more of what my hands bring.
I lean off
Plummet
Into wings.

Over the course of my great inner transformation that took over twenty-five years to begin to emerge from the fog of my mind, as my perspective of myself and my purpose actually took on a silhouette, I must have become visibly open. I attracted several women who all wanted to do step work with me. With the same trepidation I felt as a one-eyed six-year-old monster when around those frightened neighborhood girls, I relived the feeling of being a monster with every single woman who looked to me for help. It always felt like a trick was only to be revealed. I would be somehow found out as a monster. It was a combination of not trusting them, not trusting me, thinking they didn't trust me, and fearing I'd prove untrustworthy. Of course this whole raveled up knot had nothing to do with anything except that I needed to unravel it and move on. I talked to Jean and Carolyn about my fears. Their message was the same. *Just keep going.* I did. A lot of time my fortitude was rooted in their belief in me. I never stopped questioning my motives. If anything I questioned with a greater intensity. I was on a great spiritual leap and the exciting thing about it was I knew it while I was still on it. I never stopped wanting resolution on my identity. I worked with every woman who wanted to work. There was 100% success for everyone who physically and mentally applied the process. Every single one of them came to a freedom of the bondage of self to the degree of their ability to be honest. Each of them showed me who I am.

As unresolved as my physical image persisted, my spirit's mission edged into undeniable success stories the most breath relinquishing of which was my own.

I was writing and selling my booklets of poetry. I had hired someone to create a website. I was on line. I read my poetry from Manhattan to all across NJ. My writing told the truth. I was well taken. Nursing school proved to me; nothing really worthwhile is one bit easy. The expectations were mountainous with assignments of 500 page, usually very interesting but interminable, readings with twenty to forty new medical terms that were in themselves a new language, three to five pages of drugs to look up, and forty to eighty questions to answer on average per week. Then there were quizzes and tests constantly with hours of lectures and clinicals that required pages and pages of care plans that showed the professors our improving assessment skills. Nursing school was by far the most rigorous undertaking I've ever embarked on. My hard work paid off. I graduated with honors. At the nursing graduation, with the help of a classmate-friend who had made it through those battlefields of endless assignments, tests, care plans, and clinicals with me, I had secured the great honor of reading a poem I wrote named "Being A Nurse". There rose great applauds and then a standing ovation. From where I had come, for what I had done, how could I not believe there was a God in loving favor of me. I was expanding, in spite of myself, into wings.

THE GREEN FLECKS IN YOUR EYES

Remember your essence
That is the first flicker of your flame
The ignition of your breath
There can be no heart that pumps precisely the same
No one has the flecks printed in your eyes
This life is your spiritual flight

Don't get your feet caught in the shoes others wear
Their coats are made of rain and metal shards that
Slice their skin and wash the blood clean so
They can't see their own bleeding energy

Climb to the mountain top where
The rocks hang out off the edge
Feel the wind
Close your eyes
Listen to the open fields inside your head
The turkey vultures crackling wings

Your soul is given to you for free
Your body is a rust proof car to carry it in
Don't leave or lend even a suitcase from within to
those artisans who steal pieces of your framework for
blueprints that erect into faces not worthy to
be a backdrop for the green flecks in your eyes

EVEN AS I had come to this edge before, it seemed I had never been so alive. I could see the other cliffs from where I flew off before. Each time I left a bluff I flew with no view of a verge out ahead. I learned; you cannot picture spiritual growth. The moment you picture it you create a frame, a limitation. Spirit has no beginning, no end, no boundaries of time. All I can do is be awake. Be more than awake. Be alert with abandon, ever poised for flight. All of life is a spiritual experience while I keep busily distracted by weight and measure.

The NCLEX was a bitter-sweet end to an ordeal I never, at any point, felt I could surmount. My mother, my most important backer; this was a physical healing taking place between us ~ that she approved, backed, supported, and even cheered me was a deeply heartfelt miracle to me. We both hung by our fingertips in anxious fear I might ultimately fail. Neither of us had tested a fragile belief in my ability to achieve such an intellectual endeavor. Mother even told me she didn't understand my doing so well grade wise. She concluded it must have been an inferior program that I was in for me to do so well. Until this time I had been slated to the role of the family's mentally ill, hopelessly ignorant, and ultimately useless. It had been my badge to wear. I didn't know how not to wear it and my mother did not know how not to act on it. Now I was taking the state NCLEX exam. Every student in my class and every class was afraid of this test. Nervous is a weak word.

I stayed overnight across the street from the testing center. My dear friend Carolyn came with me. In the morning I went across to the test center. As expected, we were treated like a bunch of cheaters. I'll never get used to that. As I sat for the test I couldn't believe the amount of drug questions. Only a pharmacist would know these answers! I was beside myself. The test shut off at 75 questions. At least forty were on drugs, their effect, and teaching. I was sure the test shut down because I got so many wrong I'd never be able to save myself. I went back to the room. When Carolyn opened the door I busted out crying. I failed and now the job I had lined up would be lost. My income was cut off two months prior when I graduated. I had to wait two interminable days to get my true results. I couldn't breathe as I turned on my computer and punched up the information to upload a totally black screen that read, in small white block letters—Congratulations you passed! My whole body began to shake. I just stood there. I wanted to print and frame the page but there was no print option on the black screen. I didn't know what to do. Then I felt it. The relief swept over me. The proud feeling of having passed swept over me. The vindication from an incorrect definition of who I am; what I'm capable of, swept over me. I called my mother. *I passed; is all I said.* My mother screamed my father's name; *Susan passed!* Then she said; *Thank God!*

My journey into the upright and moving position of nursing was long from over. I had a month before I started. Women squeezed time in with me to do fifth steps. It was like they thought I was leaving forever. Nursing had proven to be an overwhelming responsibility that barely left time to pee. Perhaps they were right. I was leaving a life I had known for many, many years. I'd not be back. There may be no such thing as time as something real but there is only one direction in which to move. That is forward. I'd not be back. I met with several women to hear life stories, fourth, and fifth steps, and to bounce back to them the answers they came with but couldn't find on their own. Each of them left with a golden egg that sent them forward not to return from whence they had emerged.

Twigs and Straw

Know why it takes a life time?

There is no part you can hold.
You'll think you have to leave your breath behind.
That would be a wisp of wind.
There is more to it than raising the hair on your skin.
The river doesn't flow without reason.
It is in the falling the bird discovers it has wings.

There is no part you can picture.
Does the black liquid you drink that
warms your bones before the Christmas flame
give you what you dream of?
Be glad for what you do not receive.

There is no return.
When half the distance is behind you
you'll have twice the vision.
Be a teacher to those still completely blind.
The human spirit is real.

There is no pain free path.
You will crash with earth.
You'll fly.
You'll be glad it takes a life time.
The twigs and straw you claw are only for
something to measure against as you let go.

There is no greater gift.
It is all about letting go.
The boat your spirit sails is you.
Be a ship on your journey of discovery.
Be unencumbered.
This voyage is all yours.

As I ENTERED the nursing world of medicine I envisioned a huge group of caring people coming together to help the sick and injured. I had always been on the downside of the bedrail. I had encountered some mean nurses but for the most part they seemed to care.

After a grueling orientation that introduced me to both the gentle and the brutal, I hit the halls running like a rabbit anxious for its life in a hollow filled with coyotes and foxes. I hadn't arrived one moment before I could barely handle what I met. I never had had contact before with people the likes of these. Everyone was type A. Everyone was intelligent. Everyone was arrogant. It seemed everyone was a self-glorified hero. Anyone at any moment might throw you under the bus if it would make them look good. No one trusted anyone else. There was a drought of good words for anyone while the waterfall of contempt sprayed off the cliffs of self righteousness. The competition between employees was as natural as breathing.

The hazing that takes place for the induction of acceptance as a nurse is not surpassed by any college fraternity or sorority. I learned; don't underestimate the meanness wrought of human ignorance.

I was being introduced to work in the operating room of a great institution. My eyes were blasted by what goes on behind closed doors. The O.R. was so big, the nurses needed to be divided into clusters. Otherwise we'd not be able to be honed enough to meet the needs of so many specialties. I was coaxed into the general-vascular cluster and soon after, the coordinator decided I was trouble. I had stuck up for myself a couple of times against nurses I felt were attacking me. They were! I quickly came to learn it is a grave danger to stand up against anyone with more experience. They are considered right just like a cop is considered right because it is assumed he is more alert to the on-goings by virtue of his position and training. This coordinator grabbed me aside and told me I couldn't learn fast enough. She snarled; *I was stupid; that I needed to go work on the floors; that I wasn't cut out for the O.R.; I asked too many questions* which for some reason was an admission of stupidity (I was told several times *never ask!*) I thought that ridiculous so I continued to ask questions and got a reputation for being stupid. Well, I knew how to wear that badge.

In nursing school we were taught knowledge is power. I clearly witnessed the undermining use of that power in this place. Knowledge was used as intimidation, humiliation, and, very nearly for me, termination. Nurses were the meanest people I had ever met. They far surpassed any person who had ever hurt me because they had no excuse. They were intelligent, professional, adult women who were of reasonably sound mind and good physical health. They had the upper hand and they had taken an oath to help people. That doesn't end at the bedside. A nurse, to me, wasn't a nurse at all if he/she put limitations on her skills whether it be time, place, or person. Comforting is the first oath of a nurse. Teaching follows right at the heels. A nurse to me is a nurse to all. Nurses kill each other. There is a defined line demarcated there.

Working with nurses was like entering a battlefield of open assault every day. In the end I switched to a split shift. It immediately suited my personality better. I was no longer in a cluster. I never liked gangs. I began to go everywhere and be attached to nothing. How perfect can something be? Not more perfect than this for me. I needed to move freely to flourish. I made some friends but kept my distance. One thing is for sure; in order to survive in a snake pit the first requisite is to realize you are in a snake pit.

I talked to Jean a lot. I talked to Carolyn. In the beginning I drove home crying a lot. Nursing school could never prepare me for this. Nothing I was taught there applied in the O.R.. I was beginning from scratch and no one gave me a break. This was an unexpected and unimagined hell. A dungeon of self glorified rattlers.

It was incredibly uncomfortable to work with 100 women. Women are defensive. I tried being friendly and was shunned. Women don't want to be friends. Old fears rose in me. I thought maybe there was something wrong with me for wanting to be friends with these women. A twisted root from an unhealed fragment of me thrust its blade up under my ribs. Like a death that brings up every loss ever felt, it has always been so hard to let go. Forgive. But, I held a steady pace. I kept talking and writing about my new ordeal. I had no motives but to succeed. I listened to my anxiety. If someone gave me anxiety I moved away from them. If someone didn't, I relaxed. I sought a purpose. I believed I was in this place for a purpose. I could see a huge hole that needed to be filled. I had never associated with women. This was a strange and new continent for me. I was face to face in a mirror I had never seen.

The swirl threw out two stars. One was named reconciliation. That was for the never understood little girl in me. The second one was love. This is where I could actually break past the fog of my mind into the tranquility of unconditional love. Unconditional love is the prerequisite to purity of service or service with the pure intention of Divine will. That is what Mrs. D. had.

It was pretty bold of me to think I could be of Divine service in this place. But why not? I learned over the years by proven outcomes that if I align my will with God anything is possible held in check only by the degree to which I believe it possible. I believe in possibility.

The pain amongst the staff was palpable. As my head cleared and as I acquired enough skills to get by at my job, I decided to take a suggestion that Carolyn gave me; *Wherever I am, try to bring harmony to the situation.* To do this I had to make friends with my environment; with everyone in it. This was no small task but, I believed, with God's help it was possible. I believed, if I could weave a thread of love throughout these halls that strand would change these halls forever just like the immeasurable tweaking of a crystal changes where the light refracts for all time. All I needed to do was tweak the gem. This understanding was like endeavoring to actually change the tide; stop the movement of the wave. I was a marathoner. I could do this. Words echoed from rehab; *Who if not you? When if not now?* I was choosing to love everyone into loving.

How could I nurse nurses when they are all so heaped in suspicion that I question the first letter of my intention. I couldn't have been ready for this one moment sooner. In my poetry I wrote I wanted to be . . .

As Water

As water takes the shape of its container

Flows out

Drains through dirt and rock by drops
pooled back in purification

Sustains by unchecked abandonment unto
its own fulfilled diminishment

Evaporates to give rain

Quenches any thirst that drinks of its endurance

I pray that I am of use

My insides tore out. I worked the core of my fears. I searched back over my life. I worked with people and found more and more of myself. I set my physical boundaries by the voice of my spirit. I went to meetings and shared. I kept none of what I experienced to myself. It had been a couple of lifetimes since I had kept secrets. I lived by my ever-flow. I wanted to come to my purpose in this place of high strung people that were grossly over-burdened by the certified baggage they chose to lug around and measure themselves and each other by. I had come to consider myself immeasurable.

Jean would say; *You're gonna change that place.* And I'd think; *How?*

Imagine pushing a wave back; calming the tide. I had to believe in myself. I had thirty years of work on motives under my belt. I knew how to keep my course straight. I knew how to defeat devils. I decided I'm going to be who I am. I am not going to be beat down into a fearful child. I am going to bring love (love is understanding even when I disagree) into this battlefield of emotional measurements that make everyone miserable. I began to push a wave of harmony. I began to learn the names, honor, respect, love, and show worth to everyone. Not one person, including me deserved less. I would be the first ripple of a new tide. You know what happened? The wave I pushed against receded. Little by little toes began to walk the tight rope of illusive and rhythmic movement of an in-coming sea. All that I consistently offered began to be returned.

The millionth Track

By long and arduous mathematics
The brilliant minds deduct:

Of every one million tracks I trek
I may be quite lucky if I leave one.

At such infinitesimal possibility
I better be certain I leave the right one.

No matter how subtle, I want any difference I have the purpose to make be one of Divine intention and not of some limited thought of my own. That is the only way it can be a betterment to the whole plan. Self will must be smashed.

To ponder back at the fifty plus years it's taken; the thirty plus years of applying the program, to see with the shimmer of clarity I've gained, that is the most I can do in my time. My purpose is clear. For those who want to align the spirit residing within their frame with the body that gives it breath, I can take them through the process. There is no glamour. There is no certification or award. There isn't even recognition. There is no visual from the world. There is no one to hear you but those few who seek to hear. The message is not of what the majority speak. It is unspeakable, inconceivable, undeniable, and more real than the burn of a torch on the back of your hand.

Mine is a journey to raw humility where there is no other reason but service, no excuse to say no, no fear of disclosure because you can be seen clear through. There is but one motive; to open a channel where Divine love flows so that anyone who moves into its substance must take at least one drink of understanding. As fleeting as that recognition might be, change is irrevocable. This is humility so raw I need no name, no certain cloak, no desk between; a place of no resistance where principle reigns and no personality slows my pace. This is the raw humility of a miracle observed. Imagine the lack of fear of love. That is God.

A benevolent journey is ever reconciled and given reason by the ever intensifying thirst for spiritual freedom born of the clarity wrought of a singleness of purpose to be of Divine use.

Such freedom comes of humility, the one and only Divine conquest of spirit being human.

The blending of Divine spirit and human mortality is a gift that delivers the one and only mortal quest; freedom of spirit, the very sky open to the joy of dying to live.

MILLION LIPS KISSING

The essential is not apparent.
A fish does not see its pond's edge.
How can one be expected to imagine the ocean?

Only chew small bits of wisdom.
Tidal volume of breath can be measured.
Can the number of galaxies be deduced?

Move one foot and then the other to the shoreline.
Look out at the white-caps on a restless sea.
This is the best explanation.

In the constancy of motion is stillness.
The white-cap is there and then it disappears.
The ocean is never diminished.
Below its million lips kissing the sky is
a sample cup of what love can produce.

I've never gone off course in my quest to find myself; to find the Divine enlivened in me. I've been dragged by others and I've dragged myself. I've been abandoned by others and I've abandoned myself. I've been raped by others and I've raped myself. I've been loved by others and that has been the hardest of all, to love myself. This journey is not for the spiritually weak.

It is . . .

The Great Expedition

Through the bearing straight of unnerved endings
Undone in the coiled feuds of ancient misleadings
Shaved away like a carbuncle rasped from a hull
Serenaded into drunken fits of rage
Drown in the resolve to leave a masterpiece epitaph
Birthed into the tsunami called life
Fully surrendered, the heart is a flower-seed tossed about.

The expedition to some higher land only serves the
witness, the witness of mortal demise.
Traveler, bear no burden on.
Let the sleeves be left tied to a tumble-weed that will never tumble roped
    tight.
There is no one to spelunk ahead.
Not one soul can dive to the bottom of your deep.
Work a pencil and parchment to keep it mapped is all.
An atlas is the process for this unplanned foray.

When night is day some clock-wise beyond
What is inside is all dug out.
The expedition is well landmarked.
Nowhere in actual sight, but the soul is gathered and conspicuous once
    and for all.
From that cavernous center, explode out.

The darkest forest, the longest river, the mightiest mountain does not
    reflect
The star filled night, the thunderous waterfall, the interminable gorge
    that makes up the undaunted heart.

Only the most careless explorer chances a charting in this wooded wild.

I DON'T WANT to fit in. I want to ride my bicycle for seventy miles, alone. I want to hike to the top of The Gap, gaze out from the cliff, and talk to God. I want to write my poetry. I want to clear my soul of all the debris that's been thrown there. I want to wear my problems out and shake them from my sleeve.

My passage is not neat and tidy. Neat and tidy is for the fearfully weak. I'm full of scars. Every scar is an insight. If I should be defined, find me in a Thesaurus where synonyms and antonyms come together; I am a monster and an angel; one born with great mental deficiencies, a genius; a tomboy and a girl; a rebel and seeker of truth; a drunkard and a visionary; a slut and a prudent observer; a liar and one who speaks from the heart; an athlete and a writer of song; I am strong and fragile; emotional and stoic; I am ill-equipped and fully prepared; over sensitive and humble; one filled with rage and rapture; androgynous in spirit and form with a singleness of purpose; I am kind and hardened of heart; a teacher and a student; beyond human aid and in human need; the sage; a mystic; a poet; a woman; I am alive; I am the ocean and one drop of rain; I am nothing and everything; none of the above and all of it at once; I am freedom from the bondage of every self by being every self at once; I am the infinite traveler only passing through the thin skin of time.

And this I give to you . . .

NAMASTA

~The Light in me Honors the Light in you~

I have found
many times we need to go out and come back.
There is only one ocean.
We are each a part of it and, that entire ocean at once.
In that sea we are never separate.
We only come more acutely awake in the
ceaseless heave of one wave, one breath to the next.
The constancy of the tides ensures our ever mixing.
The grandeur of the surround promises our endless possibilities.
For what light in each other we honor, our bodies are the prisms
    through which that light refracts.
Our movement is the opportunity for sublimity.
Let us be all and nothing.
Let us be the whole and each of the parts apart.
Then, there can be no light that shines on one thing that does not
    matter.
There will be no need to refract light because we will be light.
When we shine out without a notion of return
we will own compassion.
There will be no crosses only oceans and tides to illuminate.

8/7/09

Most recently I came to work with a woman, a nurse from my new place of employment. She is incredibly beautiful and every fear I ever had for women emerged like one hundred dragons in the yard. Every grain of my instinct to survive screamed to run and I knew I'd never heal in this life if I did not hold my ground clear past the last fallen ash of this volcanic internal eruption.

God has given me a teacher. God has given me someone to teach. The myths and assumptions I err by, she sweeps and dashes aside. She pulls me from under the wave of terror of my own demise and I am made right sized. I am only human, a servant of Divine purpose in only as much as I can let go of my illusion of control or a need to control. I don't even need to know. Just open. Just be a channel. God is the flow.

Sweeping light has come through us, to us both. That I can move beyond my own campsites, forgive all the men, all the women, and especially me; to see, and know, and say, I am a blizzard of snowflakes, each distinct and separate, fallen into a great tapestry that has been laid out in the sun and diminished into clear liquid to quench the lawn. That the transformation of that white blanket has turned what was once frozen into a lush, green lawn removes all the weapons against me because every me defined is dismissed.

The woman I travel this short passing with is outside the safe rooms where I have relaxed in comfortable acceptance. If our meeting had come years ahead I would have committed some form of suicide to quell my fear of myself entwined. As our relationship has evolved I have experienced again, it takes but one person to turn the key, raise the shade, and present the glorious view.

The parting of who I am and who I am defined as is done. I am free. I am Susan. That is my fingerprint, the all of it all.

River Drop

It is not one root, one tree.
It is the forest.
It is not you, me.
It is humanity.

A river springs from one drop.
How many drops to create that flow?
Don't seek visibility.
Endeavor rather to strengthen the surge.

There is a waterfall up ahead.
The effervescence of that breathless drop is a rainbow.
Don't be a splash that evaporates along the bank.
Paddle to the middle.
Strengthen the current.
Catapult into colors off the edge.

Fulfillment is wetting every bottom rock.
Sustenance is planting buoys for who is next.
Consummation is being in the eternal movement.
Take long strokes in what has no beginning and moves ever forward in what has no end.

How far around I have taken my route to find my path! It is my dream to be God's channel. It is not impossible. God is love. I have decided to love all people. That decision has changed my world. When I am made new, my world is made new. What I reflect is what reflects back. Without error a place of rasped turmoil has taken some ease with a touch of harmony.

Miraculous.
Simply Divine.
This is where I begin,
at the end.

The Hammer

Be still.
Listen.
When you are silent long enough
it becomes very clear when
the hammer
hits the nail
square on the head.

I WOULDN'T SAY it comes together. It's much more like, it falls apart. With great relief, it all falls apart.

To put this endeavor of purpose we measure with what we call time into some semblance of perspective I found a reasonable explanation in a book I recently finished; There is a Swedish folktale that gives definition to this inconceivable notion; *High up in the north in a land called Svithjod, there stands a rock. It is a hundred miles high and a hundred miles wide. Once every thousand years a little bird comes to this rock to sharpen its beak. When the rock has thus been worn away, then a single day of eternity will have gone by.*

In the time I have, to have endeavored and overcome just one human frailty and to have found a purpose in that, may be to have surpassed what is equal to two days of eternity. For a great task, indeed it has been, in a sequence that hasn't even the time to be thought.

SED

7/4/2011